WHISPERS
OF TRUTH

WHISPERS
OF TRUTH

A True Story of Abuse, Corruption, and Miracles

Pamela Pearsall

Values Count, LLC
Prescott, Arizona

Library of Congress Control Number: 2017908477

Second Edition

ISBN 978-1546766230

Printed in the United States of America

DEDICATIONS

*To my many supporters who have defended me
and stood by me through thick and thin.*

*I also dedicate this book to my sister, who is my hero.
It's nice to have a person in your corner, who no matter what,
takes your side and fights your battles with you.*

To my brother, who has always been kind and thoughtful to me.

To my husband, who is a hero on so many levels.

To my children, who are the best a mother could ever wish for.

To my grandchildren, who are really the best ever!

To Dad, the man who raised and loved my brother, sister and me.

*Finally to my mother, a strong example, an overall perfect person
who has risen above huge challenges and come up smiling.*

DISCLAIMER

Everything I have recounted in this non-fiction book is true, but not entirely factual as to the events, locales, and conversations. These items are from my memory. Most names of those I deem to be creeps have been changed so that I don't get sued. In some cases, I have compressed events and even changed some identifying characteristics and details of physical properties.

My grandchildren know I'm always right, but my children and husband let me know that sometimes my perspective can be biased. So when you read this truth-based book—which reveals some appalling behavior—understand that this is how I experienced a critical part of my life.

The purpose of this memoir is to tell my story as well as entertain you. The author and publisher shall have neither liability nor responsibility to any person or entity for any loss or damage caused, or alleged to have been caused, directly or indirectly, by the information contained in this book.

If you do not wish to be bound by the above, you may return this book to the publisher for a full refund.

Contents

WHISPERS
OF TRUTH

1

ETHOS

September 2008

THE CROWD OF SUPPORTERS MOANED as results flashed on the big screen television.

"Want me to pull up your race for assessor?" the volunteer asked as she fiddled with the computer.

"Yes," I responded with a hesitant whisper. The worried buzzing, churning sounds of the crowd, the violinist playing—all echoed, making it difficult to be heard. It didn't look good for Georgene's supporters; she was running for a seat on the county board of supervisors.

"Georgene may lose in her race. She worked so hard," I said to my sister while I waited for my own campaign tabulations to display on the large monitor. My hands were clammy, mixed emotions swirled. I felt disappointment at the possible loss for my friend, excitement with my own likely win. The results finally displayed. "Was that right—did I win?" My husband, Bob, grabbed my sweaty hand and squeezed. My sister, Bev, grinned.

"We did it!" Bev shouted.

The results indicated a win for me, a landslide victory! I ducked into the hallway, barely noticing Matt, a local photographer for the newspaper, who followed. My fingers trembled, making it difficult to dial my mother's telephone number.

"I won," I told her, my voice husky. I smiled and tried not to jump up and down with excitement. Matt took photos.

We were in northern Arizona high country, a small city called Prescott.

Returning to the lobby, I could see the election results for the board of supervisor's race refreshed on the screen. The monitor indicated an even larger spread between Georgene and her opponent Carol Springer.

My sister draped her arm around me. "I think it's a loss for Georgene."

"I'm sort of embarrassed," I said.

"You should be. You'll end up stealing her victory party," Bev laughed.

There were no tables or chairs in the room. The crowd stood huddled around the large monitor. Each person focused on election results that flashed every few minutes. The chances for Georgene's win grew slimmer with each refresh. The volunteers stood in silence.

I navigated through the crowd until I reached a pyramid of long stemmed crystal glasses stacked on a white linen tablecloth. My throat felt scratchy. Most of the time I forgot I had paralyzed vocal cords, but pain reminded me. My larynx ached from all the recent speeches. I deserved this win; I had abused my voice for months.

I filled a glass with tea, and the ice cubes rattled as I dropped each in. The drink was cold and soothed the pain. I smiled at the violinist playing in the corner and maneuvered my way back to Bev. My feet were tired, months of high heels and door knocking can do that.

I took an ice cube from the glass and rubbed it on my throat. It felt hot. The right vocal cord twitched, letting me know there was still a little life in it—not much, but a little.

"I was sure Georgene would win. I can't believe this," I whispered to Bev.

"Whatever. Let's enjoy your victory and worry about Georgene's loss another time," she said with a grin.

Georgene came up to us and hugged me, her face drawn and tired. She was ten years older than I, but tonight she looked much older.

"I'm sorry," I said, my arms hugging her back.

"At least one of us did it." She held back tears of disappointment. "I had a speech and a song, but I just can't. I really thought I'd win. I'm going to leave, but things are paid for. You stay and get my money's worth."

"Awkward," Bev whispered to me with a teasing smile as Georgene left.

One by one Georgene's supporters filed out, each offering me polite congratulations for my victory as the new Yavapai County Assessor. Beverly was not at all interested in letting Georgene's defeat get in the way of our exuberance. We had worked hard, and now was our time to savor our victory.

"Let's sit down," I said to Bev as I removed my high heels and walked around in my nylons.

Exploring the property, we found some tables on the side of the building's patio. The cold air smelled of decaying leaves and wood smoke. Sitting, at last. Laughter, joy and love filled the rest of the evening. My sister and I had won. Together we knew we'd always win anything we took on. This was our secret superpower.

"We did so much right," Bev said. I nodded, looking forward to taking over as the assessor and valuing the whole county. But at that point, I had no clue what I was in for and how I'd be facing the challenge of my life—corruption in our Yavapai County government. I'd need my superpowers, big time.

"Georgene's team did everything right too, yet lost," I said, sipping the iced tea.

"Well, some of our win is due to luck, some the scandals the current assessor was mired in, and of course your vast beauty and charisma—but most of all my boob," Bev said, referring to her breast cancer.

I sighed. "All true, especially the vast beauty and charisma part." I looked at Bev: bright green eyes, hair extremely short but growing back after the chemo treatments, her body lovely and perfect. I was glad she'd chosen a lumpectomy rather than a mastectomy. I looked very much like her except she was a natural blonde—my blonde came from a bottle. It was hard to tell us apart with only eighteen months between us.

Here is a photo of me: Pam Pearsall—happy, because I won the election for Yavapai County Assessor. At the time I believed winning the election was a good thing. If I'd known what would happen during the next eight years—I'd have looked much different. Imagine the photo with me rolled up in the corner rocking myself back and forth in fear—plus tears, lots of tears, running down my Tammy Faye Bakker mascara face. That should have been the photo.

Hinshaw, Matt. *The Daily Courier.* 3 Sept. 2008.

This photo appeared on the front page above the fold of the local paper, with the following caption:

"Pam Pearsall, the unofficial winner in the Republican primary for county assessor, ducks into a back room of the Hassayampa Inn and screams joyfully into her cell phone after seeing the first round of election results Tuesday night."

#

We dismantled my living room—six metal desks, computers, and chaos—as we shut down my home appraisal office. The appraisers who worked for me packed up, moving their workload into their own homes. We would miss each other; after we'd worked for years together, it felt like we were extended family.

Scott, my best friend, and current business partner, brought his daughter Constance over to visit and help him finish packing his desk.

"Let's take a break and go into my family room," I suggested to Scott and Constance.

"You take office January 1st?" Constance asked.

She's growing up so fast, I thought to myself, *twelve years old. It seems like yesterday she was learning to walk. Wow, had it been twelve years since Bev had asked me to help with food at the funeral for Scott's wife?* That was the day I met Scott and his baby girl Constance.

"Yep, I won in the primary election. No one is running in the general election. Waiting is hard; it's like you're chomping at the bit to get started," I said looking at her pale blue eyes. "Can I French braid your hair?" I asked on impulse. I loved braiding Constance's hair, but she wasn't always in the mood to let me.

Constance nodded and sat at my feet on the carpeted floor. I grabbed the brush from my purse and started. She felt like a niece to me. She was an easy-going, happy child. She'd traipsed around with Scott and me on so many appraisal jobs, rode in the truck, or played as we typed up reports.

Scott, wrapped into a large flannel plaid shirt, chuckled, "Pam has gone to the dark side, Constance. Pam is the tax man now."

"Just refer to me as the MAN," I said. "Scott, come to work for me, be my chief deputy. It's good enough money, and you will be home nights and weekends. It would be good for Constance," I said as I twisted her blonde hair into a tight braid.

"No way!" Scott said "I hate the government, I hate taxes, and I hate appraising, too, but I can do that for a few more years. Then

I'll do the Reiki thing."

I'd heard it all before but hoped he would change his mind.

"Pam, you can always call with questions. I don't have to work for you. We can do it as a contract or consulting, or something," he added, probably sensing how insecure I felt about doing the job without his guidance.

I nodded and felt like crying. What had I been thinking? I'd now be giving up my appraisal company and moving into a government job, a politician with this absurd voice. I couldn't do it without Scott and without a voice. I'd hoped Scott would change his mind and come along with me. "Okay," I said with a sigh. "I'll call you with questions if I'm not sure about something."

Scott picked through a box on the coffee table. The box held paperwork for his latest appraisal orders. I wondered if he'd ever re-marry. He claimed he wouldn't, but I knew he got a lot of attention. He typically wore a baseball or cowboy hat to cover his slightly balding, brown wavy head of hair, but when he went country western dancing, the ladies lined up to dance with him. They were attracted to his broad shoulders and large hands and such amazing blue eyes. Mine were pale blue, but Constance's and Scott's were neon blue.

"Can you and Constance come for Christmas?" I asked, afraid I'd start to cry if I didn't change the subject.

"Christmas afternoon, after we're done with Grandma," Scott said with a smile.

"Any time after two o'clock works for me." I loved Scott as much as my own brother. It wouldn't be a nice Christmas if he couldn't be there.

#

Christmas morning, tiptoeing down the stairs, I smelled eggnog and cinnamon. *Ashley must have started breakfast,* I thought. I was heading to the kitchen but was distracted by the twinkling lights of the tree. As I gazed at the tinsel, the shiny ornaments reflected the colors of the lights. *What a pretty sight,* I thought, trying to ignore my queasiness.

Sweeping aside Christmas memories that only my sister and I shared, I vowed that this Christmas would be nice and tried to ignore the flashes of fear that simple smells and familiar scenes caused. *I love Christmas,* I thought and smiled, pretending it was true. Warmth filled my chest. I grabbed the back of a chair to keep from falling on the way to the bathroom. Then my stomach lurched. I controlled my desire to run and walked normally towards the bathroom not wanting any undue attention or concern from my husband or daughter.

I shut the bathroom door, bent over the toilet and my stomach contracted several times. Fortunately, I'd not eaten, so no mess to clean up. *Think nice thoughts, Pam. Count your blessings, Pam,* I counseled myself. I sat on the floor, my head against the cool porcelain toilet—it felt good. *Life is full, I'm blessed with kids, husband, Mom, sister . . .* My body cooled. I began to feel better.

Leaving the bathroom, I returned to the kitchen to prepare a feast for my family. *No one will notice—because of my fantastic acting abilities,* I said to myself. My kitchen was modern, bright and cheery: gray granite counter tops, oak cabinets and polished silver appliances, all items purchased with the inheritance I received from the death of my biological father, Gil Sieling.

I tried to push back the memories, force them down—forget about Gil Sieling. *Christmastime, ugh. Concentrate on today,* I told myself. My mind refused and shifted back to where I didn't want it to go: the Christmas season of 1966.

#

December 24th, 1966

It was bedtime, but Bevy was playing with her doll on the little rug that lay on a polished concrete bedroom floor. "Be quiet, Santa Claus won't come if he thinks we're awake," I said to her in my wise five-year-old voice.Bevy, my three-year-old little sister with curly blonde hair, said nothing. She decided to be obedient and climbed into my bed. She snuggled with her doll, pretending to go to sleep. She often assumed she could sleep in my bed with me.

Over the noise of the rain hitting the windows was the sound of my parents' muffled arguing. *Bevy might be scared,* I thought, and let her stay in my bed. She sometimes kicked and sprawled all over the bed leaving me little room. If that happened tonight, I could always move to the other side of the bedroom and sleep in her bed.

Will Santa come if they keep fighting like that? I wondered. My mom should settle down. Dad would probably go to sleep if she left him alone. Despite the noise of their arguing, I managed to fall asleep.

Suddenly light flooded our bedroom, waking Bevy and me. "The world is ending! Armageddon is here! You need to be baptized!" My dad was screaming. His blonde hair hung uncombed, his blue eyes alert and bright.

I was confused. I knew Santa was coming, but Dad said the world was ending. I couldn't believe him.

"I'm sorry, I'm sorry," Dad said, scooping me up from my warm bed in his muscular arms. He carried me outside through the rain. I wiggled and squirmed, trying to get out of his grasp. He didn't let go until he deposited me into the backseat of the car. He left, and I knew better than to leave the vehicle.

Dad soon returned with my sister and placed her next to me in the back seat. Bevy cried; I pulled her close to me and put my arms around her shoulders. I patted and tried to soothe her. The whole thing seemed weird. We'd never been taken from the house after being told to go to sleep. It might be some kind of Christmas test about the naughty and nice list. Maybe he would come right back and say we did well and let us go back to bed. I didn't know what to expect.

Dad slipped into the driver's side of the front seat and started the car, "Armageddon is coming, girls. That means fire will bring the end of the world, but I will save you! That's where we're going, somewhere safe," he said evenly. I heard thunder in the background.

My mother carried my baby brother and got into the front seat.

She had not heard what Dad said, so I filled her in. "Mom,

Dad said no Santa tonight. Instead, there is arms-a-getting. I don't want arms-a-getting! I want to go to sleep and wait for Santa. I'm cold!" I whimpered. "Santa won't come if we aren't home."

There was a smell of stale cigarettes from previous road trips. Now new smoke filled the car as Mom lit a cigarette. "It's okay, Santa will come. Let's go on an adventure with Dad first. Then we'll come home in time for Christmas." Mom spoke in a high-pitched whisper like I should be excited about something fun. I sensed I should not argue and thought about the scuffle I'd heard outside my bedroom door. I'd never seen Dad hit Mom, but I'd heard the smacks and seen the bruises. Even at five years old, I knew Mom didn't have the power to stop this road trip. I looked out the window as the car left our driveway and pulled onto the road. Cascading raindrops pelted the windows. Past the raindrops was a blur of distant lights.

"Please—where are we going? It's time to head back home," Mom said after what seemed like forever riding in the car. I could no longer see any blurred lights. The raindrops had long since turned into snow. Our father did not respond, he continued to drive towards Camp Verde.

It took a couple of hours to drive from our home in Paradise Valley to the Verde River. Once we arrived, Dad pulled off the main road, drove a little bit more, finally pulled the car over. He got out and left. After a few minutes of sitting in the car without him I became increasingly curious as to what he was doing or what he'd do next. I finally asked Mom if I could go check on him. She nodded. I got out of the car and followed the footsteps he'd left in the snow. I found him at the riverbank. A blanket of ice lay over the stream. The snow had stopped falling. I saw Dad chipping the ice from the creek. He made an opening that exposed the water. I sat on the bank of the river, shivered, and watched him get into the water and dip out of my sight. It was baptism!

I ran to my mother and sister. "Please, it's cold—I don't want to get baptized," I said, as I reached the open car door.

Mom cried in the front seat. She held my baby brother in her arms and, still weeping, softly talked to my sister in the back seat.

"I not get baptized," my sister said, trying to copy me as she often did. The moon cast some light through the veil of clouds. I could barely see Bevy as she shivered in the back seat, her teeth chattering. I noticed a blanket back there, but she must have forgotten about it as she shook with fear.

"It's just going to be a few drops of water on your head—it won't hurt," Mom said.

The moon now peaked through the clouds, and I could see more clearly. We seemed like outsiders in this calm, still, snow-covered forest, the stream not making a sound. Wild emotions jolted up my spine threatening to overcome me. I fought back my tears. *Don't let Bevy know you're scared.* I shuddered at the thought of being drenched in water. My feet, soaked in wet slippers, hurt with pricks and sparks of pain. Fear churned in the pit of my stomach.

"No! Baptism is getting soaked!" I cried. "I saw Dad swim when he baptized himself!" As if to prove my point, Dad walked up to the car, his clothes wet and sticking to his skin.

"I have been re-born!" Dad said with a huge smile, the moonlight through the shadows of the clouds dancing on him. I moved closer to my mother; she might protect me.

"Gil, you can baptize them by sprinkling a few drops of water on their heads. You can't dip them in the water, they'll get sick," Mom said.

The moonlight and clouds continued to make strange shadows dancing all around. "I'm not Gil, I'm Jesus," my dad said. At that moment thunder clapped—Dad grinned.

"No! You're not Jesus! Jesus didn't have kids or a wife," Mom said. I could see her hands tremble as she lit another cigarette.

"Okay, but I'm someone important! I'm John the Baptist!" Again thunder echoed as if in applause to Dad's statement. He seemed encouraged. It frightened me how the weather supported Dad's claims. He wasn't my dad—he was John? I didn't know what to make of his statement, but I did know I didn't want to get wet.

I wondered if Mom would be able to talk him out of dunking my sister and me. By the way she was holding onto my brother, I was sure that Mom would not allow the baby to be taken out of the car. Seeing my mom holding onto my brother so tightly gave me a little hope. She might do something to prevent him from dunking Bevy and me in the water.

"Whatever, John the Baptist," Mom said. "You can baptize just as well by sprinkling a couple of drops of water on someone as you can by submerging them in water. You can baptize these kids with just a few drops of water—or not at all!" She looked determined. The cigarette appeared to give her strength, or maybe she was just sick of him. At the same time, I was glad to see her stand up to him. I was afraid for her, though; in this mood I didn't know what he would do next. He might hit her.

"Please, I don't want to—I'm cold," I said, my teeth chattering so hard I thought they might break. I only had a nightie and slippers on. The snow had soaked through my slippers, and my nose was burning from the cold air.

Dad looked around, turning his head from side to side. He went to the driver's side of the car, opened the door, reached in and grabbed an empty beer can that he found on the floorboard. With that, he left us in the car and headed towards the stream.

"It will just be a drop or two of water, it won't hurt," Mom said as we waited for our dad to return. She had no idea that my baby brother and I would both develop pneumonia from this night.

"I'm not gonna be baptized," Bevy said in a stubborn voice.

I didn't want Santa Claus to get mad because Bevy wasn't being good, so I smiled at my sister and said, "It won't hurt, it is just a drop or two of water, then we go home." I tried to use the excited voice Mom had used earlier to pretend I thought it would be fun. Bevy didn't look convinced but didn't say anything more.

Dad returned to the car. "Pammy, stand still," he said. Then he tilted the beer can over my head and drizzled some of the liquid on my scalp. I let it run down my forehead and didn't wipe at it. I smiled in my sister's direction to show her it didn't hurt and wasn't a big deal.

Dad then did the same actions for my sister, my brother, and finally my mother.

We rode home. The baby cried off and on, breaking the silence. I took my wet slippers off. Together my sister and I cuddled in the blanket, trying to create more body heat. We still shivered, and our teeth chattered, but cuddling helped. It took time, after we got home and were placed in warm beds, to lose the chill and feel warm again.

The next morning company arrived, and to my surprise, Santa had come to our home in Paradise Valley during the night, and the world had not ended as promised. Gifts were opened, food eaten. I played with my sister and cousins. We dragged our new wagon up the hill, piled in, and zipped back down the hill. Up and down the hill in the wagon all day. I had a cough, probably due to the outing the night before. Even so, I enjoyed the company of my cousins, aunts, uncles and grandparents. It was a typical Christmas day as Christmases go—except something seemed strange about my dad, something I couldn't explain or even understand. He seemed very sad.

Bevy and I prepared for bed. We were tired from the festivities of the last few days. We snuggled into our new flannel nighties we'd received the previous day from Grandpa and Grandma. It seemed only minutes had passed when we heard the skirmish begin. *Not again!* I yearned for sleep, wanted quiet, and was frustrated and scared by the noise coming from my parents in the hallway outside our bedroom door.

Bevy got out of bed. "No Bevy, get in bed. Be quiet," I whispered. I picked her up and tried to put her in bed with me. She squirmed out of my bed and left our room. I worried she would get in trouble for leaving our bedroom when we were supposed to go to sleep. So I followed. But before I could catch up to her, we found Mom pinned to the wall by Dad. His hands were around Mom's throat, and her face looked purple, her eyes bulging. Dad, distracted by our presence, turned his head in our direction. I was horrified. Mom looked like a gruesome cartoon character. I was so afraid. My tongue grew so large in my mouth, and I was unable to form a syllable, let alone a word. I wanted to demand that Dad stop right now and be good. I wanted to tell him he had been bad and needed to go to bed, get some sleep. Instead, I stood petrified for what seemed like an eternity. I said nothing.

"I—I'm thirsty," Bevy said. At that moment Mom took her right leg, pulled it up quickly, and connected her knee to Dad's crotch. He let go of her neck and grabbed his groin. He fell to the floor.

"Go back to bed!" Dad shouted as he lay on the floor. Mom ran in the opposite direction. I heard the thud of the front door as she left. I grabbed Bevy's hand and ran with her back to our bedroom. The light was still off, and I pulled Bevy into my bed. We sat huddled together and said nothing. Then I had a coughing spell. I'd grown increasingly ill throughout the day, and as dark approached my coughing increased. I could hear my brother in the other bedroom coughing as well.

I'd later learn Mom had run next door. The neighbors insisted she wait at their house for the sheriff to arrive. They thought this was just a marital spat.

The deputy called for backup; he didn't want to respond to the call by himself, because domestic spats can be the most dangerous of calls. It was the Christmas season, assistance was in short supply.

Help for my mother finally arrived. Not in time to prevent what happened, but in time to respond to it.

Wedding Photo of My Parents:
Gilbert and Judith Sieling, 1959

#

2008

Ashley, my youngest daughter, entered the kitchen with her older sister Heather. "Oh, the house is so beautiful. I love the garlands wrapped around the staircase and all the candles," Ashley said. "Mom, you always do such a great job at Christmas. None of my friends' parents go all out like you do." Heather agreed.

"I love Christmas," I said with a smile, knowing I was fibbing. At Christmas time I tried to turn my home into the kind of place where people would want to enjoy the holidays. With great effort, I could enjoy the day with them.

"I love Christmas, too," said my twenty-two-year-old daughter Heather, and she kissed me on the cheek.

Later the family gathered around the tree, and we began the tradition of unwrapping gifts. I opened a large package which contained a "Rosie the Riveter" framed poster. This had been my leadership symbol for the campaign race. Rosie reminded me of my sister during her cancer treatments because both wore bandannas. The caption "We Can Do It," scrolled on the poster, was a vow Bev and I made: she would beat cancer—I would win the election. We had put Rosie's image on all our campaign literature.

I gave Ashley a wink and said, "I'll hang this in my office."

The next gift I opened was from my husband, another framed poster. This one of a person walking on a rope bridge. The bottom of the poster read *The Courage of Integrity, the highest courage is to dare to be yourself in the face of adversity. Choosing right over wrong, ethics over convenience, and truth over popularity . . . These are the choices that measure your life. Travel the path of integrity without looking back. For there is never a wrong time to do the right thing.* "I will hang this in my new office, too," I said, jumping up and giving my husband Bob a hug.

My big family and several friends, including Scott and Constance, had come for Christmas dinner. We'd enjoyed each other's company. After we said our goodbyes, the excitement of the day was over. The house smelled like pine needles. The fireplace felt warm and cozy. I got a lozenge out of my purse and hung it at the end of the stairwell on the last post. The stairway looked so cheery wrapped in Christmas garlands with little lights, and red ribbon spun throughout.

I went to the couch and sat down. Bob smiled, asked how I'd thought Christmas went. I said I loved it, it was perfect "I just love Christmas time," I answered. He turned his focus on the television and continued to watch the Christmas movie. I loved Christmas movies, that part was true, but tonight I couldn't concentrate or follow the story-line. My own Christmas story, the one I wanted to forget, kept rushing to the surface of my memory—despite my attempt to shove it back into the recesses of my mind.

#

Just my luck, a complaint the first week. I hung up the phone with the Arizona Department of Revenue. Someone had complained to them that the Yavapai County Assessor's Office was giving favors to grazing properties. The department realized I was a brand new assessor and suggested I look into the issue. If the complaint were valid, I'd need to address the problem and fix it.

This was an important issue. If the ranchers received favors, as the complaint alleged, it unlawfully shifted their property taxes from them to everyone else. It meant the other taxpayers had paid more than they needed. The whole purpose of an assessor was to assure the tax burden was spread fairly. No one should pay more than they legally were responsible for. So if this complaint had merit, it would be bad, really bad.

"Are these the agricultural files?" I asked Kiarra as I pointed at the oversized two-door metal filing cabinet. Even with the drawers closed, I could see papers poking out of it.

Kiarra, a frumpy middle-aged woman, stared directly at me but did not acknowledge or respond to my question. I slid the top drawer open. Kiarra stood up from her desk and hurried to the cabinet, her gray head bumping the metal shelf in her cubicle. "What do you need?" she asked, attempting to close the drawer I had just opened.

I raised my eyebrows, looked at Kiarra and tried to figure

out what her deal was. I held the drawer in my grasp tightly so it couldn't be closed. "Are these the agricultural files?" I repeated evenly.

"Yes," she responded, "I can get you whatever file you're looking for."

"No, I'm all right." I looked at the open drawer, a disheveled mess. Files were shoved tightly every which way, papers jutting out. I pulled three random files, shut the drawer and headed back to my office.

I had barely sat at my desk when Kiarra showed up in my doorway. "I'm the agricultural appraiser," she said. I nodded my head. "If you need anything, ask me, but don't ever go into the files directly . . . I'm—" she paused and awkwardly laughed. "I'm protective of my files and don't want anyone in them."

I looked at her. "Um, hmm—well, there are some concerns, and I'll be going directly into the agricultural files to do some research. We can discuss the department, your files, and my concerns once I'm finished with the research," I said clearly and slowly. Kiarra scowled at me, stared for several minutes, acting as if she had more to say. I ignored her as she continued to stand in my doorway. I opened one of the files and began reading and turning the pages I found in it. Kiarra finally walked away.

The file contained a mishmash of documents. There was no organization to the papers. Partial leases, documents dated over thirty years ago. I tried to cross reference the parcel numbers with the assessor's database but, to my horror, I discovered that many of the parcels no longer existed. It seemed this file had not been updated or looked at for over thirty years. My heart felt squeezed as if there were a Charlie horse in my chest. On the campaign trail I'd heard gossip of favors and laws broken by the past assessor, but I'd not believed most of the rumors. The next two files were in a similar shape. *Seems like at least this complaint is legitimate*, I thought.

I got up from my seat, walked to the rear of the office, and before I could get back to the agricultural filing cabinet, Kiarra's supervisor Betty greeted me. "Kiarra really is protective over her files and doesn't allow anyone but her in them," Betty said in a hushed tone.

"Kiarra is really going to be outside of her comfort zone the next few weeks then," I said. I walked around Betty and pulled the agricultural file drawer open.

Again Kiarra rushed to the cabinet and this time managed to push the door shut. "I'm responsible for these files and can't allow anyone in them," she said, standing next to her supervisor and holding the filing cabinet drawer closed. Betty stood beside Kiarra in an act of solidarity, her arms folded across her chest.

"Duly noted," I said, and retreated to my office.

No respect, I thought. I was comfortable with that. Respect from the staff was something I could achieve. I understood that I'd basically overthrown the office, won the election and ousted their leader. It would take time for them to learn to trust and rely on my leadership. *New assessor, old staff, loyalties, egos. I get it,*

I was a General Certified Appraiser, licensed to appraise anything from vacant lots to high rises. My licenses, designations, and experience exceeded Kiarra's—or her supervisor's—or anyone in the assessor's office for that matter. With this election, I had the responsibility to take on any agricultural issues I might find. I knew the staff would learn to respect me. They would help me to run an excellent assessor's office. It had to be soon because I needed them. I couldn't do this without them.

"Can you lead a project and help me do a lease-study? I need guidance to create policies in the assessor's office that helps curtail sham agricultural operations from receiving tax benefits they don't deserve," I said to Scott, my old business partner, and friend.

I knew I was appealing to Scott's sense of fair play. He hated the government's giving favors to some on the backs of others. Actually, he hated the government in general but especially the inequity in taxes. With Scott's help, I would get the agricultural problem resolved. My cheeks flushed as I thought of thirty years of neglect! My first week in office as the assessor, and I had a project.

"Sure. I need leases for the properties you want to be studied," Scott said. "I could throw them on a spreadsheet and analyze them. We could go over your existing policies, and I could help you tweak them. But you don't need me. You just want a crutch."

It was wonderful to hear Scott agree to help me. He'd grown up on a ranch he'd inherited when his parents died, so he knew ranches. Scott and I appraised them together, but I'd never appraised one by myself. I knew he was right; a lease-study was an easy task, and I could figure out the policies. But I wanted Scott around. I wasn't ready to be on my own.

I called the Arizona Department of Revenue and admitted their complaint had merit. Values hadn't been updated for about thirty years. These property owners had been given tax breaks not legally deserved, and their taxes had been shifted to others. The law was clear these properties were supposed to be inspected once every four years and the values were to be updated annually. We clearly hadn't been doing that in Yavapai County. I promised to act on what was discovered and asked if they could do a lease-study for the entire state. This would aid us in our update for grazing values. They agreed.

I smiled and leaned back in my chair. I admired my office, especially the framed poster of Rosie the Riveter I received from Ashley. It hung on the wall in front of me. The other poster, with the integrity quote, hung on the wall behind me. I looked at Rosie the Riveter—red bandanna with white polka dots, her arm raised up flexing her non-existent muscles, the caption "We Can Do It!" I knew I couldn't protect my community from cancer, mental illness, alcoholism or anything like that, but I could prevent an unfair assessor's office—and I would! I was glad to discover a problem I could fix. I was going to make a difference. That felt good.

If I'd seen the future, I would have been filled with dread, but I was naive. I believed public servants upheld their sworn oath of office. I never considered any of the elected officials I knew would breach the trust citizens had in them. I'd learn.

#

I love math. Math doesn't talk back, math is what it is; you're right, or you're wrong. Close isn't good enough. So it was funny to me to discover the *three—four* issue. I wanted so badly to tell my sister or husband. But it was complicated. How would I explain it, in a way that they could see the humor?

We sat in my office, I was behind my desk and four employees in green fabric-cushioned chairs sat in front of me. They looked at me blank-faced when I explained their problems in a straightforward, simple way, but they didn't get it. They had to understand, but they didn't. This made me want to giggle, but I held a straight face. Scott was the only one who'd get the silliness of the situation. He'd have to be the one I laughed with when I told, although I assumed he'd find it more ridiculous than funny.

I shut the door to my office and made the call "They rate everything from a one to a seven, based on the quality of construction," I said, once he finally answered the phone. Now I leaned back in my chair, gazing out my window into the parking lot where I saw the green hedge just outside my window and cars in neat little rows.

"Hello to you, too," Scott said with a laugh.

"Yep, so guess what?" I said, wanting to give him the punchline before I got interrupted with work.

"What?"

"The houses rated at threes or average are coming in at a higher value than those rated at fours in several market areas!" I giggled. "The staff doesn't understand why this is happening." I burst out laughing because it was such an obvious mistake.

"Let me get this straight. Your office rates structures on a scale of one through seven. Seven being the highest quality of construction and one being the least quality—and your computer system is spitting out higher values for lower quality buildings than it is for higher quality buildings. Is that what you're telling me?" He didn't sound amused.

I just laughed. Scott got it.

"That is ridiculous!"

This made me laugh even harder because I knew he'd react like that. It was the silliest mistake I'd seen so far since I'd taken over the office.

"Yep, I took office in January, but the assessor before me—Victor Hambrick—his values were mailed out in February because it takes so long to do them. Then they get approved by the Department of Revenue. After I took office, we mailed his notices out. My values will be mailed out next year after I have time to work on them and get them ready. These values we just mailed out have my name on the Notice of Value, but Victor actually was the one who—"

"So, on the notices, you recently mailed out, homes rated three are valued higher than those rated four. You have some appeals, and that's how you discovered the issue?"

"Yep, I'm looking at an appeal, and then I ask Kiarra, an appraiser that works for me, to explain what I'm seeing. She says, 'It's because it's rated a three and their neighbor, who's value was less, was rated a four.' I asked her a couple of times if she didn't see a problem with a poorer quality home coming in at a higher value. She didn't seem to understand my question. So I said, 'Okay, if you have two houses in the same neighborhood exactly the same, except one has granite counter tops, wooden floors, and the other one has Formica counter tops and carpeted floors, wouldn't you think a buyer would pay more money for the granite counter tops and wooden floors? Would you think it would cost more money to build the higher quality home?' She agreed, but then told me the computer is the one that got the values messed up."

"Seriously, she thought it was the computer? Like, no clue that garbage data in, garbage data out?" he asked.

"Correct, Scott. It must be right because the computer said so. These really are great employees that want to do things right; they just didn't understand."

"So how are you going to train them? If they incorrectly rate a home a three, when the house should actually be rated a four, they're screwing up the mathematical model, and they're screwing over all the property owners of homes that are legitimately threes!" he said, sounding both exasperated and pissed off.

"I'll require they all take some more classes, and we'll do

some quality of construction audits—plus I'd like to move to ratio studies by market area and make their staff evaluations and raises linked to correct data input. What I thought was amazing is they didn't understand the problem was with their rankings! Even an appraiser trainee should realize that. Also, when I tried to explain it, I was told they were doing the above average houses a favor by rating them a three or just average and thus coming in at a lower value for them!" I sucked in the air waiting for Scott's explosion.

"I think you're going to find a lot of similar things. The government doesn't pay enough to get truly qualified appraisers, and they typically promote from within so even your higher ranking employees don't know what they don't know. It's a good thing you got the job." He paused and took a breath. "As a General Certified Appraiser you're going to catch this stuff, and you'll be able to clean it up. They just don't understand. Math is math. If your staff does favors, it screws up the whole mathematical model. Ugh, it pisses me off that they think their job is anything but appraising—objective, independent, and ethical. I'm sure you'll teach them that."

Wow, a compliment from Scott about working for the government. Was hell freezing over, or what? We finished our conversation, and I invited Scott over for my birthday dinner. I needed to get back to my important job, and Scott could go slough off—I assumed that's what he was doing now that I wasn't there to crack the whip.

Hell freezing over, I thought and grinned, *is there really a hell?* I knew that life could be tough and perhaps that's hell. It was as close as I'd ever want to get. I thought of the time I lived through my own hell. I pushed the thoughts out of my mind. I had work to do, and I wasn't in the mood to think of hell or living through hellish events. Helping my staff learn to run the best assessor's office, that's what I needed to do.

#

I stood by our office manager Marion's desk, looking at her computer screen as she explained building permits workflow processes to me. Suddenly, Cherry, an appraiser, interrupted us and announced the county uniform shirts were too thin.

"Too thin?" I asked. *They're standard cotton blend polyester material; you just don't want to wear uniforms,* I thought. "Uniforms are here to stay, for both professional and safety reasons."

A month earlier a call had come in from an elderly woman who complained that a man had stopped by and wanted to see her house. He had no uniform on, so she asked for his ID. The name on his identification badge had been covered up with whiteout. When I looked into this complaint, I discovered that several appraisers believed they had a right to not reveal their names to the public—some kind of government secret identity right. Many had used whiteout to erase their entire names; others had covered their last names, and finally some had scratched their names out.

I made it clear to my staff that their names had to be displayed on their badges. Several employees then went upstairs to human resources, inquired about their rights, and were stunned to learn I was correct. No secret identity rights existed for them. This was not the FBI; it was the assessor's office. I blame these misunderstandings on television and the fact that we don't pay well. We hire entry level employees and then promote from within; out of sixty employees, fifty-five excelled, but five employees were ridiculously inept, with entitlement issues and a lack of work ethic. It must be said, too, that firing government employees is difficult!

Subsequently, I ordered collared three-button shirts with the county seal embroidered on them and required that the appraisers wear these and have name tag identifications on lanyards while in the field. Now property owners could see a car with a county logo on it, a person with a county shirt on, and view identification whenever someone from the assessor's office approached them. Seemed like common sense to me. But I received a lot of pushback from the appraisers.

"The shirts are too thin, Addie's wearing one today and it is showing her . . . everything!" Cherry said with a grin. She reminded me of some mean girl in school tattling on a friend and thrilled to do it.

"The shirt is too thin?" I said. *Why didn't she just put an undershirt on if the shirt is too revealing?* I wondered. "Is she showing her chichi?" I asked and laughed because in my vocabulary *chichi* means style; maybe not wearing an undershirt was Addie's style. I realized, too, that *chichi* can also be slang for breasts, which actually fit in the conversation quite well.

I walked over to Addie to see what Cherry was talking about. I should have told Marion and Cherry to stay where they were, but I didn't; they followed me to watch my response to the thin shirt and the chichi report. Addie looked up at me when I approached her cubicle. I didn't think the shirt looked revealing—it was a shirt, a regular uniform shirt, not transparent. In the office light, it looked fine.

"See, you can see right through it!" Cherry said in a high pitched voice that could probably be heard throughout the office.

Quiet down, Scary Cherry, I thought, pursing my lips. (I'd call her *Scary Cherry* when I talked to Bev later, a name that meant someone you don't want as your enemy—the gossip queen.)

"Shush," I said, feeling sorry for Addie. Mostly I was irritated with myself for the whole situation. We were standing at Addie's cubicle staring at her as if she were our birthday cake. The entire office staff was now looking in our direction. It was bad enough that I hadn't handled it discretely; now it was a major deal, and I knew it would be the topic of the day. "Her shirt is okay," I said and stomped back to my office, embarrassed at my poor leadership.

About an hour later, Marion peeked into my office. "I need to talk to you," she said, and walked in and shut the door. "Addie's upset with what happened this morning and wants to go home for the day." Marion was an elderly grandma type, sweet and kind.

"Tell her she can go home or come in and talk with me."

"Oh no, she wants to file a complaint with human resources, or Betty wants to."

"Betty? Why Betty?" I asked, wondering why a supervisor—not Addie's or Scary Cherry's supervisor—would think she was supposed to file a human resources complaint.

"Well, Addie's afraid to submit one and Betty cares," Marion said, her teeth clenched and hands on her hips like a scolding mother.

"Let Addie know she can go home or walk upstairs to human resources," I said, feeling defensive. "Betty needs to focus on her own job. She isn't Cherry or Addie's supervisor, so she needs to get back to work." *Betty hadn't even been there to witness it, so how could she report the incident?*

I decided to start a one percenters club in my mind—the one percenters of the office that played, complained, failed to focus on their own job, told others how they should be doing their jobs better, and basically were trouble-makers. Scary Cherry and Betty both made the list that day. So much of my time was taken up with interpersonal office relationships, and I was tired of it. It not only took my time but that of my staff.

Addie left the office and went home crying. Betty stopped in a couple of times to let me know how upset she was with the incident. I decided I'd give Scary Cherry a verbal warning on how she conducts herself in the office and I'd follow-up to assure there were no more false accusations or bullying—because that's what it felt like to me: Scary Cherry was bullying Addie.

Then I looked up from my office to see Regina Ani from human resources. *Damn! I'm not going to get anything done today,* I thought and smiled up at her, trying to appear composed. I motioned for her to come in. She did and closed the door.

Regina was about my age and loved to cook. She was Hispanic and was easy to talk to. She got right to the point and said "Did you say you wanted to see someone's *chichi* today? Or that Addie is trying to show us her *chichi*?"

I shook my head, denying it, but she got the quote pretty much correct. I could tell from Regina's body language—her folded arms and serious voice—that if I'd admitted it, it would be bad. "No, I didn't say that. There was an accusation that Addie came to work today wearing her uniform shirt and that it was too thin and therefore revealing; so I said, 'Let's go take a look.'" *I wish I'd said that. It would have been actually professional. I suck. I wonder what chichi means in Spanish?* I watched Regina to determine if she believed me.

Regina didn't seem to believe me, but I don't think she wanted to call the elected assessor a liar. "If you'd said you wanted to see her chichi that could be considered sexual harassment," she said.

In fact, I didn't say I wanted to *see* Addie's chichi, I asked if she was *showing* her chichi. But I wasn't about to admit anything. It sounded more and more like chichi meant breasts. Addie hadn't shown chichi, nor had I asked to see any; so I was clear no harassment had occurred. I was, however, embarrassed that I'd let the incident go so far and that I'd allowed Addie to be bullied—if that is what this was. My job could suck some days, and this day was one of those sucky days.

The next day I called Addie in and apologized. I let her know that I felt Cherry had acted sophomorically. Addie vented about a few of the appraisers and told me they ganged up on her. That sounded like grade school to me, and I wondered if it was because this was such a large office or if it was this particular group of people. I wouldn't tolerate bullying, and I'd have to figure out how to watch for it and not allow it. I didn't want to be like some grade school teachers I'd seen who clearly should have noticed bullying but pretended not to, or even on some level encouraged it.

#

December 26th, 1966

My dad barged into our room, flipped the light on. "I don't want to, please," he said. His bright blue eyes sparkled, his blonde hair messy. My sister and I sat on my bed and looked at each other. My five-year-old mind was confused. *Was he speaking to us? What didn't he want to do?* Bevy got off my bed, ran away and hid in the closet—maybe remembering a few nights ago and the road trip to baptism. It was easy to see her in the closet, so she was not fooling anyone, though she must have thought she was hidden. I continued to sit on my bed. Dad looked at me and screamed, "I don't want to! You can't make me!" Then he stormed out of our room.

I sat there on my bed for awhile, but I could hear my baby

brother screaming a cry that was unfamiliar to me. I knew Dad was doing something to him and Mom wasn't around to stop Dad. *It has to be me, I have to do something,* I decided. I went to my brother's room and found him in his crib screaming at the top of his lungs. Dad stood above him with a small steak knife. Dad swung the knife towards my brother, and my brother scooted away. The knife missed. I saw blood on the crib sheet and instantly knew Dad had already stabbed him at least once.

Dad yelled, "Please, I can't, I don't want to. Please, I can't. I'm sorry!" He looked in my direction, but he didn't seem to see me. A clap of thunder echoed outside.

Is he talking to me, the weather or someone else? I wondered, "Stop, please," I said "Dad, please don't," I said again. He ignored my pleas and continued to poke the knife into the crib. I ran over, grabbed his leg and pulled, trying to get his attention. *Stop, you need to stop,* I thought. I hit at his leg, but he was focused on the crib and my brother. Dad continued to scream that he was sorry. He screamed things like "Please don't make me!" over and over. He yelled and he cried, but he kept poking and jabbing the knife into the crib, mostly missing my brother, sometimes stabbing him—it was confusing. No one was making him poke the knife towards my brother, I couldn't see anyone. *Who is he talking to?* Dad wouldn't answer me. He didn't even seem to see me.

Dad jabbed the knife a few more times towards my brother until my brother stopped crying. Dad continued to cry and call out, "Please, I'm sorry, no don't make me." Thunder continued to clap seemingly in praise of Dad, and encouraging him to continue. Dad finally noticed me. He kicked the leg I was hanging onto and knocked me away. I fell off his leg and hit the floor with a thud. Dad left the room. I got up, ran to the crib and looked in. My brother was quiet and appeared to be sleeping. There was blood on his onesie sleeper around his tummy and neck. The blood was puddled on the crib sheet and seeping down the skirting of the crib, dripping down to the concrete floor and area rug. My brother looked very white or sort of gray.

I ran towards my bedroom to see if he was going to poke Bevy or if he was finished. I found Dad in the bedroom talking to Bevy. "It's your turn, you have to take your turn," Dad said in his sweet voice. Bevy was still in the closet, Dad reached in and grabbed her arm, pulling her out. She wiggled and tried to pull away, but he had her firmly in his grasp. He bent down over her, holding her tight.

"Dad stop, don't!" I yelled. No thunder claps to applaud my pleas, just the wind howling outside and patters of raindrops as they hit the window. He ignored me. I ran to him and hit his back as hard as I could repeatedly with both my fists. I grabbed at his arm and pulled, trying to keep the knife away from my sister. He yanked free from my pull and didn't seem concerned with my hits. I looked around the room to see if I could grab something to thunk him with, a toy or something get his attention off of Bevy so she could run and find Mom.

He held Bevy down, poked the knife towards her neck. He continued to jab the knife in the air towards her. He again called out "Please, please, I don't want to, stop, don't make me, please I can't," but even as he argued and begged with people I couldn't see, he continued to point the knife, jab it into the air and poke it towards Bevy. Thunder claps continued to roar in what seemed to me to be a pattern of celebration to his cries. Dad mostly jabbed at the air while she struggled, kicked and squirmed. I hit his back with my doll as hard as I could. I tried to grab at the knife. Then I saw the blade slice her neck. It seemed to happen in slow motion, one smooth slice. For so long he'd jabbed and poked but missed nicking her skin or cutting her. Slicing her neck the way he had seemed to surprise him. He gasped and started to cry. The pleading with unseen entities started up again. "Please, I can't I don't want to, don't make me, I'm sorry, I'm sorry." He must have loosened his grip because she broke away from his grasp and ran from the room. Blood covered the neck and chest area of her pink flowered flannel nightie.

Dad now looked at me. "It's your turn," he said with a whisper.

"Please, please, no," I said and started to cry. *Why do this? Where was Mom, why wasn't she here to make him stop?* I wondered.

"Please, please," was all I could say. He didn't have to poke me with the knife, I didn't need a turn, he could just stop.

He started again, begging and pleading, saying how sorry he was. I ran away from him, but in a few steps he had me. He held me hard against my bed and jabbed the knife into my direction. It burned as it struck my neck the first few times, but then the pain suddenly ended. I stopped struggling and fell to the ground. I might have fallen asleep. When I woke Dad was gone. I was surprised to see blood on the walls and all over the floor. Bevy had returned to our room.

"It's Mom's fault!" three-year-old Bevy cried. Scarlet red blotches now obliterated the pink flannel flowers around her neck and down the front on her nightie. Red liquid dripped all the way down to her bare feet. Each time she took a step, a bloody foot print left a mark. I looked down at my own blue-flowered nightie, and the blue flowers down the front were also hidden by red spatter.

"Mom's fault? No!" I said, trying to figure out why Bevy would think it was Mom's fault when clearly Dad was responsible. Then I remembered that Bevy had earlier saved Mom's life when she distracted Dad by asking for water, giving Mom the opportunity to defend herself and get away. It was odd for Mom to leave us alone with Dad for so long. Yes, Mom had run away, I wished she'd come back, but Dad was the one being bad.

"Yep, Mom's hiding in the bushes making him do it!" Bevy said. I went to the window where Bevy stood and looked outside. There was a shrub just outside the window. Bevy pointed at it. "She's in there."

"No, she's not!" I said. The view of the bush was clear. There was no way a person could hide in it.

Bevy looked suspiciously from me to the plant, back at me, then asked, "Then who's telling Dad to—?"

"I don't know—but I don't hear anyone talking to him. I don't hear Mom, do you?"

Bevy shook her head no. We heard the front door close. Someone was back, Mom or Dad. We didn't know which. Bev ran and hid by the dresser. My heart pounded. I held onto the bed and stood frozen. Could I hide? I thought I would fall down if I moved. The room was spinning. My brother had been quiet for a long time. Maybe this was help. Maybe—

My dad walked into the bedroom. He had the gun. I had been told never to touch it and knew it was kept in the glove compartment of the car.

"Please, please don't. Santa is going to be mad!" I said, knowing exactly what he was planning.

He began to cry. Through his tears, my dad looked at me. I knew that he was aware I was Pammy, but as parents sometimes do he accidentally called me Bevy. He said, "Bevy, stand still." Then he said one last time, "I'm sorry!"

With that, Bevy whispered at me from her hiding spot two feet away, "Run!"

I didn't run. I was tired, dizzy and done. My dad fired the gun.

Bevy, Gilbert, and Pammy Sieling, 1966

2

FREQUENCY

2009

I SAT BEHIND MY DESK enjoying my morning phone call with
Bev. "Oh my God, I just met Mike Parks. He's a deputy county
attorney. He looks exactly like Lucifer," I said to my sister, the
telephone cradled between my shoulder and ear.

"Lucifer—as in the devil?"

"Yes, he has dark hair, mustache, and beard—gives me the
heebie-jeebies," I said.

"I thought the devil had blonde hair and blue eyes," Bev said
and then laughed, knowing I would get the inside joke. I knew she
was referring to Gil Sieling.

I laughed too because I agreed the devil probably did look
like our father. "Remember Dick Dastardly from the cartoons? He
always had his dog named Muttley with him?" I asked.

"Yes, he had that long mustache and the top hat and a big
chin, but no beard," Bev answered.

"Okay, that is what Mike Park looks like but with a beard. He
gives me the creeps. Best part, he had a little dog with him. He
probably really was Dick Dastardly when he was younger, now he
has grown a beard and has changed his name," I said.

"Right, he was a cartoon character when he was younger,

now he is a deputy county attorney," Bev said. "So what did Dick Dastardly, also known as Mike Parks, want with you Pam, to tie you up to a train track or something?"

"Pretty much. He wants me to call Yavapai Downs, you know that horse race track, that you can go out to and bet on a horse? He and some other guys pretty much let me know I better call it a school so it can get a tax break and other stuff," I answered.

"Are you still joking or did he really ask you to do that?"

"I'm paraphrasing—but it sucks how people ask, then demand, for me to do stuff like that. Especially when they have a personal self-interest—and some political power. Then they act all offended when I refuse. Check this out, Supervisor Tom Thurman, who's the main person pressuring me to call this property a school, when he darn well knows it hasn't been a school for years, was literally like the director or chairman of the board for the Yavapai Downs race track at the same time he was a supervisor for the county—conflict of interest much? Assholes!"

Bev cracked up hearing my bad language. I hardly ever used bad words—I saved them just for Bev. I liked to show her just how bad I could be. We finished our call and I got back to focusing on work issues.

#

A Few Weeks Later

"Bev, let me put the phone on hold," I said, then ran and shut my office door. "Beverly, you will not believe this—it's funny in a horrible way. Mike—you know, the guy I call Dick Dastardly? He left me a screaming voicemail this morning." I tried to keep my tone muted.

"Wait a second. I need to light a cigarette for this one," Bev said. I could hear her chuckling.

"Yep, this is good. Dick Dastardly was literally screaming,"

"Okay, cigarette lit, ready for the story. Dick Dastardly, that's the deputy county attorney guy named Mike, right?"

"Right," I said, sucking in air and tucking my feet under me. "Well, you know that guy James Arthur Ray? He claimed to be a

This is what I think Mike Park sort of looks like, but with a beard.
He probably has horns too—but I can't swear to that; I'm just speculating.
Above Dastardly is his dog Muttley.

spiritual warrior? He had that sweat lodge in Sedona. People paid big money and came up to do a ritual and to spiritually grow. A couple of them died. The whole thing was just unsafe! It was horrible."

"I do know about that, I've been hearing about it all week."

"Our Yavapai County Sheriff is heading the public relations effort on this because that part of Sedona is in our county. Sheriff Waugh invited the media to the board of supervisors room in this building for a press conference. The county put up a professional looking backdrop with a county logo on it. It looked great. I saw it as I left work Friday night."

"Okay,"

"Apparently, we had a door where they checked identification to assure only media got in. Several television stations came up to Prescott. They taped it and everything. Made national news."

"Wow."

"So my employee, Kiarra, she's kind of—interested in things—"

"She's nosy. Now continue," Bev said with a laugh. She loved gossip.

"Apparently Kiarra's daughter worked for the hospital where they took the sweat lodge victims. So Kiarra, I think, wanted to impress her daughter with how in the loop she is. Kiarra has a key to the county building because she's an employee of mine—"

"She didn't!" Bev said with a gasp.

"Bev, it gets worse. She brings her daughter through the back door on Saturday morning, and they go right into the press conference."

"They get kicked out?"

"Nope, because once you get through the front door security, you can go through the lobby to the restrooms and back to the board of supervisor's room if you want,"

"Okay."

"Anyhow, Sheriff Waugh must have given his speech, and then in the question and answer period little ole Kiarra raised her hand."

"What? Oh no," Bev said, starting to giggle.

"Yep, she raised her hand and said, 'My name is Kiarra, and I'm from the assessor's office.' Then she asked, 'Was the sweat lodge built with a permit?' Remember, this structure was basically a temporary tent. Kiarra knows it didn't have, or need to have, permits. In fact, she could have looked it up in our office on her own computer. Poor Sheriff Waugh was totally blindsided with that question. I bet Kiarra's daughter was so proud."

"Oh, man—"

"So the headline around the nation is: *Arizona Sweat Lodge did not have a permit.*" I opened the top drawer to my desk and rummaged for a throat lozenge.

"Oh—I saw that! I thought that James Arthur Ray had broken some kind of county rule by building his sweat lodge without a permit," Bev said, sounding serious.

"It didn't need a permit. Tents and temporary structures don't get inspected by the county's development service department. But dear sweet Kiarra gave the media the headline! This has ticked off Dick Dastardly, hence his angry screaming message at me this morning. He's so mad. I'm supposed to call him back . . . but I'm afraid," I said in a whisper. I knew I was procrastinating. "What am I expected to say—*oh—really, she shouldn't have done that? I will let my employees know not to sneak in where they are not wanted and ask a stupid question from now on. Thanks for bringing this to my attention.*"

Bev laughed. "Wow, a deputy county attorney ticked because your employee gave a reason for the families of the victims to file a lawsuit against the county. How unreasonable he is! Well, Sis, you made my day look pretty good, so you're doing service by having such a bad day for me."

"I'll remember that. At least I gave you a laugh. Makes it all worth it, to give you joy," I said and ended the call and got back to the business at hand.

I reluctantly dialed Dick Dastardly's number. *Don't answer, don't answer,* I thought, willing the line to go to voicemail. Mike answered, heard who it was and verbally attacked. He demanded Kiarra's career end, he demanded my head on a platter, and he used adult language to express his anger. The conversation ended with me apologizing and promising to keep his office apprised to what actions I took towards Kiarra.

After careful review of the situation, human resources was prepared to support Mike's decision to fire Kiarra. I spoke to Julie Ayers, the county administrator, and she made it clear the decision was mine to make. Discovering Kiarra had over twenty years of service with the assessor's office, I decided—even if Kiarra was a pain in my neck—her behavior didn't rise to the level of losing her job. I gave her a thirty-hour suspension without pay. She huffed and puffed and stomped, but she served her suspension and returned to work. Once she returned to work, she appeared more willing to please me, at least for awhile.

#

A Month After Kiarra Returned From Suspension

"Guess what they're doing now?" Kiarra asked as she waved a letter in the air.

I looked up from my computer. "Come on in," I smiled, trying to appear friendly. I motioned for her to sit down. We'd had a rocky start. I wanted to mend some fences.

Kiarra took the seat in front of me and handed me the letter. I opened it and read. It appeared to be from a rancher to a property owner. He offered to rent cows to the property owner and promised a reduction in property taxes which would more than offset the cost of renting cows.

"Rent a cow, for property tax savings?" I asked, appalled.

"Yep, that's the deal," Kiarra said. "This property owner reported that this rancher sent these letters all over West Yavapai County. The rancher's gonna make big bucks renting his cows so people can claim their land is agricultural."

"Do you think this happens a lot?" I asked with a sinking feeling in my stomach.

"I do! Now we have proof—it couldn't be legal, right?"

"I doubt it," I said.

Kiarra nodded and agreed with a smile.

"I'm going to ask the county attorney's office if it's legal. I'll send this rancher a letter. He might be able to rent cows, but he can't promise reduced taxes. Also, I'll talk to Mattie of the Yavapai County Beef Association to see if they condone this kind of thing. Surely it's unethical...Excellent work."

I was a bit surprised to see Kiarra reporting this issue to me and hoped that this meant she was learning to look to me for leadership.

I leaned back in my chair and looked out my office window into the parking lot. Gosh, I'd come a long way from that sick little girl that couldn't speak. *People aren't only listening, they're following my leadership,* I smiled. Life sure was better now.

#

1966

I lay on a pole and pad stretcher, carried by two men through the front yard of our home. The storm had returned; it wasn't raining now, but claps of thunder broke through the many conversations going on in our yard. The two ambulances resembled bread delivery trucks, and several police vehicles with red lights lined our street. Dad stood sixty feet away. He was quiet and calm as a man in a uniform placed handcuffs on him.

The back doors of one of the ambulances opened. I was loaded into it and put on the cot inside. A stranger, in a beige uniform, sat on the crew bench next to the cot. His hand held my neck. *Where's Bevy?* I wondered.

"It was Dad—he talked to people, but I couldn't see them," I said, as I looked at the white light glowing behind the wooden cabinet mounted to the side.

"Shh, shh—we know," the stranger said. He sounded kind. I couldn't see what he looked like; his face was in the shadows. His hand pressing on my neck felt uncomfortable, not painful. I wished he would move his hand and stop touching me, but he continued to firmly hold my neck.

"Where's my mom? Is Bevy okay? My brother—" I asked the stranger. He didn't answer.

"What's going on?" Uncle Mike said, just outside the ambulance. I could hear him and other voices, but I couldn't make out what was being said. *Why is Uncle Mike here?* I wanted to yell for Uncle Mike to let him know I was inside—tell him what Dad did, ask him to find Bevy. But they shut the rear doors, and Uncle Mike was now out of earshot. I wished they'd let Uncle Mike in the ambulance. Despite the blanket, I was cold and shivering. My nightie, drenched in blood, was getting the sheet wet, and periodically I would have fits of coughing. The stranger beside me seemed concerned.

"Shh, you shouldn't speak. You're safe now," the stranger said. Sirens rang out, making the ambulance shake. We headed to John C. Lincoln North Mountain Hospital, located on Dunlap and Central in Phoenix. The stranger next to me held my neck the entire way.

At the hospital I was confused. Everything was quick and abrupt. As soon as we arrived, I was unloaded from the ambulance by new strangers who ran with me on the stretcher. They flipped me to another bed. Scissors carefully started to cut at my nightie.

"Please, please don't cut it—don't cut it," I said. I knew my nightie had blood on it, but we could wash it.

"Shh, you must be quiet," a stranger responded, sounding curt. She clipped the nightie at the neck in the front and continued cutting straight down the fabric. I squeezed my eyes shut; her breath smelled like peppermint as she leaned over me and grabbed a section of my nightie in each hand. She yanked, ripping the nightie all the way down into two pieces. They put the remnants, torn and blood-splattered, in a clear plastic bag. I could see my Christmas present—alone in the bag—destroyed.

I cried, embarrassed to be laid out in the center of strangers like a Halloween pumpkin on a platter—cut, shot, and exposed. Only panties left. Still cold. A female came into my sight, her hair bundled up in netting, her face covered in a rectangular white mask, like the other strangers. "Shh, shh, sweet baby girl," she said as she patted the top of my head. For a moment I believed she would make things better.

More strangers, with white masks covering their mouths, and hair covered by netting, continued to surround me. I felt scared because I couldn't see anyone's face—only their eyes. "Shh, shh, sweet baby girl, it's okay," the kind nurse said again, just as a different masked stranger grabbed my left hand and stretched my arm out. A sharp pain cut through my upper left arm.

I yanked my arm as hard as I could; I kicked my legs fast and refused to lay still. I lashed, yanked, and cried, "Uncle Mike! I'm in here Uncle Mike!" Uncle Mike would find me. I knew he was looking for me. I'd heard him before they took me from my house. Maybe he followed. Instead, the strangers dove on me, two across me, one on my chest, the other on my legs. They maneuvered and held my legs, arms, and head as still as they could, but I refused to cooperate as they inserted a needle in my arm. The pain was sharp and lasted for several minutes. Eventually, I began to feel fuzzy and calmed down. Sleep gradually overtook me.

I woke up hacking and coughing; my throat felt raw and burned. I found myself in a dull, dark, dimly-lit room, gadgets and equipment making a symphony of sounds—buzzing, clicking, air whistling. A clear plastic canopy that zipped up the front sheltered me from the room. A quiet whir of cool air breezed around me. My hand was attached to tubes that snaked underneath the oxygen tent to a glass bottle. The bottle hung upside down from a metal stand. Relieved to feel dry sheets and blankets around me, I tried to sit up. This caused sharp pains in both my stomach and the right side of my ribcage. I was weak. I settled back down and pulled at the blankets—relieved to see a blue hospital gown on me. I felt my panties were missing. *Where did they go, why'd they take them?*

The next several days I slept, awakened only by my coughing or the nurse. Sometimes I'd see my mom or my grandma, an aunt or an uncle, sitting by my bedside. When I opened my eyes, I would close them without saying anything or lifting my head.

I remember the noise of buzzing, clicking air, and the sounds of shoes. The room was dimly lit. *I don't like the dark! I want to see if my Dad's anywhere in the room! He might show up at any time!*

Someone in clunky white shoes walked into the room. I noticed her curly blonde hair hanging down to her shoulders. Glad to see a face without a mask or covered hair, I smiled, without lifting my head. She unzipped the plastic canopy and opened it up. Now I could see her better. The plastic was above, behind, and on each side of me. It reminded me of a princess bed with the plastic hanging all around. "Hi there, sleepy head," she said, sounding sweet.

"I want my mom, or is my Uncle Mike here?" I said, surprised at how sore my throat was. It stung to speak, and I reached up to touch my throat—I felt tape and gauze.

The woman smiled and said, "I'll let your mom and Uncle Mike know you're awake; they're both here."

With that, the woman closed the canopy, leaving me inside, and zipped it back down. She checked the bottle hanging on the metal stand, adjusted a knob, and then her shoes clicked as she walked away. I didn't mind having the plastic canopy zipped up and closed off to the room. For now, my private princess canopy bed felt cozy, but I wished the lights could be turned on in the room so I could see better. I fell back to sleep. I was glad to know Mom and Uncle Mike were close by.

I woke up to find Mom and Uncle Mike sitting at my bedside. The nurse was in the room looking at the gauges. "Where's Bevy?" I asked, my voice weak. My body felt so heavy and tired; it took considerable effort to lift my head and look around.

The nurse came to my bedside, unzipped the oxygen tent, and moved the front plastic out of the way, probably so they could hear me easier. "You've been very sick with high fevers," Mom said, "and you've had bad dreams. That's why you're in the hospital—because you've been sick." I knew she was fibbing, her voice was sweet but shaking.

I remembered Bevy's claim that Mom was making Dad hurt us. I hadn't heard Mom tell Dad anything, but Dad had been talking to someone; actually it sounded like he'd spoken to a couple of people. *How was that possible? I couldn't hear them. Nothing is making sense to me.*

I looked at Mom's brother, my uncle Mike. He looked at the floor so I couldn't see his brown eyes. His hands were folded together, and he moved in his seat from side to side as if he were uncomfortable. "Is Bevy okay?" I said, getting scared. I could feel my heart racing and the machine beside me beeping in sync to my racing heart—speeding up as my worry increased.

At home when last I'd seen Bevy, she was hiding by the dresser, but she wasn't hidden very well. *Did they find Bevy? Did she hide from everyone? Was she at the house alone? What about my brother, where was he? Why was Mom fibbing? Why had Dad done this? Did Mom and Uncle Mike make him do it?* Thoughts, no answers.

Uncle Mike and Mom gave each other an awkward glance but remained silent—leaving my questions hanging out there. "Are my sister and brother okay?" The pain increased each time I spoke. The nurse came into my view, and I could see how pretty she was with her deep blue eyes and blonde bouncing curls. "Your sister and brother are here, nearby. I'll take you to see them when you're feeling better, in the next couple days," she said as she looked directly at Mom and Uncle Mike. I thought the nurse gave them a mean look. Maybe she knew Mom was fibbing, and I was glad. I nodded my head, satisfied with the promise to take me to see my sister soon. My throat felt parched. With that, I went back to sleep.

Years later I would understand that Mom had tried to protect me from the truth. That day she didn't know how to deal with the situation she found herself in. She was doing the best she could: three children in the hospital, a little boy with knife wounds and pneumonia, her middle child with knife wounds, her five-year-old, me, in critical condition with pneumonia, knife and gunshot wounds. She was in the hospital for her own injuries; she'd been leaving her hospital room to visit her two younger children in the children's ward and her oldest daughter in the intensive care unit. She had been told I probably wouldn't survive. Her husband was in jail, or on his way to prison. That was a lot for her to handle. Of course, at the time I didn't understand any of this.

Finally, I was awake and had enough energy to sit up for a few minutes. I was given a sponge bath—the nurse washed me with a plastic tub of soapy water and a sponge—right in my bed! That was silly and made me smile.

"I'm gonna pretend I'm a princess, 'cuz this is probably how they take their baths," I said, but my throat was so sore and scratchy that using words made it worse.

The nurse laughed. "You're funny. You could pretend that the nurses' call button is a princess button, one that summons me, your trusty servant, at your every beck and call."

Over the next few days, whenever the day nurse checked on me, she would pretend she was my servant, and I was a queen or a princess. I would play along. Mostly I continued to sleep, but she woke me often to take my temperature or adjust the tubes and cords in my arm and hand. She looked at monitors, wrote on her clipboard.

I started to regain some strength. "Can I go see Bevy today?" I asked as the doctor removed the bandages from my neck and looked at the stitches. His breath smelled like peppermint, too. *Do all hospital workers like peppermint candy?* I wondered.

"I'm going to leave the bandages off of your neck to let the stitches have air. Promise not to touch?" I had about an inch strip of stitches in my upper left arm where the hospital workers had torn or cut it. There were stitches in several rows on my neck, another inch or so of stitches on my left side, and about five inches of stitches on my abdomen. I nodded my head in agreement, avoiding using words.

The doctor ignored my question. He was older than my dad and wore a leather band around his head that partially hid his dark hair. The leather band attached to a disc-shaped mirror that was flipped up. He moved forward on his swivel chair beside my bed and flipped the disk down. In the middle of the disc was an eyeball size round hole. I could see the doctor's eye peeking out of the hole. He had a flashlight. "Open your mouth wide so I can see inside," he said as he turned his flashlight on.

I shook my head *no.* "I–want–to–see–my–sister!" I said clearly and slowly. My heart raced, and the beeping machine attached to me went from steady rhythmic beeps to quick chirps. I felt paralyzed with fear; had they lied to me? Was my sister really nearby? The beeping machine stopped its quick beeps and made a solid squealing noise. *Odd,* I thought, *the machine matches my mood.* My head felt hot like it was being squeezed. My heart raced and thumped so hard I thought it might pop through my chest. *They had lied just as Mom lied. Where was my sister?* Several hospital employees ran to my bedside and checked the alarming machine. The doctor stood and shouted commands to the staff as they ran around. The beeping machine squealed—I fell asleep.

When I woke, my head and throat hurt, my body ached. I pushed the button summoning my day servant. She arrived quickly, unzipped my oxygen tent and leaned in to see what I wanted. "I need to see my sister," I whispered with suspicion. I no longer believed Bevy was nearby.

"Yes, as soon as you feel better; I'll take you, I promise," she said, looking straight into my eyes.

"Bring her here to me, I need to see her today, or I won't get better," I said and started to cry. Everyone was fibbing. *Why wouldn't they let me see Bevy? Was she okay?*

The nurse stared at me for a moment. She didn't seem to know what to do. She looked around the room as if she were trying to figure something out. "Let's see what I can arrange," she reluctantly said. Then she zipped up the oxygen tent, my signal to go back to sleep. I could hear her shoes clicking on the floor when she left the room.

My day nurse returned with a giant smile on her face, pushing a wheelchair in front of her. She unzipped my oxygen tent, and I sat up. "Really, you're taking me to see my sister, right?" I worried it might be some kind of a trick.

"I am!" she said. I grinned, making the skin on my neck feel tight and hurt, but I didn't care.

The nurse unhooked me from some medical equipment, lifted me into the wheelchair, grabbed a blanket and tucked it around me tight. She pulled over the IV metal stand and pushed me and the stand out of the dimly-lit room into a well-lit hallway. "You can't stay long, but you'll be able to see her," she said.

We arrived in an indoor play area with a large red toy train. Kids were climbing on the train, pretending to ride it. The train didn't move, but it looked fun to play on. I noticed a blue toy box with some toys and a little round table with a couple of chairs by it. The room looked bright and happy with its yellow painted walls. I was glad to see Bevy in a place that looked fun.

Bevy ran towards me, grinning.

"Gentle, you have to be careful with her," the day nurse with the clunky white shoes said to my sister.

"Where were you?" Bevy asked, gently patting my leg.

"I don't know, here somewhere—in a dark room," I said in my new raspy voice. Bevy's eyes grew wide when she heard my voice. She looked up at the nurse, then patted my leg again.

"It's fun here, they let us play sometimes. But most of the time we have to be in our beds." Bev pointed at a boy about ten years old, overweight, dark hair and bangs. "He's terminal," she added.

"What's terminal?" I asked, and we both looked up at the nurse.

"Terminal means he will live here the rest of his life," she answered. I liked her and believed she tried to be honest.

"Am I terminal?" I asked.

"Nope," she said with a gentle smile. "Sorry, girls, time to go." I waved at Bevy as the nurse rolled me out of the room. I was tired but happy.

#

2009

Scott, my former business partner, brought his daughter to meet me at Fujiyamas, a Japanese restaurant and sushi bar, for lunch. Constance was now thirteen years old. I took this opportunity to invite my twenty-three-year-old daughter, Ashley, to join us. We hadn't seen each other in months.

"How's the lease-study going on the agricultural properties?"

I asked. The waiter came over, interrupted, and took our lunch orders. The waiter was a young man in his early twenties and seemed very attentive to my daughter Ashley. I always got excellent service from young men when Ashley was with me.

"I'm done, just prettying it up a bit," Scott said, then took a sip of the water with lemon slice. "Did the Arizona Department of Revenue finish theirs?"

"Yes—it supports a value of $25 an acre, so that's an increase from $7.56 to $25 an acre," I said, using our time to get some business done.

"Damn! Near tripling the values—have fun with that," he said. Ashley was showing Constance photos on her cell phone—pictures of her home in Texas, her husband Adam and her cat, Arthur. Constance and Ashley looked like they could be sisters, both blondes.

"Yep, the values are a third of what they're supposed to be, and have been for some time," I said. "Luckily the taxes are phased in due to the taxable value, so the taxes will increase, but not triple. What value does your lease-study support?"

"About the same," Scott said. "Twenty-five dollars per acre for grazing is in the range of value with a minimum of eighteen dollars and a high of forty dollars. In a few years, I think you ought to move from an average per acre value to a per animal unit. It's fairer."

"Per animal unit per acre? What would that look like?"

"I'm bored," Constance said, interjecting herself into our adult conversation. Ashley nodded in agreement.

Scott's blue eyes squinted and seemed amused. He'd known Ashley since she was in the fourth grade. "Okay, let's talk about Ashley. That's always interesting. How's Ash?"

"My husband, the pilot . . . " We laughed. Ashley loved to mention her husband was a pilot, and then she'd add that she was practically a doctor, because she was enrolled in a graduate program for her masters. "He's in Afghanistan, you know, being a hero and all. We Skype, but it's hard. I'm volunteering for Mom at the office for something to do, 'cuz it'd be lonely in Texas on the military base without him. He'll be back in about three months."

"What are you doing at the assessor's office?" Scott asked

"Oh, mostly judging people, 'cuz I'm practically a psychologist," Ashley said. We laughed, and she quickly added, "No, really! I file, and I scan, and I put together the kudos for employees—you know if they do a good job on something—for morale building. I put together fun things to recognize a job well done. I also put together thank-you items to present after work, such as take the firefighters a basket for appreciation or make a basket for the police department. Things like that. Things that help bond the employees, so they like each other outside of work."

"She came and volunteered when her husband was in Kuwait, too," I said. "It's nice because I get to see her and we can go to lunch together." I noticed that all of us sitting at the table had blue eyes. Scott's were the most vibrant. I wondered if blue eyes were rare or typical.

"Well, you can always type up some of my appraisal reports for me like you used to. I'd pay you to do that," Scott said.

"I do school, too—but sure, that'd be great 'cuz it would help offset the cost to get here from Texas and get back home," Ashley said, smiling at the waiter as he approached our table.

I changed the subject. "Okay, so—quick and not in a boring way—animal units per acre?" The waiter delivered our food. *I love sushi*, I thought, looking at my California rolls.

"Basically a section of land—Ashley, that's 640 acres—can only provide enough feed for one cow for one month," Scott said, moving his plate to the side for the waiter to retrieve, then continued his lecture for Ashley. "It should be valued less per acre than a section of land that could provide forty cows enough grass for a month. Make sense?" Ashley nodded. Scott continued, "In property down in Wickenburg that is rocks and dirt, the poor cows would starve if you put more than a couple of them on a section of land. It shouldn't be valued the same as property located on the Verde River with tall lush grass that could support twenty cows on a section, right?"

I understood and smiled at him.

"So let's take your twenty-five dollars per acre value. In Yavapai County the average carrying capacity for a whole section of land is eight cows—that's average. Your $25 value is an average, so what is that per cow, Ashley?"

"Twenty-five dollars divided by eight," Ashley said, looking dubious. Scott nodded, and we both looked at her.

"Come on! A person that's practically a doctor should be able to do this math," Scott said.

Constance laughed and pointed at Ashley.

"About three dollars and thirteen cents per cow or per animal carrying capacity," Ashley said in a voice that conveyed she wasn't entertained by our conversation any longer.

"So you look at the carrying capacity, and for every animal unit—or cow—that the land can support on a section of land, you add three dollars and thirteen cents to the per acre value. That's a much fairer way to evaluate these properties, and it still conforms to the statute," Scott went on.

"Yes, it is. We'll work towards that," I said

We finished lunch and said our goodbyes. Scott and Constance headed off to see a movie. Ashley and I went back to the office to finish out the day at work.

#

1967

"This is how you draw a three-dimensional box," Uncle Mike said, as he drew two overlapping squares and put a line from each square's corner to the corresponding square's corner.

Uncle Mike had jet black hair, much darker than Mom's. His was short, parted on the side and swooped to the left—a boy's cut, Mom called it. His eyes were chestnut brown with gold flickers. They would squint up and almost disappear when he smiled. Uncle Mike had a little pouch for a stomach that hung out in front and slightly over his belt, not as big as Santa's, but almost. He was as kind and giving as Santa. At least that's how I'd always thought of him . . . before. Now I wasn't sure, I didn't trust him, or Mom for that matter. She'd lied, said I'd had a nightmare and that's why I was in the hospital.

"Why were you at my house?" I asked, feeling suspicious.

"At your house, when?" Uncle Mike asked. *He knows when— he's stalling,* I thought. I looked at him waiting for an answer. *Is he gonna be honest or is he gonna try to tell me I'd just had a nightmare and that's why I'm in the hospital? I bet he'll lie. Just like Mom.* "It's a long story," Uncle Mike finally said with an awkward grin.

"I heard you looking for me. I tried to let you know where I was."

Tears suddenly appeared and ran down my uncle's face. "I'm sorry," he said.

"You were there to help?" I asked. *Had he tried to help Dad? Does he believe in "arms a getting" like Dad?* I wondered. My Dad had said *I'm sorry* over and over as he prepared for "arms a getting;" now Uncle Mike was using similar words to explain why he was at my house.

"I should have helped, I should have come earlier. I'm so sorry—I just didn't even know or believe. If I'd come earlier I could've helped," he said. This was confusing. *What was he saying?*

"Why were you there?" I asked again.

Uncle Mike realized I wasn't going to let it go. "It's weird, the whole thing is weird," he said. I nodded in agreement, glad he seemed to be finally talking to me like a person. "Your grandma called, in the middle of the night. Woke me up. She felt like something was wrong, wanted me to go check on you guys, but I said 'No, everything's okay.' She pleaded and called a couple of times. She wouldn't give up. I'd talk her out of her fears, hang up, then later she'd call again. I tried to call your house, but the phone would break up into static – I guess because of the storm." Uncle Mike wiped his eyes and pulled out a handkerchief and blew his nose. "Finally, your grandma said if I wouldn't go check on you guys, then she'd have to. I didn't want her driving all the way from Yarnell to Paradise Valley in the middle of the night in that weather. So I agreed to check. I thought she was just paranoid because your Dad was acting a little off when we were at your house on Christmas. Well, I pulled up to your house, and there were ambulances, police cars, and your dad in the front yard. Honey, if I hadn't argued, if I'd listened to Grandma . . ."

Then Uncle Mike started to sob, his shoulders heaving, his hands covering his face. This was the first time I'd seen any adult show any response over what had happened, and it made me feel loved.

"Then I kind of got paranoid myself. It's weird how the brain works," Uncle Mike added, now really talking. I liked being spoken to as if I understood things. "Later I sat in the hospital outside your mom's room."

"Mom's room?" I asked.

Uncle Mike nodded. "She's still here in the hospital on a different floor. Your sister and brother are in the children's ward. There's maybe a reporter or a weirdo that's pestering your mom, so I've been posted in a chair outside her room—"

"Wow, a reporter or a weirdo?" I was intrigued. *A weirdo, was that like a clown?* My throat was aching from all the talk, and I was getting tired of sitting up. I lay on my side. Uncle Mike adjusted the plastic of the oxygen tent so I could still hear him.

"You're getting tired. I'm going to let you sleep. Tomorrow we'll visit more."

I nodded and smiled, but couldn't hide how tired I was. "Tell me more about the weirdo," I whispered, yawning and closing my eyes.

"No, sweet pea. I'll let you doze off. Promise I'll return tomorrow and tell you anything you want to know,"

"Promise?" I asked. I didn't hear his answer. I rolled over, so tired I couldn't keep my eyes open. *I want to hear about the weirdo or clown*, I thought, fighting to stay awake, but I couldn't talk anymore. *Mom's in the hospital, in her own room. Why didn't she tell me that?* It made me feel happy to know she was here somewhere close by. Uncle Mike zipped up the plastic sheet for the oxygen tent and left my room.

#

2010

Bev sat on my bed as I modeled my new outfit: tight Wrangler boot-cut jeans, buttoned up plaid shirt, cowgirl leather boots, a brown leather belt with a silver and turquoise belt buckle.

"Where's your cowboy hat?" Bev asked.

"I didn't want to overdo it. This is what I wore when I gave that presentation to the Yavapai County Beef Association," I said. I tried to hold back giggles but couldn't. We both knew that in high school, Bev's style was cowgirl, not mine.

Growing up, Bev and I both had our own horses. She barrel raced and ran for rodeo queen. I loved riding my horse, *Shane Dora the Great*. I'd worked a whole summer to earn enough money for my saddle. But even when I went to the rodeo, or rode my horse in the local parades, I'd just wear jeans and a T-shirt. I never got decked out in the country attire. It just wasn't my style. I was city girl modern all the way.

"How'd it go?" Bev asked with a nod of approval. She'd insisted that I dress country for the presentation.

I sat on the floor and tugged at my boot. I liked the look of cowboy boots, but they sure were a pain to get off.

"Great! They were so nice. It was a potluck lunch. Tasted amazing. Then I gave my PowerPoint and speech and told them how the property values had to increase because they hadn't been updated in thirty years. Mattie, the president of the association, wrote all about it in their newsletter."

I walked over to my dresser and grabbed the newsletter. Grinning ear to ear, I handed it to Bev. On the front was a big photo of me in my cowgirl outfit.

Bev fell on the bed laughing. "You brat! I sit here and watch you model, look at you prance around, and you had a picture of it all along."

"I thought you'd want to see me dolled up in person. Mattie did a great job writing the article. She explained how the increases in taxes are phased in over several years," I said as I undressed.

"She also compared us to the other counties. Even with the update, our values aren't the highest in the state; we're a little above the middle of the state in values. Mattie was fair. You'd like her, she's nice, and she's pretty, too. This newsletter is going out to all the beef association members."

"Perfect. So you've spoken to their membership. You've got the information on the updated agricultural values in their newsletter. Now, I think you should send a press release to the paper. That pretty much covers all your bases."

"I was surprised the farmers and ranchers took the information on our updates as well as they did, and they were so sweet—they gave me this T-shirt." I held out the T-shirt with its slogan written across the front: *I heart beef.*

"They probably were in shock. I can't imagine having your values locked in for over thirty years, but I bet they believed that value would go forever." I nodded my head, agreeing with my wise sister.

#

1967

When I woke up, Mom was sitting at my bedside. She was dressed in colored jeans and a plain t-shirt. "Are you in the hospital?" I said, realizing that every time she came to my room she was in regular clothes. I'd never seen her in a hospital gown like I wore.

Mom looked around my hospital room and laughed as she unzipped my oxygen tent and pulled the sides apart, making it like a princess canopy. "Yes, I'm sitting right here in the hospital," she said.

"Do you have a hospital room of your own that you're staying in?" I asked. Mom nodded, shifting her eyes from side to side as if she'd like to escape my questions. "Why are you in a hospital room?" I persisted, wishing it wasn't so hard to get information out of her. *Why is she dressed in regular clothes? How is she allowed to walk around the hospital—the nurses never let me get dressed or walk around the hospital—do adults just get to do what they want in a hospital?*

"Sometimes when a person gets scared or startled, their bodies react kind of funny, and the doctor just wanted to observe me to make sure everything was all right. I'll be released from the hospital today, I think."

"I saw Dad choke you, did you get hurt?"

"I'm alright," she said, rummaging through her purse to pull out a hair brush. *I didn't ask you that! I asked if you got hurt*, but there was no way I'd talk sassy to Mom like that. I let it go. *Uncle Mike will tell me later.* I wasn't going to get much information out of Mom. I sat up and Mom brushed my long brown hair. I liked it when she brushed my hair. She braided it on both sides and called it Indian style.

"I look like an Indian," I said with a smile, looking in the mirror Mom held up for me. Braids dangled on both sides of my face.

"Yep, just like a little Indian girl. This should keep your neck a little cooler, too." I was glad because sometimes my hair got stuck up inside the bandages on my neck and got pulled when the nurse changed them. Mom kissed me on the cheek and left, promising she'd be back in the evening. She zipped the plastic tent, and I laid down, listening to the soft whir of air as I dozed off, exhausted from the exertion of sitting upright and visiting.

#

2010

I scooted into the Applebees restaurant booth seat. A man I'll call Muttley, because he did the bidding of Mike Parks (AKA Dick Dastardly), a deputy county attorney, sat in the seat opposite me. I'd invited Muttley to lunch because I'd something important to tell him. I wasn't sure how to start.

Being a tattletale wasn't who I wanted to be. When I'd been sworn into office as the assessor, I'd sworn an oath to God to stand up for both the constitution and the laws. I hadn't known then I'd be forced to either break that promise or have to stand up against powerful elected people. Lie to God and break laws, or stand up to powerful people—that was the decision I had to make. Fibbing to God wasn't something I would willingly do, but I was afraid to take on corruption.

I could feel the pulse of my heart beating in my ears. It blocked out the sounds of the restaurant. I could only hear the breath that was raggedly moving in and out of my mouth at regular, gasping intervals. Muttley sat across from me, patiently waiting for me to explain why I'd asked to meet for lunch.

"I need to show you something and let you know what's going on," I said. I placed my red two-inch notebook on the table, pushed it over towards him, then opened it to the first page. I pointed at an Excel spreadsheet with information including taxpayer identification numbers, names, description of property, taxes delinquent, penalties and totals due. In all, the sheets described over a million dollars in delinquencies. I started to speak, and my apprehension disappeared. I had begun my story.

Muttley seemed interested. "Some of these appear delinquent for over ten years," he said, looking up at me, his forehead crinkled. He let out a sigh.

The waiter, slightly overweight with a quick grin, came to our table and we ordered our drinks. As he left, I said, "Right." We both were aware of the legal requirements on the county treasurer and sheriff regarding this. Delinquencies like these indicated the laws probably were not being followed.

"It gets worse than that. A lot worse," I added, as I turned the page past the delinquency list and on to the Yavapai County Board of Supervisors' meeting agenda. I'd highlighted the abatement totals in yellow. Abatements were taxes cleared off the tax roll and deemed no longer collectible. I flipped the page over to the minutes of this meeting, showing that the item had been unanimously approved by the supervisors. Finally, I turned to the Excel spreadsheet of the properties abated.

Muttley pulled the notebook towards him and studied the items. He turned the pages, reading carefully. The waiter returned with our drinks and took our food order. "Are you saying they illegally abated all these delinquencies?" Muttley asked. He was obviously troubled that the supervisors would have excused all the listed delinquent taxes—which shifted this tax burden from these taxpayers to the rest of the taxpayers.

I took the notebook from him, turned the page to the statutes, then pushed the notebook back to him so he could see the laws. "I wanted to meet with you to go over the laws, my oath of office, and see if we're comfortable that the law is being followed." I had skirted Mutt's question, but I believed the county had broken the law with these abatements.

Tax law said the assessor valued, the treasurer billed and sent delinquency lists to the sheriff, who notified, confiscated, and later auctioned the items if the taxes remained unpaid. This was the prescribed process directed by law, but this was not what our county appeared to be doing.

"Here's the back story," I said, leaning in and lowering my voice so other people in the restaurant would not hear. "When we were doing our computer conversion project in the assessor's office, I noticed these delinquent properties. I asked the treasurer about them, and he told me there was an agreement not to worry about them." I shifted in my seat and glanced around nervously, waited a moment to let that sink in. I went on to explain, "A meeting took place years before I was elected. It included Ross Jacobs, the treasurer, the sheriff, Steve Waugh, and board of supervisor member, Carol Springer. At this meeting, Supervisor Springer told the sheriff and treasurer that she didn't like personal property taxes. So if the taxpayer came in and paid their taxes, fine, but she didn't want the taxes pursued if they were unpaid. No seizure or auctions."

My hands started to tremble, the fear returning. Saying this out loud to Muttley was startling to me. It sounded so wrong. "This happened on purpose, a conspiracy," I added.

"I'm assigned as the attorney for your office," Muttley said, "but I'm also appointed as the attorney for the treasurer's office. This puts me in an awkward position. I have a conflict."

"There's more," I responded, setting aside Muttley's conflict issue. *Whether he has a conflict or not, he's the attorney assigned to me, and he's going to hear this and give me legal advice!* The feelings of fear began to leave me.

Rather than lecture Muttley on his conflicts, I decided to tell him what I'd witnessed. "I went to Julie, our county administrator, with this and explained the problem and what Treasurer Jacobs said regarding Supervisor Springer and her directives." I paused and flipped the notebook pages to the statutes that were being broken. "Julie and I then went to Supervisor Springer directly. We asked her to explain."

With that, the waiter returned with our lunches. We pushed the notebook to the side, and the waiter set our meals down. It smelled great, my fajitas sat sizzling in the skillet they were served in. Muttley looked tired. I believed he had integrity and felt uncomfortable in this compromised position.

"I have a conflict of interest. I'm not sure how to help you," he said, picking up his fork.

I continued to tell him what I'd discovered, ignoring his discomfort at the conversation. "Supervisor Springer told the county administrator and me that she didn't like personal property taxes. When she'd been in the state legislature, she'd tried to get them eliminated. But failed. She then instructed us to work on eliminating the personal property taxes and told me to only value the personal property I couldn't ignore." *How dare she tell me to break the law! She should have run again for the legislature if she wanted these laws changed instead of conspiring to have us break these laws!*

I told her I had no interest in eliminating personal property taxes, but Supervisor Springer was welcome to attend my property tax sub-committee meetings and work with us to improve the property tax system. Though invited, she never once attended.

Muttley nodded his head, letting me know he'd heard me, but said nothing. He continued to eat his hamburger.

"I went to every county supervisor and told them about the issue. Over a million dollars was owed to our schools, fire districts, and other taxing jurisdictions. The tax burden had shifted to those of us paying our taxes. I showed the board members this notebook and told them basically what I've told you. Then the abatement appeared on the board of supervisors' agenda, and they wiped clean all this debt! Here are the laws on the process of abatement," I said, pulling the notebook from the side of the table and pointing to the process for reductions.

Mutt moved his plate out of the way and took the notebook. He read the statutes while I turned my attention to my fajitas. Still warm, I put cheese, sour cream and meat in a tortilla. I'd pretty much told him everything; the notebook said the rest.

"I have a conflict," he muttered. "First, the treasurer should have used me for these abatements, that's my job." He spoke in a low voice under his breath as he read. "I'll let my boss know, and that's all I can do. I have a conflict. I represent both you and the treasurer. I won't be able to keep you out of it; I'll have to tell him who reported this to me."

His boss, Dick Dastardly, wouldn't do anything. I couldn't see him forwarding the complaint to another county for investigation. Also, letting them know I reported it wouldn't be good. At worst, I'd see retribution. At best, they'd resentfully follow the laws.

"Here's my problem," I said. "I swore an oath when I took office as the assessor. I believe this oath was to God. I want to keep that promise. It's sacred." I gave a nervous laugh. I did believe the oath was sacred, and I was stunned that so many others who had taken the very same oath didn't take it seriously. "What more do I need to do to keep my oath of office? I've brought the problem to the county administrator's attention, to the attention of every member of the board of supervisors, complained to the treasurer, and now I've notified you."

"I'll speak to my boss, and there's nothing more you can do," Muttley said, looking up as the waiter brought us our bill.

After this disappointing conversation with Muttley, I took a copy of the entire notebook to Scott Orr, a reporter at the *Daily Courier*, the local newspaper. I also had a conversation with Dennis McGrane, the assistant to the county attorney. I'd seen him in the county administrator's office. I told him about the issue.

Our local sheriff was conspiring with the Treasurer and Supervisor Carol Springer, shorting schools and fire districts and other taxing jurisdictions of much-needed funding or shifting these taxes to the rest of us. I thought that would make a relevant news article, or perhaps require an investigation by another county, but I never saw it in the paper, nor to my knowledge were the violations ever investigated.

#

1967

I awoke to discover Uncle Mike back at my bedside. I smiled and sat up. He unzipped the canopy, moved the sides apart, and hugged me.

"How are you today, little one?" he asked.

"Ready to go home," I said, thinking maybe he'd believe me and take me to his home.

"I brought you some coloring books. I could teach you some letters of the alphabet," he said. He pulled my hospital tray over to the bed and put a plastic bag on it. He took the coloring books and crayons out of the bag and placed them neatly on the tray next to the water.

I was thirsty but hated to swallow the water. It hurt. Sometimes drinking things made me sick to my stomach, my mid-section ached from the stitches on my side and back and the strip of stitching on my tummy. Throwing up was the worst, it made the stitches pull and stretch, feeling like they may give way and break apart—opening me up like a pinata. If that happened, I was sure candy would not be what spilled out. So I'd drink slowly and only as much as I had to, to ease the crackling dry feeling. Reluctantly, I poured some water into my glass and drank so that my throat would be lubricated enough to visit with Uncle Mike.

"Tell me about the weirdo," I said, ready for the story.

"What do you want to know about yourself?" Uncle Mike said laughing. He loved to tease. He sat back down and pulled the chair up as close as he could to the bed.

"The weirdo guy that was bugging Mom," I said, knowing he knew what I meant and was playing with me.

"Oh, it was so strange! I was telling you that the night everything happened, I showed up at your house, thinking that nothing was wrong—but I needed to confirm that for Grandma. I was caught off guard when I got there and realized that Grandma was right. There actually was a problem. Your mom came running up to me. She didn't know why I was there, and I didn't know how to explain why I was there along with ambulances, the sheriff, neighbors—just chaos."

I turned to line up my pillows so I could be propped up or lie down while listening to him. He went on. "So I met your mom at the hospital, called your aunts, uncles, and grandparents to let everyone know at least as much as I knew because I didn't want them to hear about it on the news. Then I hung out at the hospital and pretty soon everyone got here. Grandma and everyone came down here to the hospital."

"Grandma?"

"She's been here. You've slept through most of the visits, and sometimes they don't allow you too much company. We have to take turns because we don't want to wear you out."

Trying not to talk, I nodded. I wanted to visit Grandma, but I'd seen how strict the hospital was. They wouldn't let me out of bed, and they made me keep my tent zipped unless I had a visitor. They'd wake me up to take medicine or change my bandages.

"So, the night we got here I was freaked out. Nothing made sense . . ." he said. I was glad he was as confused as I was.

"Your mom was put in a hospital emergency cubicle thingy, with those curtains that partition it off. They take your vitals and decide what they're going to do for you. It's before they admit you to the hospital." I shook my head from left to right, no idea what he was talking about. "Your mom said that after they left, a short guy with a bald head in white doctor's coat came in. He asked her questions and said mean things to her. She got really upset. The hospital staff actually had to sedate her after that."

"Sedate her?" I said wondering what *sedate* meant. Uncle Mike didn't seem to hear my question. It was hard to hear my raspy voice, especially behind the plastic.

"So they admitted her to a private room," he continued. "And I sat in a chair posted outside of it. I was on the lookout for this short bald guy dressed in a doctor's coat. No one on hospital staff knew who she was describing. He managed to get to her a couple of more times, though. I'd take a break, to go to the bathroom or get a cup of coffee, even fall asleep. She'd start screaming, and we'd run in—nurses and I. He'd been there—in her room—telling her more stuff and actually harassing her. But we never saw him. We would have thought it was her dreaming or confusion, but he gave her information about your injuries that her nursing staff wasn't aware of—so he had to have been real. We all figured he was a reporter trying to get information. Or he could have been some kind of weird mentally deranged person that gets off on this sort of thing. Whatever it was—it was strange! But he did give information to your mom that the staff didn't know at the time. Remember, one set of people were taking care of you, while another set of staff were taking care of your mom at the same time, so information about you kids was muddled."

I sat back up and poured some water in my cup. "Can I get you some ice?" Uncle Mike said. I nodded. I liked it cold. It was more soothing that way. He took the plastic water pitcher, left the room, and returned in a few minutes with ice water. He poured cold water into the tumbler and gave it to me, sat back down, pulled his chair near to the bed and leaned over like he was going to tell me a secret. I'll never forget that kindness.

"So, let me tell on myself now," he said. "Here's where I acted strangely. It was a long night, and I sat outside your mom's room in a chair—on the lookout for the weirdo or reporter guy. A janitor walks down the hospital corridor with a large blue hamper bag on wheels—it's full of sheets and stuff. Just brimming full. At this point, I'm tired, and I don't trust anyone. Remember, I'd already found out, because of what the reporter/weirdo told your mom, that we'd received incorrect information from the hospital about you. Anyhow, I think to myself, *Pammy is in that laundry hamper. Pammy could fit in it easily.* I stand up and confront the janitor! It's so embarrassing now, but I got it in my mind that you were dead and they were sneaking you into the morgue in that hamper. I mean how would they take you to the morgue if you died? In my defense I was tired." Uncle Mike stood up and adjusted my pillows.

I didn't know what the word *morgue* meant, but I didn't want to interrupt him.

Uncle Mike remembered to adjust the plastic so I could still see him clearly. Then he continued "So that poor janitor emptied all the dirty laundry out of the hamper to prove to me you weren't in there. It was embarrassing, but I was so relieved. So yep, it's been an awful ride."

I liked hearing Uncle Mike, loved his visits. It was nice he didn't expect me to carry on any conversation. He'd talk and talk, and when I rolled over to go to sleep, he'd zip up the plastic tent and quietly leave. Looking back now, I realize it must have been difficult for Uncle Mike to work all day, then come to see us. I now can appreciate his openness and his willingness to sacrifice time away from his young wife for these visits.

#

2010

I juggled my laptop computer, purse, and briefcase as I entered the security code granting me access to the assessor's office. Proceeding past staff cubicles at a quick pace, I headed for my office. *What's that?* I wondered and stopped to look closer. A crocheted blanket protruded from under a desk in one of the cubicles. I continued to my office and dropped off my things before I went back to the staff cubicles. Most of the staff were busy working.

At the desk in question, the chair was pulled neatly against the desk with the blanket tangled in the chair wheels. I bent over to get a better look. The employee next to the cubicle I was examining appeared to grow nervous. I stooped down, thinking I could see someone curled in the blanket behind the chair. I scooted the chair out of the way. Yes, someone was sleeping under the blanket. "Honey, wake up," I said in a motherly voice.

The girl, disoriented, looked up at me, her eyes foggy. "What?"

"Come to my office," I said, my face turning red. I stomped back to my office, angry that an employee was sleeping under her desk. Upset that her supervisor hadn't noticed and taken care of it for me. To top it off it appeared to be a premeditated nap! Otherwise why bring a blanket to work?

Within a few minutes, Gabby appeared. Now awake. Her eyes wide, her face pale.

"I was on my break," she said.

"Go home."

"I was on my break."

"Go home. We'll talk about it Monday morning." I stood, and Gabby went to her cubicle and gathered her things.

After some investigation, I discovered that Gabby watched movies on her cell phone and took naps under her desk often—not just on her breaks. Monday she was fired. I guess the tricky move with the chair propped in and hiding her napping body behind it had fooled her supervisor.

3

LIES AND WHISPERS

2011

MY FRIEND, a bright, successful real estate woman who'd started her own goat operation, asked to see me. The goats were used to eat forest ground brush, aiding in fire prevention. Carol had a natural beauty with her dark black hair, brown eyes and olive complexion. I was surprised to hear she had stopped by the office.

"Send her back," I told the receptionist.

Carol walked into my office. We hugged, and she took a seat as I admired how femininely she carried herself. She had a lovely air about her. "Do you know how in trouble you are?" she asked.

I shrugged my shoulders. *What was she talking about?* I'd no idea how to respond, so I remained quiet, waiting for her to clarify the amount of trouble I was in.

"The beef people. They think you're after them. You don't know what you're doing, and they're mad," she said.

"Really? Who? Because of the grazing update?"

Carol blew out a laugh and seemed to hardly believe my response or the situation. "You need to do something! They're making plans. They're mad. I tried to tell them you weren't like that. Not vindictive, not after people. I was told to stay out of it. They say you're just a hippie who doesn't know anything."

"Who says that?"

"No, not who, all of them. They're upset with you. Say you're gonna put them out of business. That you don't understand agriculture and that you'll be taxing them out of business."

Carol and I had gone through and graduated Project Centrl together. This was a two-year leadership program that taught agricultural issues, concentrating on concerns in the state of Arizona. Each month we spent one Friday and Saturday together in a different county of Arizona: Yavapai, Gila, Coconino, Yuma, Mohave, Maricopa, Pinal, Navajo, Apache, Santa Cruz, Graham, Pima, La Paz, Cochise, and Greenlee. A day before our class met, I would try to go to that county, visit a local assessor's office and learn about the county from the perspective of a local assessor. Typically we would go to lunch, and I felt that I got to know each assessor better. The next day the Project Centrl class would meet and hear from a town council, local leaders, farmers, and/or ranchers of the respective county.

There were about thirty students in the Project Centrl Class XXI—two from each county. Two females would share a motel room together, and the roommates changed from month to month, so we got to know our classmates well. I had shared a room with Carol in Safford and we learned about each other's families, her devotion to God and how she'd gotten to where she was in life. I admired her. She grew in her leadership roles with the Arizona Voice of Farmers United, and I moved up in leadership in the Arizona Association of Assessing Officers, as well as the Arizona Group of Elected Representatives. I believe our skills in leadership were a result of our participation in Project Centrl, an exceptional leadership organization. The friends I made as a result of this two-year commitment meant a lot to me, so it made it all the more disappointing to learn that the agricultural community was annoyed with me.

The first year in Project Centrl we traveled to Mexico, which borders Arizona to the south. We learned about water, infrastructure, chickens, farming, feedlots, dairy and trade – Mexico's agricultural issues. The final year we finished our training in Washington D.C., learning about issues with farming and ranching in the United States. Carol, a leader in the Arizona Voice of Farmers United, was privy to information that I was not. If she said that the agricultural community in Yavapai County was upset with my grazing updates, then I knew it was true.

"What do you think I should do? The value increase is because of thirty years of neglect, as I assumed you knew. Their taxes will be phased in. It's a small increase in taxes, twenty-seven cents per acre phased in over seven years," I said, my stomach starting to cramp. My throat felt dry.

"I can set up a presentation, and you should come tell them that," Carol offered.

"I did give a presentation to the Yavapai County Beef Association. Mattie, the president, did a whole article in the newsletter on it. If you could set something up with another organization, that would be great! I could nip the gossip. We don't want them afraid they're going to lose family farms or ranches. I'd love to do another presentation—if you think it would help,"

"The Arizona Voice of Farmers United has a lot of the same members as the beef association. It couldn't hurt if you came, spoke and did some questions and answers. I think I can set it up and get back with you. I didn't know what to do. Knew it didn't sound like you. But some really nice people are freaked out. I mean, it is a big deal to them," Carol said.

She left. Outside, through my small window, the clouds were gray and growing on this July afternoon. Our Prescott monsoons provide spectacular weather events each July. Today was no exception. The mornings start with clear blue skies. Later, innocent white puffy clouds grow throughout the day. As they grow, they turn light gray. Then they become dark gray. They murmur and rumble, a breeze picks up and gusts into wind. Finally, the clouds grow large enough to cover the entire sky and turn black, bellow, crack, and sizzle. The once unassuming clouds let forth fury. All this moisture comes to us from the Gulf of Mexico instead of from the west, like most weather. In the morning we awaken to find clear blue skies, and the pattern repeats itself.

I felt worried as I looked outside and watched the coming storm. I was an Arizona girl. My family went back three generations in Arizona; I loved agriculture. Eating is a good thing, we need agriculture to do that. Me a hippie? Me? Far from it.

In high school, like most Arizona girls, I loved cowboys, horses, and the outdoors. The Prescott culture of rodeos, parades, corn festivals, swimming in creeks—this was me.

My great grandfather Rucker had been an Arizona cowboy. My husband's great aunt was Johnie (Parsons) Fain—a ranch woman from a huge ranching family in Yavapai County. My brother-in-law had a ranch in Mexico. I wouldn't exploit family genealogy or connections, but I was an Arizona girl for sure.

It sounded like some in the agricultural community were afraid I had an agenda against rural properties. My heart was with agriculture, but the tax laws had been neglected for over thirty years. Updates had to be made so that we could be fair to everyone. Any increase in taxes to ranchers was small and would be phased in. I had to get this information out and stop any unneeded fears.

#

2011

Carol, of the Arizona Voice of Farmers United, did as promised and set up a presentation for me to explain the new tax valuations. The meeting was held at Carson's Nursery on Willow Creek Road in Prescott. I'd known the owner, Bobbie Carson, since she was a teenager. She babysat my nieces and nephews. Everyone loved Bobbie, with her broad smile and carefree attitude—now with teenagers of her own. Bobbie and I had attended the same Church of Jesus Christ of Latter-Day Saints ward, or congregation, years ago. We both helped ward members acquire food storage. Bobbie and her husband bought a farm and ranch nearby in Dewey, then moved there. Carson's Nursery was beautiful. The presentation was to be held in a room behind shelves lined with flowers, plants, and shrubs. Rose scent drifted throughout the chamber.

It was evening, not quite dark. The meeting would start at seven o'clock. I arrived with staff and a car loaded with equipment, including PowerPoint Screen, projector, and handouts. As we unloaded the vehicle, Mattie, of the Yavapai County Beef Association, pulled her pickup truck next to us.

Mattie walked over and gave me a hug. She smelled of peppermint. "Hey there, how're you doing? Can I give you some help?" she asked, as she reached out her arms to take the long round metal cylinder that held the display screen. She looked cute with her blonde hair, tight Wrangler jeans and cowboy boots. I smiled, glad to see a friendly face.

"I'm doing fine, didn't know you were coming," I said as we walked into the building together. I looked into my purse to make sure I had a bag of lozenges. I'd need some later to soothe my throat after so much talking.

We set up the equipment for our presentation. Mattie pitched in. Irritated farmers and ranchers arrived one at a time. I'd walk up and introduce myself to receive a nod, handshake, and stern face. Sometimes, if it were a friend, I'd get a hug and whispers of good luck. My hands started to feel clammy, my insides quivered. This crowd was unhappy, and I was at the center of their discontent.

It'll be okay—good thing Mattie showed up. The ranchers respect her, she understands why the agricultural valuation updates were needed. She'll help me with these guys, It's nice to have Carol here, too—she'll help with the farmers—It'll be okay, I said to myself, mustering up courage for my presentation.

Several members of the group were clearly unhappy, but they remained polite. Carol facilitated the meeting. We gave the presentation explaining the agricultural update, why values had to be updated. We reminded them the assessor's office had failed to update these values for over thirty years. We explained the dramatic increase in value from seven dollars and fifty-six cents to twenty-five dollars per acre amounted to a twenty-seven-cent per acre increase in taxes, well under market value if the property was used for another purpose. The new taxes would be phased in over the next seven years.

The citizens in attendance continued to be annoyed but didn't yell or show blatant disrespect. Still, a heavy feeling stuck in the air; the body language of audience members included folded arms, rolling eyes, suspicious glances from one member to another.

After the presentation, Mattie helped us carry equipment out to the car and helped load up. She gave me a hug goodbye. "Thanks for the presentation. You did great, I think it went a long ways to clarify the issues. Don't worry. No one likes paying taxes, but they're a fair-minded group. I'll help smooth things over," she said and smiled with kindness—or so I thought.

"I hope they understand that the tax increase is minimal and will be phased in. I agree no one likes taxes, but after thirty years of being ignored it was bound to be addressed sooner or later," I said. Mattie remained in the parking lot and waved at us as we pulled out. I saw her headed back into the building. *Odd that everyone stayed, but my staff and me; what were they discussing—regular agricultural meeting business, or me?* Later I debated about calling Carol to ask if she thought I needed to know something. But I didn't. I assumed she'd call me if there were something I needed to know. I was wrong.

There are many ways to be in the dark and feel vulnerable. This was not the first time I'd found myself in the dark alone.

#

1967

My Uncle Les came to visit at the hospital every single evening at dinner time. He was Mom's oldest brother, and he was fun. He'd watch me make three-dimensional boxes, and stars, then clap in amazement at my artistic talent. We'd talk. Actually he'd talk, but I loved to listen. He'd turn the television to a show called, *Get Smart*, a comedy about silly spies. We'd always tell the same joke: I'd say "What's this show called?" Uncle Les would respond, "Get Smart." Then I'd say, "I'm smart—you're being mean." Then he'd reply, "No, no, the show's name is *Get Smart*. I'm not saying for YOU to get smart." Then we'd laugh and watch the show. When it was time for Uncle Les to leave, I would beg him to take me with him. The last time it happened the conversation went like this:

"I can't take you with me, you have to stay," he said, looking very concerned. "Are they mean to you? Is there a reason you hate it here?"

"I can't tell you, I just hate it at night; please don't leave me," I said with my raspy achy voice.

"It makes me feel bad when you beg me, but I can't take you. If there's a reason you hate the hospital, if they're mean to you or something, I might be able to fix it. Tell me if there's something—"

"Okay, I'll tell you—but it's embarrassing," I said looking at the floor, not wanting to say, and wishing he would sneak me out.

"Out with it, little Missy," he said, then smiled, sat back down and leaned in to hear me better.

"They took my panties. It doesn't feel right," I said, my eyes tearing up from embarrassment. Uncle Les let out a deep belly laugh.

"I'll be back tonight. We can take care of this! This is an easy fix," he said and rushed out of the room, forgetting to zip me back into my oxygen tent. I crawled in and rang for the nurse. It was my night nurse, and I didn't like her. While my day nurses were fun and played princess with me, my night nurse was curt and unfriendly. She'd turn off the lights and tell me, "Time to sleep." I didn't like the dark. I was afraid Dad would visit me. No one told me he was in jail or prison, and I didn't understand he couldn't come visit. I expected him anytime and lay frightened until I could sleep. The night nurse zipped me in and left, her shoes making no noise as she exited.

Uncle Les returned later that night and woke me up. Usually, when people visited, I would wake up to find them there by my bedside waiting. This time, he woke me up and looked excited. He unzipped the oxygen tent. I sat up. "Here you go," he said with a broad grin as he handed me a package. I opened it. Inside were seven panties! "Okay, here is our top secret *Get Smart* plan, I'm gonna give you one pair to wear now. We're gonna hide the rest. Tell no one!" And he hid the package in the bottom shelf of the end table, behind some books. "When they ask you how you got your panties, just look at them like you don't understand the question, or they'll take the package of panties away. If they take the pair you're wearing, when no one is looking just get another pair from the package. Our secret joke on them! It'll drive them crazy." With that, I hugged him. He solved my biggest problem! "Oh, when you're out of these," he added. "I'll get you more. I'll keep you supplied 'til you're out of here, little Missy."

#

2011

Working with a staff of sixty people daily often brought challenges or sometimes just surprises. This was one of those times.

I looked at my cell phone, it was my sister Bev. I smiled. "Just a second, I want to shut my office door," I said into the phone as I walked over to the door and closed it. "I'm all yours," I said, returning to my chair to settle in.

"You're practically famous now!" she said laughing. "I heard you on the radio—everyone heard you on the radio."

"When? I wasn't on the radio today. I don't think . . . what was I talking about?" I said. "Maybe they took an old interview and reworked it and played it again." I looked in my drawer for a gumdrop or something. Out of lozenges. I'd have to stop by the store at lunch time.

"You like chickens—can't live without your pet Sebastian, the chicken, even put her in diapers and sleep with her at night," Bev said through giggles.

"You heard me on the radio say that?" I said, wondering if the radio had taken me out of context and done some kind of spoof —or was it something else? I found a lemon drop, something to suck on.

"It was on the radio today, two radio personalities asked what you can't live without, and some callers called and said *oh I can't live without my mom.* Some called and said *Oh I can't live without my husband.* Then a woman called and announced she was Pam, worked for the assessor's office. She stated she can't live without her pet chicken, Sebastian, who she puts diapers on and sleeps with. You're the only Pam I know that works at the assessor's office, so I figured it was you. I bet everyone that heard it thought it was you," she said, laughing.

"Oh no!" I laughed, knowing that anyone that knew me would recognize that the person on the radio wasn't me, my compromised voice pretty distinctive. "Wait a minute! There is a Pam that works here; she does have a pet chicken," I said in my most excited voice, so Bev would understand how good this story was.

"Okay, let me get a cigarette—hang on," she said. I looked at some emails and waited for Bev to get back on the phone. I really needed to go to the store for some lozenges. Maybe I'd get Chloraseptic sore throat spray. That might help a little. Despite the complaint of my vocal cords, I was determined to finish our conversation, then try to spend the day without using my voice much more. "Okay, I'm ready—tell me, tell me, tell me," Bev said.

"There's a woman here named Pam. She's in her late forties, doesn't look mentally ill or anything. One day she found her little baby chick was sick. She did what any normal adult woman would do—she shoved the baby chick into her bra."

"Oh no, she didn't!"

"You can't even make this stuff up. She shoved the little chick in her bra and smuggled it to work. All day long staff heard the chirps of this poor, sick bird cuddled inside a woman's bosoms."

"Oh, that's just 'fowl,'" Bev said laughing.

"Yep, everyone just thought it was a cell phone chirping. So the bird does what you'd think a bird would do. She goes to the break sink, right out in the open, and begins to clean herself and the little chick up. That's when she and the birdie are busted."

"Busted, you're punny!"

"It wasn't bring your bird to work day, guess she kinda got confused. So anyhow she got in trouble for that. My guess: she was on the radio today."

We finished our daily chat. I ran to the store and stocked up on throat soothers, then went home and put an ice pack on my neck. After about an hour I felt better and went back to work.

Having a regular job which required a fair amount of speaking, I'd need to remember to keep my desk stocked up with an inhaler, lozenges, and Chloraseptic.

#

From Prescott several members of my staff and I headed to Florence, Arizona. I sat in the car reading a book as my chief deputy drove. I looked forward to the statewide assessor's meeting. I always learned new information when the assessors, chief deputies, and some staff got together and debated back and forth on current issues and challenges. It was a nice change to mix with colleagues and co-workers and gave me a chance to know them.

We'd traveled through Camp Verde, Strawberry, and now drove along the East Verde River, located just north of Payson. I was surprised to receive a cell phone call from Larry Gavin, the Director of the Property Tax Division of the Arizona Department of Revenue. "I wanted to give you a heads up on a memo we're sending out to all assessors regarding the lease-study we did last year. You didn't rely on that lease-study when you updated your agricultural values, did you?"

Gigantic red-rock bluffs appeared east of the road as we wound above the East Verde River to the left. "Wh—What? Yes, I relied on it. That's why I asked for it." There was an awkward silence. I finally realized the phone had gone dead. Probably due to a loss of signal.

The driver and other passengers wanted a bathroom break. I helped navigate the driver to the public restrooms. *Good timing*, I thought. I wanted a break from the car ride myself. It was difficult for me to breathe and I didn't want anyone to notice. My paralyzed vocal cords were causing problems.

As soon as the car was parked, I jumped out. The cool pine breeze felt good as it brushed my skin. I reached into the car and pulled the inhaler out of my purse. I didn't have asthma, but the scar tissue in my neck had created an *infantile passageway*. According to the doctors, the opening was abnormally small, so that any inflammation, such as a cold, made it difficult to breathe.

After a few minutes in the cool air with the fresh breeze and the use of my inhaler, I could breathe again.

I walked down to the bank of the East Verde River and sat on a familiar rock slab that jutted up and over the swimming hole. A few strings dangled from a low hanging branch. The strings had once been part of a rope that encircled an inner-tube. People would swing and jump into the river from it. You had to swing far enough out and drop just in time to avoid hitting the rock slabs underneath the stream. It was tricky. If you were successful, you landed in the deep cool swimming hole. Some missed and hit the slab—causing bruises and broken bones, or perhaps even death. That's why the swing was cut down. I had never swung from the inner tube, although I had witnessed my sister do it many times. It had looked tempting but menacing.

It felt odd to be back. I had spent many summer days as a teenager in this very place.

I thought about the cut-off call and Gavin's announcement about the upcoming memo from the department of revenue. I wasn't surprised to learn about the memo because I had heard rumblings that the director had an influential friend who was unhappy with the agricultural grazing updates in Yavapai County. There'd been multiple meetings with Director Green, Gavin, and others from the Property Tax Division of the Department of Revenue in attendance. In these sessions, they had received political pressure to call their lease-study flawed.

After that meeting, it was rumored that Gavin, the Director of the Property Tax Division of the Arizona Department of Revenue, refused to put the "flawed" label on the lease-study. Instead, he'd agreed to send a memo stating that assessors were not to rely on the study for individual appraisals.

As I sat by the river, I had time to contemplate the timing of the memo, it seemed odd. It came a year after the updated valuations were sent out. So the rumors had been growing. *Could this mystery political "friend" have that much power?* I had to wait and see what the memo said. If the memo stated the lease-study wasn't to be used for individual appraisals, as the rumors predicted, then I was fine—because I relied on their lease-study only for mass estimates, not individual ones. *Who was this mystery political friend? Could it be Bill, the county administrator? Maybe Barney, the guy on the Executive Board of the Yavapai Republican Party, Mike, the deputy county attorney—or was there someone else?*

My travel buddies joined me on the slab. For a while we enjoyed the sounds of summer: trees rustling, river gurgling, insects chirping, and birds singing. I sighed. It was time to leave our haven and continue the trip to Florence. Despite our pleasant break, this agricultural thing kept festering in my mind. Then, as we left, I glanced back at the East Verde River and shuddered with a sudden memory of the Verde River and my father in the dark of night and the cold of winter. I preferred the light of day and the warmth of summer.

#

1967

Panty issue solved, I still had another problem—the dark. I'd sneak the television on because it offered light. Although I usually couldn't see it very well through the plastic of the oxygen tent, I could hear it since the speaker was on the call button. If the night nurse discovered the television on past nine o'clock, she'd turn it off, but she couldn't take the remote control away from me because it was hooked to the call button. So I could sneak the television back on later. She would sometimes talk in a mean tone to me, but I didn't care; it was worth it to have some light to sleep by. She'd threaten that I wouldn't get ice cream or pudding for dinner the next night if I didn't mind her and leave the television off. I'd rather have the light on at night than pudding or ice cream with dinner, even though cold deserts felt good on my throat.

Just before the television stations went off the air, I would always hear a woman read Psalm 23:

The Lord is my shepherd; I shall not want.

He maketh me to lie down in green pastures: he leadeth me beside the still waters.

He restoreth my soul: he leadeth me in the paths of righteousness for his name's sake.

Yea, though I walk through the valley of the shadow of death, I will fear no evil: for thou art with me; thy rod and thy staff they comfort me.

Thou preparest a table before me in the presence of mine enemies: thou anoints my head with oil; my cup runneth over.

Surely goodness and mercy shall follow me all the days of my life: and I will dwell in the house of the Lord forever.

I loved to hear her. Those words helped me feel less afraid and sometimes I could go to sleep even in the dark.

One night, the night nurse came in, turned off the television and scolded me. "Tomorrow is Popsicles for dessert. You won't get any if you keep this up. You need to go to sleep and leave the television off. It's nine o'clock now and time for you to go to sleep." She stomped out of the room, her shoes making no noise even as she stomped.

I lay there, afraid, trying to see through the dark, make out the shadows. Would Dad come here? Why hadn't he already? The shadows looked like a man crouched down, ready to leap at any second. I tried to remember what the lady said at night. *I will fear no evil; for thou art with me.* I said it in my mind, but I still feared Dad, and I wasn't at all sure anyone was with me. I knew enough to understand the lady was talking about God when she said *thou*. I'd been to Presbyterian churches a couple of times when Dad and Mom would stop fighting and make up. Dad would quit drinking for a couple of weeks. When he'd start drinking again, we'd stop going to church.

As I waited, afraid, I said to myself over and over, *I don't fear anything, God's with me,* and watched the shadow of something that looked to be a man ready to attack as soon as I dozed off. Despite saying the lady's words over and over in my mind, I couldn't calm my fears. I lay there in terror.

Finally, a calming voice entered the oxygen tent with me. At first, I thought it was the television, but it was off. It was a man's deep voice similar to Uncle Les's voice, yet a little deeper and more peaceful. I wasn't afraid, and the voice calmly asked: "What are you scared of?" As he asked the question, my fear left, and I felt a calm joy. I sensed I was loved and that God knew who I was.

I'm afraid I'll be killed, I answered without my voice. It pleased me to realize I could communicate without having to speak. *Then, you would be with me—always.* As he said it, I understood if I died I'd be with God, and it would be good. *I don't know why you allowed this to happen,* I thought. I had to convey my confusion regarding my dad, how he'd acted, why it had been allowed, and no one stopped it. If God was aware of me, loved me, why? All this poured out in a simple thought and I was sure he understood.

I allow people to act on their desires; otherwise, how could I know them? I don't interfere, but I was aware, and it made me sad. That satisfied me; I felt loved. I could sleep in the dark even if the shadows could jump up and attack. I'd be with God, and that wasn't bad. I turned over and went to sleep, never again afraid of the dark.

#

2011

I'd formed the Yavapai County Property Tax Sub-Committee to explore and discuss current tax laws in Arizona. The attendees were to assist in coming up with wanted and needed revisions. As the assessor, I'd work, with their help, to get these changes into state statute.

"So if I understand, and please correct me if I'm wrong, we don't want to support a clawback provision?" I said, pretending I wasn't sure. The audience burst out laughing. This was a relief because for twenty minutes now I'd been yelled at by multiple attendees. They'd raise their hands, I'd call on them, and they'd shout about their opposition to a clawback provision. A clawback provision was a provision some states had with rural properties. Basically it provided for a tax break while properties were in agricultural use. The assessor kept track of the reduction in taxes over the last five years or whatever period of time identified in law and when the property sold for any use, other than agricultural, the new purchaser would pay back the taxpayers the savings that had occurred over that period of time; we were scheduled to learn about it tonight.

Our past committee meetings averaged about thirty people over the last six months. We'd worked hard and had accomplished a lot. Tonight attendance was more than expected. The room was too crowded, with standing room only. The meeting hall was functional—walls white, an American Flag in the corner, thirty-five chairs lined up in neat little rows. About a hundred people crowded in, and barely fit. Working with this many people was difficult. The new participants seemed hostile and had not worked through the process we'd been going through.

Committee members had researched how California handled agricultural properties; the committee wanted to know what the Williamson Act was, and what was a clawback provision. We'd planned to hear an informational presentation on these topics tonight. Instead, sixty new citizens had showed up to our meeting, angry and stating that they were not interested in a clawback provision. *Okay, good to know. Let's move on,* I thought, wishing I had a microphone. I hadn't needed one for thirty people, I really should have had one for tonight.

"So, we're going to move on," I suggested. "Let's break up into four groups—about twenty-five in each cluster—and come up with our top issue and possible solutions. We'll present to the entire group in thirty minutes."

I directed the groups into their respective areas and provided butcher paper for them to put notes on. When they presented, we'd be able to read their decisions as a group. Then I reminded them they had thirty minutes to come up with ideas and a consensus.

"Can I talk to you for a minute?" a man asked. He had weathered skin that comes from working in the sun every day, a cowboy hat, jeans, and boots.

"Sure," I said and put my cold hand on my throat. It felt good. My throat was throbbing. A hundred people and I hadn't used a microphone. What had I been thinking? I should have taken a break and found a microphone; instead, I'd tried to talk loud enough for everyone to hear. My throat rebelled. I wished the meeting was over, so I could go home and put ice on it.

I might just have to disband this committee, I thought. Tonight was impossible with all these people. The new people didn't understand property taxes, and they were rude to the original board members. They'd missed too many prior meetings. Why had I kept it open to the public? *I can't do this!* I rubbed my throat, knowing I'd have no voice for the next couple of days. I'd have to take some time off work. Tears from frustration welled up; my committee was a failure. I couldn't wait to get home.

The cowboy continued, "I wanted to tell you . . . " He looked around and lowered his voice, "I wanted to tell you the reason so many of us are here tonight. Mattie made phone calls and said we better get here and stop you because you're bound and determined to regulate agriculture out of this state."

Had I heard him right? Did he say, Mattie? "Mattie? As in the Yavapai County Beef Association Mattie? She called you?"

"Yes! She called all her members. I thought you should know because I like you, and I don't believe you know what's going on." He looked directly at me, but keeping his voice low.

"I don't what?" I asked, feeling stupid. I'd no idea what he was talking about—*What was going on? Mattie was a friend, why would she call people and send them to my committee meeting? Had he misunderstood something? Did she really tell people I had an agenda to end agricultural activity in Arizona? Was this guy making this up?* My throat was starting to close off; it was becoming hard to breathe.

"You'll figure it out," he said, "but Mattie is behind it. I wanted you to know. I don't feel comfortable saying more, just . . . don't trust Mattie." Then he went to his group to work on his assignment.

I left for the bathroom to use my inhaler. That only helped minimally; it still took a lot of effort to breathe. Because of scar tissue, exerting my paralyzed vocal cords caused swelling, so it was hard to get air into my throat.

I stepped outside, and the fresh air felt good. I sucked it in, and instantly my throat opened enough to breathe more easily. I leaned against the red brick of the building, admiring the stars. The dark is fantastic in Prescott; you see so many stars! I thanked God for letting me live in such a beautiful place with such a beautiful night sky. I reflected on tonight's meeting. *Did Mattie actually sabotage my committee meeting? Why would she do that?* I'd felt honored that Barney from the Executive Board of the Republican Party had attended. Now I wondered if his attendance was connected to Mattie's phone calls.

#

A Month Later

I was excited to serve on the board of the Arizona Group of Elected Representatives, AGER, as the representative for the assessors. Today I sat with the AGER board around a large, round, highly polished maple conference table. We listened to various proposals and bills, then voted to support, oppose or remain neutral on each of the proposals.

The various personalities around the table were fascinating. The guy to my right, middle-aged, liked to be heard and wasn't a great listener. The man at the head of the table, middle-aged also, liked to get along with everyone. All the women on the board, five total, remained quiet and polite, speaking only when asked their opinion on something. The young lobbyist giving the presentation spent her time explaining the bills from a neutral point of view. We listened. On some issues, you could tell the Democrats from the Republicans just by watching them lean in or out, or fold their arms around their chests.

We heard a lecture on civil discourse, and I smiled to myself. This was going to be fun. I liked being part of something that would make a positive difference for the citizens of Arizona. My heart beat quickly, but I tried to sit still. It was exciting to work with other county officials throughout the state. I'd seen these people on television or read about them in the newspaper. Here I was working with them on legislative items that impacted counties. With barely a voice, I'd been voted by my fellow assessors last month to represent them on this committee. Now here I was.

On the balcony, after the meeting, I enjoyed the smell of

orange blossoms. Trisha, the lobbyist for AGER, asked. "Are you having meetings on behalf of the governor's office?"

"No," I said. "The governor's office? In the name of the governor's office? No. I don't even know Governor Brewer."

"The governor's office called AGER—said you were holding meetings that you indicated were at the request of the governor's office. They want you to knock it off."

I fought back the tears. The smell of orange blossoms was not so pleasant now. *Why was this happening? I'd never act like I had some kind of friendship with the governor and was conducting meetings on her behalf.* "I didn't—I've been having meetings simply to understand my constituent's desires on property tax reform. I never said it was on behalf of the governor."

I went on to explain to Trisha that I was on an ad hoc committee for the Arizona Association of Assessing Officers to come up with suggestions for property tax reform for the 2011 legislative session. Then I was appointed to the newly formed tax policy committee as part of Senate Bill 1035. We were supposed to report back to Governor Brewer by December—but we hadn't had those meetings yet. "The governor knows about that committee," I added. "The meetings I'm having in Yavapai County with my constituents are to help me understand what they want in reform! I've never said that these sessions were for the governor or that the governor asked me to have these meetings for her." My stomach felt heavy, and my throat felt dry. I reached into my purse to see if I had a lozenge or a lemon drop.

Trisha looked from right to left, lowered her voice, and said, "I used to be the lobbyist for Arizona Beef Association before I came here. They, um—they were having problems with membership. I'm gonna tell you something, but I'll deny it if you ever repeat it."

I nodded, and she continued. "A lot of people in Arizona agriculture belong to both the ABA—run by Mattie—and they also belong to the Arizona Voice of Farmers United. Well, membership in Mattie's organization, the ABA, is waning because a lot of people don't like Mattie. You know she shot those pet dogs, and she just has a bad reputation—"

"She—killed pet dogs?" I said, shocked. I held my hand just under my throat on my upper chest and pushed my hand to open my passageway a little. My throat felt like it was trying to close; my skin tingled. I'd liked Mattie. *Mattie shot dogs and had a bad reputation?* I'd never heard any of that.

"Yes. She shot two of her neighbor's pet Labradors. Look it up in the *Verde Independent;* they did a pretty good job of covering the story. At any rate, the membership in ABA is dwindling. Agricultural people are renewing membership for the Voice of Farmers United—but not ABA. Now remember, I was a lobbyist for ABA, that's how I know." Trisha looked again from side to side then lowered her voice so that the board members in the conference room or out on the balcony couldn't hear us. "The best way to drive up membership is to give members a threat, so they're claiming you're going to increase property taxes so high they'll lose their ranches. Your reputation will be destroyed! They're going through the state holding meetings. They're claiming they'll fight to keep assessors like you from killing off the ranching industry in Arizona, but they have to have membership to fight bad guys like you."

"I went through Project Cntrl, a leadership program that taught us about agricultural issues in Arizona. I like agriculture, I'm not—"

"It's not personal. They're using you to drive up membership, and you're probably going to be thrown under the bus. Politics is a blood sport."

My left hand grabbed onto the balcony railing. I was feeling hot and dizzy. *This makes sense, but it's so calculated! How can I affect property tax reform if Mattie is whispering lies?* "Do you have any idea how I could counteract this?" I asked.

"Nope. That's the power of a whisper campaign; there's no way to fight back." Trisha leaned in and gave me a hug. I wiped at my tears. They tasted salty. It hurt to know that Mattie was behind this. *How could I have been so stupid?*

Back in my office on Monday, I received a letter from State Senator Yarborough. It said my appointment on the newly formed

Tax Policy Committee in no way entitled me to conduct meetings in Yavapai County for the governor's office and I was to stop making such claims. I sent out an email to everyone that had attended any of the property tax reform committee meetings in Yavapai County, clarifying that the meetings were for us to come up with property tax reform ideas and in no way were they held on behalf of Governor Brewer or requested by her office, nor were they about my position on the Tax Policy Committee as part of Senate Bill 1035. The Yavapai County meetings were for us, and we would work together to attempt to change property tax laws. I sent a copy of this letter to Senator Yarborough. I never heard back from him.

I shut my office door and looked out the window. I spotted a spider. I'm not a spider expert, but it appeared to me to be a brown recluse. It was bigger than a penny, sandy brown with a darker brown violin-shaped marking on its back. The spider was working on making its gray web bigger, to surround a moth tangled up in the web. *Poor moth,* I thought, *how scared it must be.*

I grabbed my cell phone and dialed my sister's number. *Pick up, pick up, pick . . .*

"Hi there, how's it going today?" Bev said.

"Bad! You're not going to believe it! Mattie shot two Labrador retrievers to death. One was a thirteen-year-old yellow lab, and the other one was a three-year-old chocolate lab," I blurted.

"Today?"

"Oh, no. Sorry. She did it in March. Pull up the *Verde Independent* on your computer and do a search on her name. It'll come up."

"Okay wait. I'm gonna pull it up and also light a cigarette," Bev said. "Oh my, so it's range law? Hmm, looks like the Collier's gate was left open, and their dogs escaped. Oh man, they heard the shots when they were looking for their dogs and ran up and caught Mattie on her horse with the rifle and the poor dead pets. That can't be legal. Killing labs—that's sick."

"Well, Mattie claims those dogs killed her calf a week before. If the dogs were chasing cattle, then it's legal if you shoot, but the

Colliers claim their labs weren't out a week before. Anyhow, they settled for some unknown amount of money out of court."

"Even so, that's only a civil crime! You'd think there'd be some kind of criminal thing for shooting in a town like that," Bev said. "It says it happened near the Safeway grocery store parking lot in Cottonwood."

"I know. It makes me really not like Mattie. Especially considering everything else." I rummaged through my desk looking for some hard candy.

"Say the word. I'll kick her ass," Bev said and started to laugh.

"No, I hear she's a pretty good shot."

"Well, she's a big shot for sure."

I then proceeded to tell Beverly about my week, how Mattie apparently was setting me up so that she could drive up membership in the ABA. How my Yavapai County property tax reform committee was being derailed. Bev sympathized and said naughty things about Mattie—which made me feel better.

Looking out my window, I noticed the moth had given up its struggle and lay there, in the web, awaiting its fate. I pitied the moth and hated the spider.

#

1967

Time seemed to stand still in the hospital. Mom, Bevy, and my little brother were released, but I stayed—eventually moved from the dimly-lit room into a room with white walls and a television set. The nurse call-button and speaker for the television were still all in one unit tied to the metal railing of my bed. An oxygen tent still surrounded me and separated me from the room. The room was brightly lit during the daytime with fluorescent light tubes in the ceiling. I liked that. But at night it was dark, with little light streaming from the corridor.

My bed was near a window. I had roommates; they would come and stay for a few days or a week; then they'd go while I stayed and stayed. The roommates had their own television sets and a curtain to separate us. Most roommate patients kept to themselves. But some times, the roommate and I would get acquainted. Once, a newlywed couple included me in their conversation. They had champagne to toast something, and they got me a 7-Up so I could toast with them.

Another roommate was my age. She was in an oxygen tent, too. I liked her. Her mom would come every day and read us both nursery rhymes and stories as we sat outside our tents. My mom actually knew my roommate's mom; they'd gone to school together. I was glad the girl got well, but I was sad that she got to go home while I stayed at the hospital.

"Why don't I get to go home?" I asked the nurses over and over.

"You know how you sleep all the time and you're so tired? When you are better you won't be so tired, and you'll be able to go home," the day nurse said. I was never well enough to be moved to the children's ward or strong enough to go play on the playground train that I knew was there.

My oxygen tent unzipped and folded back so I could be with my visitors. One time, I sat on my bed as Mother brushed my hair that had grown well past my shoulders. "What's this, why's it white like that?" Mom asked the nurse, holding a lock of my hair up in the air. I had a long clump of hair about an inch thick, from my scalp to the end of the strands, that had turned completely white while the rest of my hair remained brown.

The nurse came over to look. "I'm not sure. Emotions can affect hormones and the body's chemical levels. My guess would be it's temporary and will grow back brown. Kind of like the old myths of being scared and your hair turns white. She's been through a lot; her body's just processing it."

Mom smiled. "That's kinda cool, huh? Like Frankenstein's wife," she said, sounding cheerful. I knew she was acting. I could see her eyes as they teared up, and I heard her voice quiver.

"I'm tired, can I get my hair brushed tomorrow?" She agreed, and I climbed into bed as Mom zipped up my oxygen tent. I could see her cry as she left the room.

#

2011

It was springtime in old Prescott, trees budding out in neatly landscaped yards that front historic homes, restored and looking like they did a hundred years ago. Most yards had American flags displayed with pride. Go a little further from these downtown areas, and you find ranchettes. Further still are vast tracks of open land, consisting of federally managed land and ranches. Cows sprinkle the landscape throughout the county.

I was excited to be invited to lunch at Murphy's Restaurant by a member of the Yavapai County Executive Board of the Republican Party. *I am not worthy,* I said to myself, trying to be funny like the characters in the movie Wayne's World—but I felt pretty honored. My mom will be so proud. *I'll call her tonight and tell her,* I thought.

Murphy's started as a mercantile and general store in the 1890's. It's a classy landmark and has fantastic, albeit pricey, food. I certainly was not a regular. But I was running in this favored circle now, so I'd be eating at Murphy's—*I am in the tribe—I've arrived,* I thought and smiled, pushing out my chest and standing up straight as I entered.

I had invited my friend Missy, who seemed excited to be included. We decided that she would bring a notebook and paper to write down what suggestions Barney had for me so that I could be a better politician. Also, Missy suggested we audiotape the meeting, in case she got caught up in the conversation or forgot to write down something important.

Barney waved from a booth he was sitting at and motioned for us to join him. Missy slipped into the restaurant booth, and I slid in beside her. "Barney is a member of the Yavapai County Republican Executive Board and wanted to visit with us about some concerns they have," I explained to Missy before giving my attention to Barney.

"I invited you here Pam, 'cuz well—" Barney shifted his gaze from me to Missy then back to me. I wondered what Barney thought of Missy. Missy and I were both in our forties, while

Barney looked to be in his early fifties. Missy was a spunky, cute blonde with blue eyes. I had known her since junior high school and long ago had trusted her with my deepest secrets. Barney said, "We think it's time for you to remember who you work for."

I had no idea that afternoon I would be blindsided. I thought that Barney had ideas he wanted to share with me to help me do a better job as the county assessor.

"Wh—" I began to respond but was interrupted by the waitress. We each took a turn and ordered lunch.

After the waitress left, Barney's chin jutted out, oddly reminding me of a duck. He slowly and firmly said, "These grazing values are not gonna be acceptable. We will make it painful for you if you continue on this course."

I folded my arms across my chest. Calmly smiled. I leaned in so that Barney would be sure to hear me. "I work for everyone —even Jehovah Witnesses, who won't do a thing to get me re-elected, but they own property in Yavapai County. I work for the Democrats, who aren't gonna help me get re-elected, but they own property in Yavapai County. Barney, I work for the ranchers, who won't be doing anything to help me get re-elected, but they—"

Barney's face turned red. *Was he angry?* He stood up. "Are you leaving?" I asked. I scooted out of my seat to follow Barney as he walked away. "Are you leaving?" I asked again, trying to raise my voice, but finding that impossible. As Barney scurried away, I thought he looked like a platypus whose parts didn't fit together. At that instant, I spotted a man sitting in the booth directly behind me.

"Pam, what are they trying to get you to do?" Tom asked. He was an acquaintance and a very active Republican who was sitting with a group of people. "It's my birthday," he added with a broad smile.

Barney did not look back, but he continued to walk away and quickly was out the door. I could hardly believe he'd left before the food even arrived. *What was I supposed to do with his order?*

"What are they trying to get you to do now?" Tom asked again, this time motioning towards the door.

"Same stuff—favors for some, tax shifts for others."

"That's a bunch of crap," Tom said with a frown. The people sitting at his table nodded in agreement.

"Happy birthday," I said. Tom nodded, grinned and turned his attention back to his guests.

I returned to Missy and sat across from her. I whispered, "Did you record everything?"

Missy nodded. I smiled, glad that in Arizona it was legal to record conversations as long as one of the people being recorded knows about it. In this case, both Missy and I knew our conversation had been recorded, so it was legal—that struck us funny. We laughed and enjoyed our expensive lunch. Then we packed Barney's lunch to share the next day.

#

Not only were things happening on a county level but the Tax Policy Committee, part of Senate Bill 1035, finally met in Phoenix. I'd bought a new blue dress that hung barely below my knees. It had a long gold-colored zipper in the back that zipped from the top all the way down. Sexy in the back; professional in the front. My black high-heeled shoes were over four inches high. I carried a tan designer purse. I was ready and felt great. I stood straight as I walked from the state Capitol parking lot to the House of Representatives building. I'd prepared for years with research and meetings with constituents. I was very clear on the reforms I'd like to see. I had a briefcase full of ideas with examples from other states. I'd hardly gotten any sleep the night before, thinking about actually being at the Capitol and working towards reform.

Inside, the room had a lower section for spectators and an upper area for the committee. Desks sat in six tiers. A nameplate that stated *Honorable Pearsall* identified my desk on the highest level near Representative Jack Harper's desk. I took my seat, hiding the fluttering in my stomach and my giddiness. There were a few other assessors on the committee, a couple of tax agents, a tax attorney and two representatives from the state legislature—Representative Yarborough and Representative Harper.

Looking down into the lower audience section, I saw Mattie with a lobbyist from Arizona Beef Association. She waved at me in a friendly manner. I waved back, pretending to be happy to see her.

Representative Harper called the meeting to order, hit his gavel on the desk and called the roll. I said *here* when he called my name. It was so cool, my name called in the state House of Representatives building for an important committee meeting! I probably was grinning.

After roll had been called, Representative Harper announced a presentation by the Maricopa County Assessor Keith Russell on how property taxes work in Arizona. *That's odd—everyone on this committee understands how the current system works: the assessors know, the tax agents know, the tax attorneys know—why have a presentation?* From my vantage point, I could see Representative Harper's computer screen as he checked his emails and read *Capitol Times*. I was disappointed that he wasn't paying attention to the presentation. Representative Yarborough sat on a lower tier and was to my right. He seemed attentive. *The only two people that might not completely understand property taxes in Arizona are these state Representatives, and one doesn't appear to care.*

Next, Joy Gomez, a tax agent, did another presentation on the process of property taxes in Arizona. Representative Harper continued to pay attention to his computer and seemed to ignore the presentations. After Gomez, Representative Harper adjourned the meeting. No further meetings were scheduled. There was no input from the committee regarding suggestions for reform.

After the meeting, I walked up to Representative Harper, "Don't we need more meetings? When will we have meetings to discuss reform?"

"I didn't schedule any, so we're done."

"Done?"

"Yes, we're done," he said, turning to speak to someone else who'd walked up. I stood confused. *We're done, but no one from the committee had an opportunity to say anything—done? We didn't do anything.*

I walked down to the audience section. Mattie came up and gave me a hug. "I'm so proud of you," she said sweetly.

"For what?" I asked. I wanted to cry, but I'd wait until I got to my car. I'd worked so hard in preparation for today. I hadn't understood. I thought we all wanted reform.

"I just love how hard you work and how far you've come. Working with strong women is great. We have to stick together," she said with a smile that seemed sweet and sincere. Mattie wasn't a friend. I'd never met anyone like her before. So beautiful, so tricky. She didn't look like someone who would kill Labrador Retrievers.

#

The Big Island of Hawaii, with its lava rocks and lush greenery surrounded us. For five years we put aside money each month, faithfully saving for a trip to Hawaii. Here it was, and we were in paradise.

My husband, Bob, had insisted I leave the laptop computer behind. He wanted the trip to be about tours, scuba diving, trying new and exotic foods, and enjoying the company of each other. I laughed to myself, understanding that Bob didn't realize a smartphone was basically a palm-sized computer—so it was easy to agree to his requests. Besides, spending private time with him was long overdue.

Five days into our vacation, I received an email from a local reporter. "I need a comment about the agricultural lawsuits that were filed today." *What lawsuits?* I slipped outside onto the wooden deck of the condo we'd rented. The view was spectacular—black lava rock, the beach, and the limitless ocean.

I phoned my office and asked them if there were agricultural lawsuits served. They responded that none had been received. I quickly let the reporter know that the suits had not yet come in. She emailed me the press release she'd received and said she wanted a comment in the next hour or she'd run the story without a comment from me.

Apparently, about ninety-five agricultural property owners filed lawsuits against the county for their updated valuations. The list of property owners read like a who's who of the county and contained its most influential citizens. *Crazy they'd send a press release before they'd even served the lawsuit.* I came up with what I hoped was an articulate comment then called Tami, the reporter, and gave her my quote.

As we finished our vacation, I ignored the temptation to monitor the newspaper and concentrated on my husband and the beauty of the island.

#

1967

After I was released from the hospital, there were still issues. Mom asked Uncle Junior and Aunt Ethel if we could stay overnight with them so they could witness what Mom saw, because the doctor seemed to think Mom was just overprotective and that she had exaggerated what she relayed to him.

"Why are you doing this?" Mother asked me with frustration and concern. It was the middle of a chilly night. We sat in my Uncle Junior and Aunt Ethel's car. Aunt Ethel was at the steering wheel ready to rush me to the hospital.

Several nights in a row, as I went to bed, I'd be okay. I would lie down and fall asleep. Then I'd start gasping loudly as I tried to breathe—gulping for air. I felt like a little goldfish who found herself out of her bowl, yet could still find a drop of water here or there if she worked for it, flipping and floundering, trying to get to something that was only barely available. Mom would grab me, screaming, and carry me out into the cold air, all in a panic. Once awake, once outside, the air was attainable, and the struggle would end.

The doctors said Mom was overprotective, imagining things. Now she had Uncle Junior and Aunt Ethel as witnesses to the nightly events.

Armed with her witnesses, we went to the hospital. They convinced the doctor to admit me for observation. That night, as I went to sleep in my hospital bed, I started to flail, struggle and gasp. I gulped and wheezed, but my throat refused to allow the air to pass easily. My mother was vindicated. Her reports had not been an overreaction.

"Her left vocal cord is completely paralyzed," the ear nose and throat specialist said. "The right one is about ninety-eight percent paralyzed. When Pam relaxes and goes to sleep, they fall on each other, and oxygen is restricted from passing through until she wakes up and is exposed to the cold night air. It's getting worse, and soon she'll be doing this even when fully awake. We need to do surgery soon—sew the left vocal cord, so it stays stable and won't fold in. Also, we must put an opening in her windpipe to allow the air direct access to a breathing tube. The surgical procedure is called a tracheostomy. We basically surgically tie the paralyzed vocal cord over, and then we'll put an opening in her windpipe. A tube will be placed through this opening to provide an airway and to remove secretions from the lungs. There is a metal collar that she'll wear and the nurse will instruct you on how to keep all the parts clean. Pam will have a speaking valve to cover with her finger when she speaks."

The doctor sounded serious. I liked his white coat but thought the leather band on his head with its mirrored disk made him look silly. Mom's eyes teared up, her face ashen. "Will she be able to speak?" Mom asked, her voice quiet and shaky.

The doctor shrugged his shoulders. "She might be able to, but she might never be understood. It's a very precise surgery. If I don't sew the vocal cord far enough, she'll have problems breathing without the tracheotomy, that's what the opening is called after the procedure. If I sew it too far, she won't be able to produce enough sound to be understood. One step at a time. We'll do the tracheostomy, then review and evaluate. If at a later time we find she can breathe without the tracheotomy then we can surgically close it. First, let's concentrate on the breathing. She has to be able to breathe."

"I have another question. Because of the gunshot wounds, is her spleen gone or damaged?" Mom looked in her purse, pulled out a looped-handled red lollipop, handed it to me, and gave a weak smile.

"Spleens, they fall apart when . . . it's still there but . . . damaged. It won't work," he said.

"Will she ever be able to have children?"

"Oh sure, that's not a problem. Spleens don't have anything to do with the reproductive system. Spleens help with the immune system. She could be sickly, though. We can work with penicillin and try to keep her away from others that are sick."

4

PUSH OR PULL?

1967

Weeks after the tracheostomy surgery, it was finally time to leave the hospital. Mom had met a man—now her boyfriend—Jerry. They both picked me up from the hospital.

"Grandma's with Bevy and your brother because they've already met Jerry. He wanted to meet and get to know you," Mom said. I thought he looked like James Garner in the *Maverick* television series.

The procedure I'd undergone left my throat tender with an opening in it that made it easy to breathe through. The opening was encased with a medical apparatus consisting of a couple of tubes. One was larger and stationary. The other one slipped in and out of the larger tube and could be removed for cleaning. A metal plate on the front of my neck held everything stable, while strings tied in the back of my neck kept the plate and tubes from shifting around.

We went to the Pinnacle Peak Patio—a steakhouse in north Scottsdale, a fun Western restaurant. As soon as we sat down, a charred cowboy boot on a platter passed in front of us. Jerry laughed, "If you order your steak well-done that's what the waiter brings you," he said. Looking up, he added, "This is their collection of clipped ties. If you come dressed up in a suit and tie, the waiter will cut your tie off with a cleaver and hang it from the ceiling." He pointed to the ties dangling from the beams. I looked up and saw red, blue, polka-dotted and striped ties—ties of all colors dangling from the rafters leaving no empty spots. I couldn't begin to count them all but assumed there were kazillions.

The patio had picnic tables with benches. A band played country music like, *There Goes My Everything, Don't Come Home A' Drinkin' With Lovin' On Your Mind,* The aroma of mesquite wood and steaks on the outdoor grills wafted over us as we sat at our table. I liked Jerry. *Where's Dad? I wondered. No one spoke of him.* I didn't ask. He wasn't here with us. I was all right with that.

Mom and Jerry held hands.

I clapped and put my finger on the opening in my windpipe. "A love story!" I said. I'd seen James Garner kiss the girl on TV and wondered if I'd see Jerry kiss Mom tonight. I didn't.

"What do you want to eat? You can have anything. I bet it'll beat that hospital food," Jerry said.

"Just orange soda," I said, with my finger covering the opening on the metal tube. It took work to speak. The contraption was bulky and warm on my neck. I started to get tired.

"Okay, orange soda and I'll share my steak with you," Jerry said.

Once the orange soda came, I sipped it and tried to use my manners so Mom would be proud. Later I lay down on the bench and went to sleep. *I'm probably not supposed to lie down at a restaurant,* I thought, but I was so tired, and Mom and Jerry didn't seem to mind.

#

2012

Let's look at the lawsuit, and their press release, I thought, sitting at my desk where the Rosie the Riveter poster challenged me with its caption "We Can Do It." The taxpayers of Yavapai County had been shortchanged because the calculation on agricultural properties hadn't been updated for over thirty years. No matter the pushback, I'd continue to value these properties fairly and not give favors to special interest. I'd represent the taxpayers of the County, ensuring that the burden of taxes was kept as small and as equitable as possible. When favors had been given to ranch owners, it had unfairly shifted the tax burden to ordinary taxpayers. *Yes, Rosie, we can do this.*

The lawsuit—Arizona Beef Association versus Yavapai County—had pages of ranches and parcel numbers, a total of about ninety-five plaintiffs including the Spider Ranch—the Spider Ranch? *Crap! Wasn't that the county attorney, Sheila Polk's, family ranch? Crap, crap, crap!*

Oh great, there's Mattie's ranch! In fact, she was the front of the entire lawsuit, the go-to person. *It's really time to unfriend her from my Facebook, probably should block her too. I bet she timed that press release about this lawsuit on purpose to coincide with my trip to Hawaii—dang that dog killer.* Seemed anyone powerful and important here in our county was named with her in the lawsuit. *Really, they're suing over an update that was about thirty years overdue? Are they really all fooled with Mattie's propaganda, her agenda to increase membership? Is that it? A twenty-seven cent per acre tax increase phased in over seven years, hardly seemed worth lawsuits and legal fees.* My thoughts were interrupted by the phone.

"This is Donny Stanley, could we schedule a meeting? I have a problem with the assessor's office and my agricultural properties." *Was there going to be any other kind of problem in Yavapai County this week?*

"Sure, what kind of problem are you having?'

"Well, hmm, the appraiser, Kiarra—I don't wanna get anyone in trouble, ma'am—but the fact is, she doesn't get out of her car and look at anything. She seems to be on some kind of power trip and denies that I'm ranching on my properties! But I'm ranching! I'm a developer, too, don't wanna lie about that, but the properties I'm talking about are being used for ranching. So I wanted to meet with you about that."

I smiled, thinking that a pleasant road trip would solve this. I could show a rancher I'm not out to get him. Sounded fun. "Sure, can I meet you somewhere tomorrow? Then you can show me your ranch and the parcels she's denying."

"Really? You—you'll come see?"

"Sure, but I'll need to meet you somewhere. Then I'll follow you in, or ride with you. I'll bring the file—you can show me the cows," I said, and we both laughed. I laughed because it sounded like *show me the money*. I think he laughed because he was relieved.

This was a chance to wear my cowgirl boots and Wranglers. I'd hike the fencing if needed on Stanley's ranch. On the way, I'd enjoy the drive through the historic hillside town of Jerome. Many of the homes there are over a hundred years old, and they hang on the cliff-side—in some cases sliding down the hill. Once a thriving copper mining town, by the 1950's Jerome had become a ghost town. Now it was an artsy tourist destination.

After an hour's drive, my chief deputy Ron and I arrived at Donny's office in Cottonwood. Donny Stanley was a well-mannered rancher who never forgot to say please and thank you. He told stories; Ron and I enjoyed his company and laughed at his jokes. I showed him the maps of the parcels in question. He explained his grazing plans, pointed on the maps where the fencing was and the access. Then he loaded Ron and me into his car, and we drove to his property. I followed my maps as Donny drove. I marked fence lines as I saw them and noted the cows in the enclosures. According to Kiarra's notes, fencing was missing—but here it was.

"Can you stop? I'd like to get some photos," I said, grabbing the camera out of my purse. Donny pulled over, and I took several photos and jotted down information regarding the fencing, clearly visible, that had been noted as missing in the files. Later Ron and I drove back to the office.

#

"Kiarra, can you come see me when you have a minute?" I said lightly as I walked past her cubicle. Kiarra and another appraiser named Bridget showed up in my corner office about ten minutes later. I motioned for both of them to sit down. They looked at each other and remained standing. "Donny Stanley's property," I said, but before I could finish Kiarra interrupted.

"We were there today," Kiarra said, "and he still doesn't have fences, so we're denying the agricultural classification." She had her right hand on her hip as she made the statement.

"You were there today? So were we; he does have the fencing up. I took photos. You know, when I was an appraiser, I found that vacant land could be tricky. It's out in the middle of nowhere. You can get confused and be at the wrong site. I understand how easy that is, I've done it. But Donny does have the fencing up. I've marked it here on the map and here's the photos," I said without malice.

I understood how easy it was to get confused. When I appraised with Scott, I'd gotten turned around myself until I'd become an expert with legal descriptions, a compass, and map. Scott had made sure of that. He'd given me a compass one Christmas as a gag gift. I wasn't angry at Kiarra; she just needed more training.

Kiarra rolled her eyes, flipped her head back and chuckled. She shook her head and said, "There's no fencing. He doesn't qualify for agriculture."

"These properties qualify for agricultural classification, and they are approved. We were there today. You either missed the fences or were on the wrong property," I said firmly. I was starting to feel angry. I'd had enough of Kiarra's attitude. *Is this some kind of power trip? Does she have it out for Donny? I'm glad I went and saw the fences for myself; if I hadn't, I would've believed her. Does Kiarra even know how to read a map and a compass?*

"There are no fences," she said in a snarly voice as she left my office and stomped away with Bridget following her.

That's it! I decided.

The next morning I asked a representative from human resources to wait in my office as I went to get Kiarra. I walked to her cubicle, "Kiarra, I need to see you in my office."

"Can't right now, I'm going into the field," Kiarra said, gathering up her clipboard, measuring tape and purse.

"No, I need you to come see me in my office now," I said, my hands clenched in fists. I turned—in my high heels—and walked to my office. *She better follow.*

I got to my desk and looked at Regina from human resources. I liked Regina; she was my age, and I loved her ideas about cooking.

"She'll be here in a minute," I said, hoping I was right. As we waited, Regina caught me up with her family, and I told her of the challenges I'd had with Kiarra and my reorganization plan.

It took five minutes, but Kiarra finally arrived. Her eyes widened when she saw Regina.

"Please shut the door and sit down," I said, directing Kiarra towards a green swivel chair to the side of my desk.

"Is everything ok?" she asked, looking from Regina and then to me.

"I'm transferring you to the commercial department. Your new supervisor will be Lucille, and this is effective as of now." I handed Kiarra the new organizational chart with her new position. I also handed her a seating chart showing her where her new seat assignment would be in the office. "The move to the new cubicle will happen today," I added.

"Don't I have any say in this?" Kiarra asked in what appeared to be disbelief. She directed this question to Regina.

"The assessor is in charge of this office and can assign you to any department she needs. As long as you work for the assessor's office, it's up to her," Regina said. I was so relieved to have Regina with me.

"There's nothing I can do about it?" Kiarra asked, her eyebrows raised, her chest puffed out ready for combat.

"No, not as long as you want to remain working here. If you want to work in the assessor's office, it will be in the commercial department," I answered.

"I like the agricultural appraising! I don't want to...be transferred," Kiarra said, her eyes tearing up.

I sat without comment and looked at her with a blank stare, waiting for her next remark.

"Can I ask why?"

"Sure. Kiarra, you've been disrespectful to me several times since I was elected assessor. I tried to give you time, sought to earn your respect. Now I'm done. I was elected to run this office. People will be given agricultural classification if I say they qualify. I'm not going to argue about it with you. I'm going to do lease-studies and look at agricultural files when I want to. I shouldn't have to beg you for permission. You rolled your eyes at me yesterday—that was the last straw. I'm frankly not going to take it, so you're being transferred to a new department. Your disrespect, the mistake with fencing, all of this will be documented and put in your file. More problems could result in your losing your job."

Kiarra looked at Regina, her eyes wide, her face turning red. "I'm, I'm . . . there's nothing I can do?" she asked again.

Regina took over. "There's plenty you can do. You can be a good commercial appraiser. You can understand that Pam is the assessor and you will treat her with respect, or you can go find yourself a new job somewhere else. You have plenty of choices. What you can't do, what the assessor is no longer going to tolerate, is you running the show. If you want to run the show—run for the job of assessor and win; otherwise, you're a worker bee."

I was shocked at how supportive Regina was.

"Kiarra, don't gossip about this. You're a commercial appraiser now," I said. "Anyone asks why—you can direct them to ask me. If I find out there is gossiping or murmuring, you'll be called back to my office, and it will be documented."

"Can I have the rest of today off? So I can process this. I'd like to compose myself. Decide if I still want to work here."

"Sure, take today off, make a decision if you want to work here, for me or not. If you decide to come back tomorrow, you'll need to change your attitude and work with me, " I said.

Kiarra stood, no longer puffed up and proud, but slumping a little as she left the office. I hugged Regina and thanked her for her help.

#

1967

After I had the surgery and was released from the hospital I lived with my grandparents in a small town called Yarnell, Arizona. Mom worked at Motorola in Phoenix a couple hours drive away; she needed money to support us, but more importantly she needed to have health insurance.

The tracheostomy had created an opening in my windpipe. I now had a contraption called a tracheotomy, that consisted of a collar tied around the back of my neck with a metal plate in the front. A hole in the center attached to a metal tube called the outer cannula. This snaked it's way through my windpipe and kept the hole open, making it easier to breathe. There was a smaller metal pipe called the inner cannula—this fit inside the first wider tube (the outer cannula). The inner cannula was removable. Grandma pulled it out and cleaned it with pipe cleaners and rubbing alcohol after each meal.

The new device made it difficult for me to swallow or bathe. To talk, I put my finger on the opening on the front metal plate, forcing the air to go out of my mouth rather than escape through my neck. My throat was tender, and pressing against the plate on the front of my neck rubbed the skin around the opening raw. I tried to listen and obey and spoke only when I had to.

Months earlier I'd looked out my hospital window and watched the school kids line up at their school bus stop. I had daydreamed that I could be one of those kids. Now finally, I was going to school, just like them. The Yarnell school was small with only two rooms, three rows of desks in each room. Each row represented a grade—first, second, and third in the first room. The other room had fourth, fifth, and sixth grade. I was in first-grade. I sat in the first room, first row, third seat back. My brown hair hung to my waist. I usually wore it down and curled at the ends, I hoped I could hide my throat by putting most of my hair in front of it. Grandma wanted to French braid my hair because she said it looked neat and would stay out of the way of the metal pipes—but she'd let me wear it any way I wanted.

"Let me stay at school and eat, like the other kids," I pleaded. "Please. I'll be good. I want those Necco candies like the other kids have, and a lunch box with Cinderella on it like Melissa's." I spoke holding my index finger to my neck as I'd been taught. And I crossed my fingers on my left hand for good luck.

This request would be difficult for Grandma to fulfill because she had to use a suction machine three times a day to remove secretions from my breathing passageway and lungs. I called the machine "the suck machine." It was a metal, football sized cylinder canister with a cord and plug on one side and a long plastic flexible tube on the other end. Several inches of plastic tubing from this device was inserted through the hole in my neck. My throat, still tender and sore from the recent surgery hurt with the pushing and pulling of the plastic tube. After the tube was inserted and in place, a switch on the suck machine would be flipped into the "on" position, and the motor started. Whirling, grinding vacuum noise emitted while it sucked out mucus and yuck from my body. It wasn't just irritating to my tender throat, I could feel the flexible tubing inside my throat and in my chest. It was a dull pressure. I believe this must be the origin of the term "that sucks"—because this literally sucked. This sucky event played out after each meal I ate. So, while other kids got to eat lunch at school, Grandma would pick me up, feed me lunch at home and clean my tracheotomy. She'd use the suck machine, take out the removable parts, pour rubbing alcohol over each piece, brush it down with pipe cleaners, dry everything and reassemble it. When she was finished, it tasted and smelled metallic and sour. All the other first-graders ate lunch at school, and I wanted to be like them, so I kept asking Grandma nightly if I could please eat lunch with the other kids.

Grandma placed about two inches of water in the bathtub and put a little metal plug in the tube of my neck. We were careful not to get any water near my neck and used a wash rag to soap me up and rinse me off. I was told I could drown if water got inside the hole in my neck. Grandma was careful to keep the water far from the hole. After my bath one night, I got a surprise. Grandma said "I'll pick you up after lunch to take care of you, so you can go ahead and eat at school. No Cinderella lunch box, though. But looky here!" She waved a pack of Necco candy in the air. I danced and jumped up and down, I was so happy. Grandma grinned. She was such a wonderful person, and actions like this meant so much to me as I grew up. Even now, if I have a bad day I go buy some Necco candy, and I feel as if Grandma is with me as I remember her love.

I was excited the next day at school. I could hardly wait for lunch knowing that those Necco candies were in my lunch bag.

At lunch, I sat at a picnic table in the school playground where students ate lunch when the weather was good. That day it was cold, with a slight breeze. I pulled my sweater tight and could hear mourning doves cooing. Melissa, with her cur blonde hair, came and sat by me at the picnic table. I smiled, thinking maybe we'd be friends. In class Melissa always sat in the first-grade row, in seat one. There was another girl at the picnic table with us named Debbie. Debbie had dark hair and dark eyes; she was quieter than Melissa. Most everyone was more reserved than Melissa. In class, Debbie sat in seat four. "Say something," Melissa said to me in a mocking tone. Debbie smiled.

I hated to speak to anyone because it was uncomfortable. My neck was sore, and the contraption I wore was heavy, sweaty and smelled gross, like the dirty pipe cleaners Grandma used. I knew I would sound raspy. In class I never spoke, just listened. I hesitated. Melissa repeated herself, "Say something!" This time, she said it loud enough that other kids in the playground looked over at us. An older blond boy, about ten years old, walked close to our picnic table, probably to hear better.

Reluctantly, I placed my finger on the opening. "What do you want me to say?" I asked, in a raspy whisper. Feeling awkward, I tried to sound friendly.

"See, I told you she isn't a real girl," Melissa said to our classmates. "She's what you call deaf and dumb!"

The boy shook his head. "No, it's called deaf mute," he said.

"Whatever—she's a voiceless moron," Melissa said, and that's how it started. The rest of the school year, Melissa and other classmates used this nickname for me often—sometimes in front of adults. I never heard anyone ask them to stop. Sometimes Melissa sang it, at times Debbie joined in.

Grandma picked me up after lunch to take care of the tracheotomy. "How was lunch?" she asked excitedly.

I began to cry. "They hate me, they're mean," I tried to say, but forgot to hold my neck, so sound just gurgled out, and words didn't make sense.

Grandma got the gist of the situation. The next day a new outfit lay on my bed, a gift from Grandma, a pretty blue dress. I knew Grandma loved me and felt bad for me, but I felt embarrassed and ashamed. I didn't want Grandma to feel bad for me; I didn't want anyone to feel sorry for me. I promised myself I would never complain or let anyone ever know if my feelings were hurt. I wouldn't cause any more problems.

After that, I didn't speak unless I had to and then only to adults. I wanted to be a real girl with a real voice. For some reason, the children began to believe I couldn't hear them, and the taunting eventually faded.

I missed my sister Bev and was glad on weekends when she'd come up, and we could play together. Grandma and Grandpa had a big boulder in their front yard that we loved to climb, so we'd sit up there and play with our dolls. I loved being with my brother, sister or cousins. Playing with them was a welcome relief after being the social outcast at school.

#

2012

In high spirits I walked up the concrete steps to the old Maricopa County Superior Court building, entering through an arched entry and carved double doors. I'd be in court all week representing the assessor's office in this lawsuit. The building was built in the late 1920's, and I admired the old Spanish style architecture—but that wasn't why I was here. I didn't have time to inspect the marble or the dark paneling and amuse myself by looking at the period details that were so charmingly old—contrasted against the recent ill-conceived modernizations.

I turned my attention back to my excitement over the lawsuit. It would be fun to watch Kate, our lawyer, fighting for the taxpayers against these expensive lawyers who were representing lying tax agents at Phoenix Cement. What their client's tax agent had done wasn't merely tax avoidance—it seemed to me to be tax evasion. Now they were suing. They'd been caught failing to report sixty million dollars in assets! *It'll be interesting to see what the judge thinks of them,* I thought as I proceeded through security.

In a few moments, I found myself in a grand entrance foyer, marble stairs to my left and an impressive, ornately decorated elevator to my right. *Maybe tomorrow I'll come early so I can take my time to marvel at this interior.* I chose the staircase and went up a flight of stairs. Down a corridor, the area wasn't as impressive. It looked like it had been remodeled in the late seventies; *What were they thinking?*

I walked into the restroom and looked in the mirror. My makeup looked okay, but I needed more lip color. Reaching into my purse, I grabbed the lipstick and a throat lozenge. I noticed a white sheet of paper folded neatly inside—a neatly typed prayer my sister Bev had given me. The words served to quiet my fears. They asked God to allow whatever was in the best interest of the citizens and taxpayers of Yavapai County to prevail in court this week. They asked God to be with us and to allow the Judge insight and wisdom. I appreciated Bev for thinking of it. This prayer helped to remind me to focus on the taxpayers and what was right for them.

The beauty of the construction in the restroom caught my attention. *Is that gray Alaskan marble wainscoting? They really went all out when they built buildings back in the twenties. Okay, stop it, and focus on the court case, not the building.* I loved buildings like this as much as I loved old cemeteries.

I made my way to the courtroom and sat next to Kate, the attorney the Yavapai County Board of Supervisors had hired to represent us in this case. I observed the room's paneling and woodwork. They seemed to be part of the original construction, and at odds with the 1970's, remodel. Kate smiled warmly in my direction. *What a spitfire brunette*, I thought. *I bet she'd look great as a redhead.* Sitting down you couldn't tell I was half a foot taller than she.

Kate leaned over and said in a whisper, "Scoot over one seat. We'll let Kirk sit here." I got up and moved to the end of the table, leaving the place between us vacant for Kirk, our expert witness on business personal property. I sighed. I wanted to sit next to Kate, drink in her intelligence and her spunkiness.

This case was important—sixty million dollars important—because the tax agent for Phoenix Cement, a local concrete plant, had not reported over sixty million dollars of taxable business equipment. After our audit, we discovered they'd underreported these items, yet they still moved forward with this lawsuit claiming they were overvalued. *The truth is, they're undervalued. Why would a company such as Phoenix Cement risk an increase?*

Kirk, our expert witness, walked into the courtroom with a young male attorney. They looked like twins—both in their late thirties and both about six feet tall. Kate moved over one more chair, leaving two chairs—one for Kirk and one for the young attorney. Kirk took the seat next to me and smiled, but seemed nervous. I liked him, but I let out an exasperated sigh, still pouting for losing my place next to Kate.

Kirk had a piece of paper in his hand. He twisted it, turned it, then picked up a paperclip and started to turn and unbend it. *Stop it, you're making me feel jittery, and we haven't even started yet!* I hoped he'd receive my message telepathically. Pulling my purse to my lap, I grabbed a handful of throat lozenges from it and placed it back on the table in front of me. Then I pulled out the folded paper from Bev and read it again. I put the sheet back into my purse, feeling better about today and less irritated with Kirk.

"Can I have one?" Kirk asked, leaning over and whispering to me. I loved his southern drawl; it made him sound like a country boy.

"Sure, does your throat hurt?"

"I have a little cough, I think it's the change in weather," Kirk said.

"I'm well stocked so help yourself." I pulled my purse to my lap again, took out three packages of cough drops from different manufacturers, and set all three bags on the table in front of Kirk—so he could have a selection.

"Wow," he said with a laugh, "you take cough drops seriously."

"My husband said we should buy stock in them. I try to keep plenty on hand." I didn't have a cough, but they seemed to help my throat open up when it felt like it was trying to close. Now wasn't the time to explain my throat problems.

Darren, the young attorney, sitting by Kate, whispered something to her. Then he turned his attention to Kirk and explained, "When Kate asks questions of their expert, if you hear anything you believe is wrong—or think of something that should be asked—pass me a note."

"Kate's doing the opening and all the questioning?" I asked.

"She's doing the opening and most of the questioning. But Kirk and I have worked together on this, so when it's his turn I'll do the questioning," Darren answered. Kirk seemed to shrink and grow pale at the thought of having to testify as our expert.

"Have you ever testified or been an expert witness before?" I asked, turning to Kirk. He shook his head and seemed to grow green, his blue eyes wide and sweat droplets starting to appear on his forehead.

"How long before he testifies?" I asked Darren and motioned towards Kirk.

"Probably two days. Wednesday he'll likely testify."

"Did you sleep last night?" I asked with my attention now back on the sweaty Kirk.

He shook his head. "I couldn't sleep. I kept fretting, playing in my mind everything that could go wrong," he answered with his cute southern drawl.

I wonder if he's prayed. Does he believe in God? Isn't he from the Bible belt? He probably is religious. I can't ask. The thought that Kirk could benefit from prayer kept nagging me, especially when I reached in my purse and felt the folded paper.

All day Judge Fink listened attentively. The witnesses were called, sworn in and then questioned. Watching Kate was exquisite—much like observing artwork or listening to my favorite song. She stood behind the lectern, asked questions, presented exhibits, smiled, frowned—everything in perfect concert to make her points, better than television or a movie. *If she'd been Marcia Clark, O.J. would have been convicted of murder!* All day their expert appraiser was on the stand, questioned by their attorney, then grilled by Kate. He held up well enough. At 4:30 p.m. we were excused and scheduled to come back the next day. Kirk's turn on the stand was drawing closer. He seemed more shaken up the nearer it got to his turn.

A couple trial days passed; each day felt the same as the last. They consisted of parking, hiking to the building, going through security. I tried not to get engrossed in the history of the building or the architecture, so I paid attention to the testimony and watched Kate.

Poor Kirk turned more and more sweaty, pale and shaken as time drew nearer to his turn as a witness. The idea of how prayer could help him was a constant thought of mine, but I remained silent. I prayed for him, but that didn't seem to help. Finally, during a break, Kate and the twins—as I liked to call the attorney and Kirk—huddled together, preparing for Kirk's turn on the stand next. Kirk looked like he was going to vomit.

I couldn't help myself any longer. I blurted out, interrupting the huddled conversation, "Are you religious?" I felt awkward, but I was no longer able to hold my tongue. I'd directed my question to Kirk, but all three responded to me by nodding in agreement. I pulled out the folded piece of paper and explained how it was a prayer my sister had written for me. I asked Kirk if he'd like me to write a prayer for him. I told him he could put it in his pocket and if he felt scared while he was on the stand he could place his hand in his pocket, and it would be like praying, but he could stay focused on the questions.

Immediately color returned to Kirk's face. He stood straighter; he appeared braver than I'd seen him, and he replied he'd appreciate it very much if I'd write out a prayer for him. I returned to the attorneys' table, wrote a prayer and gave it to him. Later I saw him wipe at his eyes as he read it, which made me embarrassed. But when he got on the witness stand, he was a rock star!

The young attorney fumbled a little—not as seasoned as Kate—and I found that frustrating. Then, during the next break, he asked if I planned to write him a prayer, too. That struck me funny as if my prayers were somehow better than he could write for himself. I did feel honored, though, because I'd done nothing for this case but sit and watch. They were doing the heavy lifting, and the least I could do was write out a prayer. So I said a silent prayer that the words I wrote would fit this guy, hoping they would ring true and help him feel confident.

In the handwritten prayer I wrote, I used the phrase that he was a "gladiator for the taxpayers" and asked God to please help him be inspired. There was more, but that was the gist of it. I gave it to him, he read it, nodded, folded it up, grinned, and put it in his pocket. From there forward both the twins were amazing. Kirk seemed to know his stuff. He was humble and sincere, and the young attorney seemed on point, confident and inspiring. There was a cross-examination and more. It was a delight to watch as Kirk explained economic obsolescence and why it didn't apply in this market to this asset. Finally, wrapping up the day and excused from court, we gathered our belongings and headed out.

The young attorney pulled me aside. "How did you know?" he asked as we walked together towards the staircase.

"Did I know—what?" I said.

"That I watch the television show *Scandal*, and my friends and I tease that we're gladiators. It's from the show. You stated I was a gladiator in the prayer; how did you know?"

"Oh no, I didn't know. But you're religious, right?" I asked

"Yes, my wife and I go to church every Sunday. I'm very spiritual."

Good, I don't want to be the kind of person, the kind that shoves my beliefs at you. "Well, I just . . . prayed," I said, stammering and searching for the right words. ". . . and I think God gave me that phrasing so you'd know he was aware of you and . . . to remind you that he's got you covered." I felt a little guilty about the misgivings I'd had about him earlier. I really had no idea why I used that particular word. I couldn't wait to get to the phone and call Bev. The conversation gave me goosebumps.

Later that year, Kirk wrote an article in his trade magazine about the written prayer and the Phoenix Cement case. He told me that the magazine tried to cut out the prayer part of his article—because they are not a religious journal. Kirk told them if they wanted his article they had to include the portion regarding the prayer. They printed it as he gave it to them.

We won that case for the taxpayers. The judge ruled for a $30 million dollar increase in the valuation after depreciation and a $3 million dollar valuation increase penalty for one year, in addition they faced a ten percent tax penalty. He added a $35 million dollar increase with a $3.5 million dollar valuation penalty increase for another year, and again another ten percent tax penalty. An increase of this magnitude was unheard of. I'd never seen a company go forward with a lawsuit claiming they were overvalued after it had been revealed they'd underreported assets by millions of dollars. Of course, this case would be appealed and was far from over, but the taxpayers in Yavapai County were well served. When Phoenix Cement paid these penalties, it would result in fewer taxes to the rest of the taxpayers. The schools, fire district, county and all other jurisdictions would still get their entire budgets, and they'd receive more from Phoenix Cement and less from the other taxpayers. When you're caught cheating there should be a consequence, and it was nice that those of us that had played by the rules would receive the benefit.

#

1968

Jerry, my new stepdad, worked for General Electric and we moved to Auburn, Washington for his job. Mom said it would be nice to get a fresh start away from the media. My Uncle Mike and his wife, Aunt Sandy, also moved to Washington and lived near us.

"I pledge allegiance to the flag . . . " I said in concert with the class, my right hand on my heart. The other school children had their left hands down at their sides; mine was up, with my finger on my windpipe blocking the opening so that the words could be heard.

"Stop!" the teacher shouted. We obeyed and looked to see what had elicited such a command; she had a frown on her face, her arms folded across her chest. Once she caught our attention, she said "Pam, that's not appropriate. Do it correctly. You can do it right. I'm not going to accept this." All eyes turned to me.

"What?" I said. *Why was she mad? What was I doing?* I turned a blank face towards her, not understanding what she wanted me to do. Chinook Elementary School was a new school for me, with a new teacher. Back in Yarnell, this was how I'd said the pledge. That teacher never seemed to mind. I guessed in Auburn, Washington, schools were different.

"You'll say the pledge of allegiance correctly with your left hand at your side and your right hand on your heart—show the class," the sour teacher said as she walked from her desk towards me.

I can't, I have to cover my tracheotomy, I thought silently as I looked at her, but said nothing.

"Use your thumb for your throat—your hand on your heart," she said, placing her right hand on her heart in a downward angle and stretching her thumb up to touch her neck.

My face burned from embarrassment, as the entire class looked at me. I placed my left hand at my side and held my right hand at an angle, covering my trachea with my thumb. This hurt because the tube in my neck pushed at a funny angle. I recited the pledge, apparently adequately enough to satisfy the teacher. The students did not giggle or laugh but remained silent. I sat down and looked around, expecting to see pointing fingers or whispers. Instead, the other students were looking down. No one looked at me and no one whispered. It seemed they were embarrassed, too.

At lunchtime, I pulled out my new metal Cinderella lunch box and headed to the cafeteria where we'd eat lunch. Chinook was a big school; second grade took up an entire classroom, not just one row of a room, like in Yarnell. In fact, there were several classrooms full of second graders. We also had a library and a nurse's office. I'd be able to eat at school and go to the nurse's station after lunch where she could help me clean and suction out my tracheotomy.

I took a seat by myself at a table and opened my lunch box. I was excited to eat at school instead of racing home to Grandma's like I used to. Carol, a girl from my class, sat down next to me. "I hate our teacher, she's mean," she said. I nodded in agreement. Soon the table was full of classmates eating and chattering. The cafeteria filled with kids, all talking, yelling, dishes banging, feet tapping. It was fun—but there was no way I'd be able to speak above the noise level. I smiled when anyone looked at me, but I didn't speak. The kids at my table seemed fine with that.

After going to the nurse's station and getting my tracheotomy cleaned and suctioned, there was a little recess time left, so I walked by myself to the fence surrounding our playground. I stood at the wall, leaned against it, and watched the kids play on the swingsets, the monkey bars and in the tetherball courts. At the Yarnell School, we didn't have monkey bars, tetherballs or much equipment at all. A boy named Danny walked up. I recognized him from my classroom. "Hi," he said.

I looked at him but said nothing. *Please go away,* I thought. I wanted to be left alone. It was so nice to be away from Melissa and her moron tauntings at Yarnell School. *Was Danny going to replace Melissa and be my new tormentor at this new school?* My palms grew sweaty, my heart started to race. *Go away, go away! Here we go again, it's gonna start again, the name-calling, the teasing.* I wanted to run home, stay home.

"Why won't you say anything?" Danny asked with a smile that looked kind. *Go away,* I thought again. Suddenly my right hand was on his face. My nails tore down his cheek, leaving three sharp creases. I could feel his skin under my nails. The creases on his face filled with blood, deep bloody scratches. His eyes turned wide and filled with tears. "Why?" he said and ran away.

Eventually, the bell rang, signaling it was time to go back to class. I walked as slowly as I could to my desk. Danny was there, the blood washed off, scratches starting to scab over. The teacher walked to the green chalkboard and picked up the chalk. Then she stopped, looked at Danny. "What happened? Who scratched you?"

My heart cramped, my stomach turned.

Danny shrugged.

"Someone scratched you. Does anyone know what happened?" The teacher looked over the entire class. I looked around wondering if Danny had told anyone. The other students stared down at the floor or around at other students, but no one raised their hands. No one spoke up.

Why didn't he tell? I deserve to be in trouble. No way I'm gonna tell.

At the bus stop, I walked up to Danny and whispered with my finger on my windpipe, "How come you didn't tell?"

"Why'd you scratch me? It hurts." He pointed to his face, which looked jagged and a little swollen. His eyes were narrow and suspicious.

I shrugged. I had no excuse. He'd done nothing to scare me. I knew he didn't deserve my hurting him. There was no way to explain it.

"I'm not a tattletale, that's why," he said and stormed away to the other side of the group of kids waiting for the bus. When we boarded the school bus, he sat as far away from me as he could.

#

2012

I instructed the staff in the land department to go through each parcel in the Arizona Beef Association lawsuit to determine if each actually was being used for grazing, and if we had the improvements listed correctly. To my dismay, after two weeks of research, they reported many properties were not being used for grazing, and there were many structures located on parcels that the assessor's office did not have records of.

I sat at my desk and reviewed a thick stack of satellite imagery.

This agricultural issue seemed bigger than I'd imagined, and it appeared to get bigger the more we dug into it. Each photo revealed improvements that we'd missed. *How could this have happened? Why wouldn't these structures be on the tax roll, and why would people include these properties in a lawsuit if they aren't even being taxed on the buildings?* I picked up my phone and dialed the supervisor of the land department.

I asked Betty, the supervisor, "Please come over to my office when you have a second." An attractive, tall brunette showed up at my office within five minutes of my call. She took a seat on the other side of my desk.

"I'm going through the photos; I hadn't expected such a mess," I said, pointing to the pile of photos her department had provided to me earlier in the day. "Kiarra wasn't doing her job!"

Betty cleared her throat and leaned in towards my desk. She pulled some of the photos towards her and viewed a few of them. "It wasn't Kiarra's fault. It's too big a job for one person to stay on top of." She looked at me, her eyes round, her face pale. "Kiarra pretty much did the agricultural stuff, and we let her handle it on her own. Now that you've moved her to a different department, we're kind of . . ." She cleared her throat again, sat straight up in her chair and appeared to gain some courage. "To be honest, as the supervisor, I felt um—I don't know the right word—left out or disrespected when you transferred Kiarra and hadn't even let me know it was going to happen, or discussed it with me."

She had a point. I should have respected her position as Kiarra's supervisor and talked with her about my decision before I'd moved Kiarra. I did it without discussing it with anyone other than human resources. Kiarra wasn't willing to fix the problems I'd identified, But I also believed Betty had been overprotective of Kiarra, and this agricultural mess was ultimately Betty's responsibility. She shouldn't be a supervisor if she didn't follow up and monitor the quality of work performed by her department. I was considering whether or not Betty should continue to be a supervisor.

I sucked in my breath. "Okay. Now, tell me, as the director of the land department, tell me what you think happened and, more importantly, how we fix it." I tried to get to the point without any nonsense. I leaned in, lowered my voice so Betty would have to work hard to hear me, and added, "Betty, your agricultural files are a mess. They're shoved every which way. The statutes say properties are to be inspected once every four years by us. I can go to the files, pull five random records and I bet you money three of the five wouldn't have been inspected in the last twenty years! You have expired leases that haven't been updated. Now, looking into this lawsuit, we've discovered we have houses, barns, buildings that haven't been placed on the tax rolls, and you never even did a lease-study and updated the values in what? How long?"

"Our records go to 1986, and we know the values were $7.56 since then," Betty answered, her voice steady. "There was a lease-study done by the department of revenue in 1992, but we didn't update values or do anything with that lease-study like we should have," she explained matter-of-factly.

"Here's what I want first. You or your staff need to get on the internet and find some kind of filing system that you will implement. It can be four different colors or tabs or whatever. I want to be able to pull out the file drawer, look at the files, and see which files are scheduled to be updated so 25% will be updated each year. Let's say those are all in yellow files. Then the next year's are all in green files, and so on. The law says properties are to be updated once every four years, so within four years we'll have updated everything. I want uniformity in all the records. Also, we need a pocket or a metal clip to hold the lease. The format or pattern for every file will be consistent, so I can grab a file and know exactly where the current lease for that operation will be." I sat back and took a breath. Before she could speak, I went on. "Figure out a system that does this for us, and get back with me in two days. Then we'll have a four-year plan to get this all inspected. I like the color code idea, but I'm open to different ideas."

Betty sighed and seemed overwhelmed. "This isn't my fault, and it isn't Kiarra's either," she said.

"Okay, this might not have been Kiarra's fault, maybe it's not yours; it looks like it took a long period of neglect to get here, but it is what it is, and you need to get your department cleaned up. Look, let's just start with a plan on how to organize the files. Come back in two days and let me know what you come up with."

Betty leaned in, folded her arms in front of her and said, "This wasn't an accident. This was neglected on purpose, and not by Kiarra or me . . . before us." She looked from side to side as if she might find an unseen observer in my office.

She lowered her voice, "The land supervisor before me gave anyone that asked for it an agricultural classification. He deliberately kept the values frozen, and he ignored new buildings as they were constructed. This was either not worth the effort for the minimal return on taxes or . . ." She paused and then whispered, ". . . favors given political cronies. It's not fair that now I'm looking like the incompetent one when it was ignored on purpose. Kiarra was trying to clean it up but she's only one person."

"Was it Boe?" I asked.

I'd heard similar gossip. Boe had been the land supervisor years before, and I had been told he'd quit because he knew he was about to be fired for some shenanigans that may have included what Betty had just relayed to me. I knew Boe because he worked in the Maricopa County Assessor's Office as their Chief Appraiser. He was a fun jokester with a bad boy reputation.

Betty nodded her head.

"So let's say it's either all his fault, or it's not his fault, but prior administrations must have decided that it wasn't worth the effort to stay on top of the mess. Either way, we're going to clean it up. It's a priority, has to be, because so many of these files are involved in the lawsuit. And from now on I'll include you when I'm frustrated with your employees, and I won't single-handedly discipline them or transfer them without talking to you first. I promise."

Betty smiled. I liked her and hoped she'd figure out how to get the files organized.

#

1968

"I don't want to sit in front of her," Danny said, complaining about me to our new teacher. Third grade—new classroom, new teacher, mostly new classmates. Our teacher had short dark hair and a very fair complexion. A large dark birthmark covered her entire left cheek.

"I'll have none of that. You'll sit where I assigned you," the teacher said to Danny, sounding irritated. Who could blame Danny for not wanting to sit in front of me? I'd scratched him last year for no reason. If I were Danny, I wouldn't want to sit in front of me either. He'd never told anyone about how I'd unexpectedly attacked him, so the teacher didn't understand his request. "I want to make something clear. There will be no bullying. Everyone will treat everyone else with respect. No teasing, no making fun of others. Is this understood?" she added, glaring in Danny's direction.

Poor Danny. The teacher seemed to think he was a bully or being mean. In fact, he was the nicest person I knew. He probably just wanted to avoid putting himself in a position where he might get hurt again. Danny sat quietly and didn't try to explain.

The recess bell rang. "Please stay behind, I want to talk to you," the teacher said to me. I sat still in my chair. "Come sit up here," she said, motioning towards a chair next to her desk. I obeyed. "I haven't heard you speak, but I'm told you can. Is that right?" she asked in a kind voice. I nodded. "Notice anything about my face?" she asked.

I shrugged. *Of course, there's a large dark mark on your face,* I thought but said nothing.

"I've been teased my whole life because of it," she said, pointing at the ugly birthmark. "I haven't let that get in my way. I know how it feels to wish you could be invisible. Your voice is different, but I'm not going to let you get away with trying to hide. You will join in, ask questions when you don't understand, raise your hand and answer the questions when you know the answer—Okay?" I nodded. "No, you have to answer. I want to be clear, this is a safe place for you—no one will tease you. But you are not invisible, and you won't get away with not joining in with the class. Understand?"

I liked being ignored, but I placed my finger on my trachea and answered, "Yes, ma'am."

"Good. Now, about Danny. I'm not going to tolerate anyone treating anyone like they have cooties or—"

I shook my head. "Ma'am, Danny isn't being mean. Don't be mad. Last year I scratched his face, because, I don't know why. He didn't deserve it." I started to cry. I'd felt guilty about acting that way ever since I'd done it, and it felt good to finally tell on myself.

My new teacher's eyes grew wide. "Oh, I see. So no more of that. You'll be kind to everyone in this class, and everyone else will be kind too. Deal?" She grabbed a tissue out of the box on her desk and handed it to me.

I wiped my tears and blew my nose. I nodded in agreement.

"Good try," the teacher said, and we both laughed.

I wouldn't get away with only a nod. I placed my finger on my neck and said, "Deal."

After recess when my classmates arrived back in our room, the teacher took Danny outside and talked to him. After school, at the bus stop, Danny walked up to me, "Why did you tell Mrs. Argo?"

I shrugged. "I'm sorry I did that last year," I said as clearly as I could—positioning my finger to prevent the air from escaping through my neck. "I felt bad about scratching you," I added out loud.

"It was weird. You're kind of weird," Danny said in a matter-of-fact way.

I nodded—both statements were probably true.

#

2012

"Hey, ready for some good news then some bad news?" I asked into the telephone, leaning back in the chair and putting my feet up on the desk. Outside my office window, it was starting to snow. *I'll go home after this call,* I decided.

"Okay, I want the good news first, but just forget the bad news. It's Friday, and I don't want to ruin my weekend," Muttley said in a spirited mood.

"Good news is—remember the personal property issue I brought to your attention a few years back? Told you the county was breaking the law?"

I got up and turned on the floor heater. It was freezing in my office. There was a pause.

I knew Muttley remembered, so I continued. "Well, I spoke to the new board of supervisors and, of course, told them of my concerns. They all just took their oaths of office, so I figured they needed to know about these broken laws— about the conspiracy between Supervisor Springer, the treasurer, and the sheriff."

"Okay," Muttley replied, sounding unimpressed so far.

"Supervisor Brown says he's met with the treasurer and the sheriff, and he tells me the laws will be followed going forward. That's the good news."

"Oh, that is good," Mutt said with a laugh that sounded like relief. "Spit out the bad news," he added.

"There are personal property abatements on the board of supervisors' consent agenda scheduled for next week," I said.

I knew Muttley would be upset. They were planning to clear all the uncollected accumulated personal property taxes! Since the last time they'd cleared this debt, it had probably accumulated another million dollars. Now the new board didn't appear to be following the statutes on abatements, like they promised me they would do going forward, nor was the county trying to collect these debts. This would result in shorting schools and fire districts and other jurisdictions that needed these funds, and it would shift property taxes to the rest of us.

"Oh no, they aren't!" Muttley yelled. "I gotta go, I need to call the treasurer's office."

He hung up before I could say another thing. I smiled, sure that abatements would be removed from the consent agenda by Monday. I closed my blinds, put my jacket on, unplugged the heater, turned off my office lights and headed for home.

Monday, when I returned to the office and pulled the supervisors' agenda up on my computer, I discovered the abatement item was no longer there. I sighed with relief. They weren't going to clear these debts after all. Good news; Mutt had stopped this travesty.

5

◆━━━◦◦◦━━━◆

SHADOWS DEFINE THE LIGHT

2012

I PARKED MY CAR, admired the Christmas decorations on the light post; turned off the ignition and hesitated. Here I was ready to meet with Barney again. *Why had I agreed to meet with him?* Since the last time I'd met Barney at Murphys, I'd tried to keep my distance. It had been a surprise when he requested another meeting. It was no secret he'd been pushing me to reconsider the agricultural grazing values I'd set to use for taxes. I didn't understand his interest in these values; he didn't own a ranch; well not that I knew of. I figured maybe he had powerful Republican ranching friends that he felt I needed to be more mindful of. I got out of my car and walked through the parking lot into Denny's. I'd just get a soda, I didn't think I could stomach food, I felt a little nauseous.

Inside, I took my jacket off. I saw Barney and waved. He was in a booth located to my left. I walked over and slid in across from him. I smiled and said "hi," trying to appear friendly, but my stomach cramped. Pretending to like him was challenging.

"What's wrong with your voice?" Barney, who was still the county Republican executive board member, leaned in and asked loud enough other tables in the restaurant could easily overhear.

"My vocal cords are paralyzed due to an injury," I answered in an even, soft tone. *What was his deal?* He had known the answer before he asked the question. *What a jerk,* I thought—I couldn't remember a time anyone had pressed for a more detailed answer than that. *Would Barney ask for more details?* It was ages since anyone had teased me about my voice, but I could still recall the tauntings, and I could almost hear the sing-song *voiceless moron, voiceless moron* of my classmates long ago.

"How did you get injured?" Barney asked with a sneer. There it was! Even though he made it sound like a question, he seemed to be making some kind of statement. I wasn't positive, but he appeared to be threatening me with something.

"Hmm, is that a question? Because you look like you might already know the answer," I responded, trying to appear confident, but in my mind, I could still hear *voiceless moron, voiceless moron* sung by little friends. *How did he know? Did he know?*

"I know it's time for you to leave office. Don't run for re-election. We're tired of you." He reminded me of a giant duck that maybe I had seen once on *Alice in Wonderland*, a duck with a big grin. Was it a duck? No, it wasn't a duck, it was a cat. He looked like that fat Cheshire cat with the big grin from *Alice in Wonderland*.

"No, I kind of like being the assessor, I'm not tired of it yet," I said, shaking my head.

"Oh no, you won't run again," he said with his big cat grin. "You don't want your story to get out, and I promise it will. I will make sure it does—on the front page of the paper. It will even be above the fold."

"What will?" I said, "Tell me what it is you think you have on me."

Barney revealed a manila file folder and placed it gently on the table. He slid the file to me. In the folder, I discovered an assortment of copies of old newspaper articles.

Had Barney hired some kind of background check, or some detective to get information from my past? How had he gotten these articles? How did he know they were tied to me? My name had changed multiple times since this article had come out. My adoption came with a name change and a new birth certificate. My first marriage changed my adopted name to my married name. Then I divorced and remarried, and that gave me yet another name—how had Barney figured out I was the child in the articles? My adoption papers were sealed. How did he know my maiden name, which was my adopted name, wasn't my original name?

With that, Barney took his fork, jabbed it into his pasta and took a bite, satisfied with himself.

The articles in his envelope dated back to when I was five years old. Back then I hadn't even started reading *Dick and Jane*. I'd never seen the articles, nor known the version of the attack that was detailed here. Funny—seeing these articles now, I realized I could have searched these out at any time. I picked up the first paper: the article read—*Gilbert F. Sieling was charged by information in the Arizona Superior Court with three counts of assault with a deadly weapon, and five counts of assault to commit murder.* It sounded odd, but I understood full well what it referred to. Gil had done a lot of things to my mother, sister, brother and, of course, to me. I wasn't sure what he'd been criminally charged with, but the claim in the article didn't add up. I knew he had shot me in the stomach, the bullet hit and broke, exiting from my back and my side, so that was at least one assault with a deadly weapon or maybe three if they counted the entry and exit wound injuries separately. Plus he had stabbed me in the neck multiple times. So that was at least a second assault with a deadly weapon. Or three more attacks if you counted each stab wound. But he'd stabbed both my sister and brother, too. That would be at least four assaults with deadly weapons if you just counted each weapon once for my brother and sister. But that didn't count my mom's injuries; maybe hands aren't considered deadly weapons. Then according to the article, he was charged with five counts of assault to commit murder. Seemed to me there should be more counts of assault to commit murder if you counted choking my mother. Oh well, I didn't understand the criminal legal system and how they decided what to charge for, and I really didn't care what he was accused of. It was more interesting that Barney had the articles and connected them to me.

"Wow, Barney, you seem pretty interested in me. Are you a stalker or just infatuated?" I asked, trying to pretend I was flattered by his creepy attention.

"I'll give it to the media—it will all come out."

Was he saying he'd leak this information to embarrass me? If he went through with his threat, it would mortify my mother and my sister. I started to feel hot, and my throat felt like it was swelling shut. The article wasn't about my dad. The attacker wasn't my dad anymore. My dad was the man who had adopted me and taught me a work ethic and what a father should be, a man of honor.

The articles referred to Gil Sieling, my biological father who was just someone to be pitied, an alcoholic, mentally ill or demon possessed—whichever he was, he wasn't cruel, calculating or mean. Whatever he was guilty of, it had nothing to do with me and my ability to be the assessor.

"Yep, I really would love to see that, I really would," I said with a smile. I hoped looked sincere. My hands felt sweaty, and I clenched them in fists, as I thought, *Real evil looks like Barney, a puppet master behind the scenes trying to take control of an elected official. We work, we make promises, we get elected, then people like Barney tell us to serve them—or else.* I stood. "Eat your pasta, you pig," I said as I left.

I found my blue Jeep in the parking lot, opened the front door and took my seat. The Christmas decorations on the light poles were blurred from my tears—I couldn't focus.

I sat, forlorn and upset. If the story of how I'd been shot and stabbed got out in a public way, as Barney had threatened, this would be a shock to my entire family, especially my kids. It was Christmas time again; now wasn't the right time for this to come out. I hadn't even told my kids the details. Was this the way I wanted them to find out? *Maybe I shouldn't run for assessor again. Being an appraiser with Scott was easier; it paid better and didn't expose people I loved to . . . What had I been thinking, why did I ever think I could do this?* I had wanted to appraise the county land and properties, assuring fairness for taxpayers. I was no gladiator. I couldn't stand up against corruption. Favors to a select few wealthy people had been the way of Yavapai County government. *Who did I think I was to come along and try to change that? I wasn't up to this.*

I started my car. It was cold. It had been cold that night, too, when Gil's car had no working heater. *These incidents happened a long time ago. Should I let them affect me now?* I flipped my heater on. My heater worked. I smiled and realized my life was so much better now. *Why let Barney get the best of me?* I had survived worse than Barney.

I turned the radio on in my jeep, put it into drive and started home, concentrating on the Christmas music. Johnny Mathis—*It's Beginning To Look A Lot Like Christmas*, Madonna—*Santa Baby*. I needed to distract myself and shove painful memories deep inside.

What should I do about the conflict with the ranchers? I wanted to live my life with integrity. Those who'd elected me trusted me to do a good job for them. I could agree to finish this term with integrity and then move on, ending my public career with one four year term. Then I could go back and work with my faithful partner, Scott. If I agreed to do that, Barney and his ilk would replace me with their puppet, a person who would do their bidding. It lacked honesty to agree to that. So I couldn't agree to backing off and leaving the job as Barney wanted.

Barney was going to make the past events public if I didn't agree to leave my post. It was so ugly, now that I thought about it. I didn't want my kids, my friends or my husband Bob to learn the details. My husband knew most of it, but I just couldn't tell my kids and it just wasn't anything my friends needed to know.

As I pulled into our driveway, the Christmas lights flickered from inside the living room window. I smiled to myself. It looked warm and cozy, just like you would want a home to look during the holidays—like our family home looked to outsiders years ago. *I'd survived the attack in 1966, but could I politically survive these ranchers' anger, given their clearly strong political connections?* Memories of how hard it was to physically recover from Gil Sieling's abuse came *to me. It had been painful, taken time, but I'd survived. I wondered if I ran again and refused to kowtow to their demands .*

.. *Kowtow*. If I took the abuse that Barney was threatening, would I survive politically? I was sure it wouldn't end with embarrassing my family or me, he'd probably come up with more tricks.

#

Tax Shifts Reviewed

I sat at my desk and looked at the graphs for the PowerPoint I was creating. The graph tracked the tax shifts for a typical house compared and contrasted with a 78-acre property that had been classified as agricultural grazing. With the value of the agricultural grazing land frozen at $7.56 an acre every year, their tax bill declined, and by 2009 had fallen to 50% of what it had been in 1990. Meanwhile, the residential properties' values had increased from year to year as they were supposed to. These tax bills *increased* by 80% over the same period of time! The graph (below) demonstrated what I calculated to be an improper tax shift. Because the value remained $7.56 an acre every year on grazing land, those taxes declined because values on all other properties were increasing. Voila! Tax shift.

Even now with the updated values, there was still a 65% disparity from what these ranching property owners paid in 1990 until now. Really, it should have been the residential property owners or commercial property owners that had sued—that would make more sense. They'd been the ones treated unfairly over the years.

I put my elbows on my desk and my head in my hands. Why had this happened? No lease-studies, no value updates? Had it been on purpose? Surely these agricultural property owners had noticed that their tax bills had gone down each year. They must have thought that was odd. I was trying to fix this mess; how had it resulted in such controversy?

I looked at the printed lawsuit on my desk—a massive lawsuit filed by influential people. *I bet these same people listed in the lawsuit would never think about shoplifting. I bet they give to charity. Attend church. Think of themselves as honest—but they've pushed some of their taxes to their neighbors, and now they're suing because the error was corrected.*

I lifted my head from my hands. I had to believe they didn't understand. *This had to be because of manipulation from Mattie. People just wouldn't be this unfair and selfish.* My eyes watered. *It wasn't worth causing my sister or mother public embarrassment by exposing things that would cause an uproar. I could just leave quietly and not run for re-election. Let them run their puppet candidate for assessor! He'd come in and do as demanded. Then this wouldn't be my problem anymore.* I sighed, looking at the graph again. I picked it up, then laid it back on my desk. I'd been elected to value and classify everything fairly. I remembered how each Sunday at church I'd stand with the Young Women of our ward and recite our theme:

> *We are daughters of our Heavenly Father, who loves us, and we love Him. We will stand as witnesses of God at all times and in all things, and in all places as we strive to live the Young Women values, which are:*
>
> *Faith • Divine Nature • Individual Worth • Knowledge • Choice and Accountability • Good Works • Integrity • and Virtue.*

We believe as we come to accept and act upon these values, We will be prepared to strengthen home and family, make and keep sacred covenants, receive the ordinances of the temple, and enjoy the blessings of exaltation.

I put my head back into my hands and started to cry. For several years I'd been the President of the Young Women, and I tried to be an example for the girls, aged twelve to eighteen. I'd taught them to live their lives valiantly choosing right over wrong. *I do live my life that way,* I said aloud, trying to defend myself from harsh judgment. Just because I was receiving pushback, could I just fold and quit? No, I had to stand up for truth and integrity. Not running for reelection because of a threat wasn't living with integrity. I wiped my tears. I'd run for reelection, do the best I could. Let Barney do what he would, my job was to keep my oath of office, value everything fairly. This recent tax update phased in what should have been occurring all along. I'd work hard on my presentation, and maybe the public would understand the fairness issue. If I were lucky, the media would help get out the information and maybe the people bringing the lawsuit would know they hadn't been paying their portion of taxes according to the law.

Maybe Barney will change his mind. Or get hit by a car, but that's probably not nice to hope for, I thought and giggled.

#

1969

"We're going to play a trick on Dad after your doctor's appointment today," Mom said. Her voice sounded excited.

Each week I received a shot of penicillin at the doctor's office to prevent me from getting sick before the surgery to remove the tracheotomy contraption and close the opening.

Mom drove us to a prank store full of practical jokes and costumes. The store smelled of cigarettes from an ashtray on the counter that overflowed with cigarette butts. Costumes hung from the ceiling to the floor along one wall. The aisles were filled with displays: soaps that would turn you black when you washed with them, gum that tasted bad or would turn your tongue black, jars that said peanut brittle but when opened a spring that looked like a snake leaped out. We took our time looking at the different items and laughing.

"This will be perfect," Mom said, pointing to a plastic ice cream bar that appeared to be half melted. She headed for the cash register counter.

I could barely see over the countertop. A lady with short blonde hair, red nose, and cheeks, sat on a stool and watched me. She put her half-smoked cigarette on the overflowing ashtray and rang up my mom's purchase. I put my hand over my throat and kept my mouth shut, holding my breath, trying not to smell the stale ashes and smoke. *How weird that my neck can smell that,* I thought. I dropped my hand down to test my idea, sucking the air into my trachea. *It smelled horrible!*

In the car Mom acted excited, talking rapid-fire. "After the doctor, we'll go get you an ice cream bar. Then we'll stop by Dad's office. You make sure he sees you eating the ice cream. When you come out of the bathroom, ditch the ice cream; either finish it or throw it away. Because I'm going to sneak this—" she pointed to the plastic ice cream novelty item she'd just purchased, "—onto that schematic that Dad's been working so hard on for months."

"Is there more than just getting a shot today?" I asked, knowing that I was supposed to be getting the tracheotomy removed soon. I hoped it would be very soon. It was bulky, made my neck sweat, and I hated the sour smell of the pipe cleaners after they'd cleaned the metal tracheotomy attachment. The vacuum machine thing that suctioned my throat was irritating. It would be wonderful to be a real girl, not a robot whisperer.

"Just a shot today, but we're going to talk about the upcoming surgery and schedule it," Mom said. "It's going to be so funny. We'll set the ice cream on Dad's drawings. Dad's going to remember the months of hard work it took to have all that completed, and believe you ruined it with your ice cream."

"He'll be mad at me, he'll think I'm a brat," I said and laughed with her.

"That's why it's so funny. Once he realizes it's just a plastic thing on his paper and nothing damaged on the schematic, he'll know we tricked him." We both laughed. My new dad, Jerry, did like practical jokes, and he'd worked every night on this huge piece of paper drawing circuits or something for work. He had a big thick pen, and by clicking the top of it you could change the ink from red to green, click it again, and you could have blue —the neatest pen ever. Dad would let me play with it when he wasn't using it on his work projects.

I hesitated, afraid to change the subject. "Surgery? They can't just take it out?" I asked. My hands trembled, and I felt cold.

"That's what the doctor's going to explain today, so we can make plans," Mom answered as lightly as she could, keeping her eyes on the road and avoiding my gaze.

#

2013

I went to the Embry-Riddle University, Prescott campus, for a mandatory Republican Precinct Committee meeting. This property had once been Prescott College, but in the early 1970's it sold to Embry-Riddle, and in the late seventies the aeronautical university had opened. It was a beautiful campus, student housing and cafeteria to my left, library and labs to my right —mandatory stupid meeting directly in front of me. Precinct committee members, like me, work in our respective districts to support Republican candidates, and we'd been ordered to attend.

The day was overcast, and snow covered the ground. It crackled as I stepped through it in my high-heeled shoes. I gingerly and ungracefully navigated my way to the doors, hoping I wouldn't slip and fall. Although I was a precinct committee member, I sure didn't want to attend this meeting.

Barney was already an executive board member of the Yavapai County Republican Party, and today were the elections for this board. He'd be there in his glorious self-serving manner, running for re-election, probably unopposed. Barney was the leering Cheshire Cat in his platypus body—maybe with his manila envelope that held my secrets. He'd threatened me with it just last month. Had Barney shown it to anyone yet? Would he use it today to expose me? I gulped, my heart shriveled down like a prune.

I wanted to run, go home, play sick—but this was a mandatory meeting. I wasn't sure of the consequences for skipping something mandatory.

The room had theater-type seating in tight rows cascading upward, all facing the stage fitted with a lectern and microphone. In front of the doors were two card tables for check in and ballots. The place was abuzz, everyone talking, laughing and networking.

I smiled, signed in and found a seat. I didn't feel like being friendly or visiting. *Get this vote done, this mandatory meeting over, and let me get the hell out of here,* I thought and hoped Barney wouldn't take me aside.

Then I spotted him walking to the lectern. I sucked in my breath and looked down at my cute high-heeled shoes. I reached into my purse, grabbing the bottle of water, and took a sip. Barney called the meeting to order. The candidates for the executive board were all given an opportunity to speak. I was surprised to see someone was running against Barney for his position on the board. Does he have a chance? I'd certainly vote for anyone running against Barney—*Barnyard, that's what I'll call him when I talk to my husband Bob about this later.*

It was time to fill in our ballots. They'd be counted while we were informed about our budget and other housekeeping items. Barney seemed pretty confident. Finally, the results were announced. Barney Barnyard had lost!

By the look on Barnyard's face, I could tell he couldn't believe it—I could hardly believe it either. I wanted to dance, to hop up and down in celebration. Barnyard brushed at his knees as if there was something on them, then he folded his arms, looked down, looked over to the crowd and down again. I almost felt sorry for him, but to be honest, I didn't feel sorry for him at all. How many elected officials was he controlling? He'd scolded me and tried to convince me I worked for special wealthy Republicans when I met him in Murphy's restaurant; he'd threatened me with his manila folder last month in Denny's.

I left the building, and people were lingering outside. I said hi to Emily, the wife of one of the members of the board of supervisors, and as I walked by, she asked me if I could believe what just happened. "It's such a surprise," she added.

"Yes, I'm shocked too. I thought the current president and other members were supported by the Republican clique—the inner circle guys—and kind of bulletproof."

"The real conservative types—Tea Party members—organized," Emily said. "They signed up a bunch of precinct committee members, then ran their own candidates. More of their members showed up, so the mainstream Republicans lost today."

"Man, I'm so out of the loop. I didn't know that," I said, and had to smile because if mainstream meant Barney the Barnyard and his puppet masters, I was glad they lost.

As I drove home, I sang to myself because I was happy, and I thanked the universe for mandatory meetings so I could witness the slaughter of Barnyard.

The next week I scheduled an appointment with the new president of the Yavapai County Executive Board of the Republican Party, Jim Dutton. He agreed to meet with me at the Republican Headquarters in Prescott on Union Street.

I walked into the front room of the Headquarters, and a professional looking woman with a nice smile, Sharon Brewer, escorted me into the back room with its large conference table. I sat towards the end waiting for Jim. Sharon offered me water, but I said I was okay — I had a bottle with me.

When Jim arrived, he seemed a little nervous. I didn't know him well. I explained that I was sideways with the old Executive Board of the Republican Party and asked if he was aware of issues with the assessor's office or me, or if he had any other concerns. Jim apparently didn't know of the past issues that Barney had with me. I didn't tell him about the manila envelope, the secrets Barney had threatened to expose. But I told Jim about the ranchers, the agricultural values and Barney's threatening comment that I needed to understand who I worked for.

Jim assured me that I should follow the law, and that's what the Republican Party wanted. He agreed I should treat everyone fairly and ethically. As long as I did that, he promised the Republican Party would be all right with me. Keep your oath of office, he counseled.

Jim let me know that he was a pastor in his church. I liked him. He was quite different from Barney, and I was glad to see someone of integrity at the helm. I hoped he'd be the guy he professed to be, and I hoped Barney and company would not be successful in taking him down. I had a feeling they'd try.

#

I was dressed warmly and instantly took off my coat when I entered the cozy restaurant. The air smelled of pepper. The hostess smiled at me like I'd made her night by appearing in her lobby. I smiled back, glad for a friendly face, and announced there would be two of us. She sat me at a booth, and I played on my cell phone waiting for Scott to arrive. *What's taking him so long?* I wondered because we'd left the office at the same time. When the waiter came to check on me, I ordered an iced tea. About a half an hour later Scott showed up.

"What happened? I was starting to worry," I asked, as he scooted into the booth, seating himself across from me.

"Man, it's cold out there," he said taking off his jacket. "I left my keys in the office, so I didn't have car keys. I went back to the office door but it was locked—you took off like a bat out of hell so I couldn't use your keys," Scott answered, his eyes twinkling with his snarky bat out of hell remark. "So, I went around knocking on the windows until I found someone who let me in, got my keys and here I am,"

"Wow, you could have called me, I would have come back—"

"No, it wasn't that big a deal. Betty let me in,"

"Okay, I'm starving, so let's decide what to order. Then I have lots to catch you up on," I said, opening my menu and deciding on a salad for the main course. I'd save my appetite for chocolate dessert later. Bob was working out of town, and Constance was at the movies. It was nice to have Scott to myself. I was happy he'd finally agreed to come to work at the assessor's office. It had taken a few years of repeatedly asking him, but with Constance becoming a teenager, Scott saw the wisdom of a steady nine to five job with weekends off.

"Okay, I know what I want—catch me up on your stuff," Scott said. Although his desk was just outside my office, we rarely had time to visit. Most days I had a line of people and appointments and had what others considered emergencies. Scott was working on some commercial appraisals on local rock quarries for the office. So during the day, we didn't have time to "shoot the bull," as Scott would say. Tonight was our night to catch up.

The waiter came over, glaring at us like we were the reason he had to be there. I arched a brow and smiled at Scott. I asked for an iced tea, again, and we gave our dinner orders. When the waiter walked away, Scott snorted at the rude behavior. "You'll still give him a great tip," I said with a giggle, knowing that Scott was generous and wouldn't punish the waiter for being in a bad mood. "Ugh, I have so much to tell you, I don't know where to start—it's like a movie, a conspiracy movie—I'm the star," I said.

"Start at a non-boring part. You've always been the star of your life, by the way. You know, unless Ashley is around, then she's the star," Scott said with a belly laugh.

It was true. My grown children, including Ashley, were the stars of my life, but lately, they were busy with their own lives, so it was all about me. "Okay, remember Boe?"

"Yea, he was the guy they were gonna fire for just grabbing sales prices and slapping them into the computer system, rather than actually capturing features that add to value and calculating the values out, like he was supposed to—illegal in Arizona for an assessors' office to do that. Anyhow, he caught wind that they were getting ready to fire him and he quit. Went to Phoenix and went to work with Maricopa County."

The waiter walked up, put ice water in front of us "Can I get an iced tea?" I asked, trying to appear pleasant. *This guy does not want me to have iced tea,* I decided. The waiter rolled his eyes and walked away.

"He's probably a rancher," Scott said, appearing amused with the waiter's unprofessional behavior.

"Or son of a rancher," I said laughing. "Anyhow, Boe is back with a vengeance. I'm not sure what the deal is but he's a pain in the butt," I added with more seriousness.

"Do spill," Scott said in a high pitched voice, appearing to mimic Bev in one of our gossip fests.

The waiter returned with my iced tea and actually smiled at me before he left. "See, even the son of a rancher can't resist my charm," I said. "Okay, so two really weird things happened and I know they're connected, but not sure exactly how. First I get a phone call from the Cochise County Assessor Phil Leiendecker. He informed me that Boe put together a committee of assessors to meet with the Arizona Beef Association, or at least that's what Phil had been led to believe. Boe, who's not an assessor but just an employee of Maricopa County, told Phil that he had been selected to be on this committee along with the Gila and Navajo assessors. They all came up to Prescott and—to Phil's surprise—they met with Mattie and the Yavapai County Beef Association, not the state association as he'd been told. It was basically a Pam Pearsall trash talk fest. Phil felt confused and said he'd never go to some other elected assessor's county to meet with a litigant and listen to trash talk. But he'd been led to believe this was a meeting with the state association about policies across the state and he was surprised to learn instead it was just a county association to discuss their lawsuit issues. This was so inappropriate. Anyhow, he told me he tried to explain that he saw the statutes the same way I did. Phil wanted to give me the heads up that this meeting had taken place."

"I heard that Boe intends to run for Maricopa Assessor and he's trying to get friends in high places. He's trying to impress Senator Pierce because he has a ranch up here," Scott said. The waiter delivered our meals and asked if we needed anything else. The server seemed to be over whatever had been bothering him. "What was the second weird thing?" Scott asked, and he cut into his steak.

"Boe came into the Yavapai County building the other day. He went into the elevator, I'm pretty sure he went to see the supervisors. He didn't even stop in my office and say hi. I saw Mattie from ABA enter the building about ten minutes later and head into the elevator—I don't want to appear paranoid, but I think there was a meeting upstairs about me. I mean, Boe works for the Maricopa County Assessor's Office in Phoenix, so why is he coming up here and meeting with people?" I sucked in my breath. It did sound a little narcissistic now that I heard myself say it out loud.

"I hate politics. I warned you that it's a despicable game with no honor," Scott said, in an angry tone. I was caught off guard by his response. "Here is what I think. It's just my two cents worth but here is the way I'd put things together. The ABA is coming at you on all sides. In the end, they'll have to take you out politically because they aren't going to succeed in the courts. They gotta get someone to run for assessor—it can't be Boe; he'd never win. The crap about his sales chasing and past agricultural favors would come out, so they'll get a puppet. Boe is their puppet master, or at least the assistant to a puppet master because he understands the assessor's office and he can help their candidate once they find him. You ever see the movie 'The Manchurian Candidate?'"

I shook my head, the movie didn't sound familiar.

"Well, they'll get some stupid schmuck, probably a real estate agent, that they can lead around by his nose. They'll get him plenty of funding, and they'll try to beat you in the next election. Then if their puppet wins, Boe will come run the office for them. He'll work a few years, build his resume, then he'll go down to the valley, and they'll pay him back for his service by helping him win the election as assessor down there."

I was glad that Scott didn't think I was a narcissist or paranoid. I then told him of Barney's threat. This was confirmation to Scott that the attacks were indeed coming from all sides.

#

1969

"Stick out your tongue and say ah," the doctor said, holding gauze in his hand. The familiar disk-shaped mirror attached by a leather band wound around his balding head. He wrapped the bandage around my tongue and held it down, then placed a little round mirror attached to a metal extension in my mouth so he could see my throat. I was used to this, so I relaxed, otherwise I would gag or throw up. I learned long ago to relax for shots, prods, pokes, and stitches. It hurt less if you didn't fight.

"Okay, it all looks like we expected," he said. "So—you want this removed?" He pointed to the tracheotomy contraption. "I think it's time," he added.

I nodded. *Maybe Mom's wrong about surgery. It'd be so cool if he just slips it out.* I started to feel excited. *Would I be able to go to school tomorrow—normal?*

"Yes, if she can breathe without it—let's remove it," Mom said, smiling in my direction.

"I want to explain the procedure," the doctor said, sitting on a stool with wheels. He rolled over to a counter that had several glass containers; one was full of cotton balls, another with cotton swabs; the last one with looped-handled lollipops. He grabbed a purple lollipop and handed it to me. "The tracheotomy has been in for a long time, and the scar tissue is thick around the opening. It will remain open unless we do some surgeries."

"Surgeries—more than one?" Mom asked, her smile gone, her face gray.

"Yes, even if we removed the tube outside, the outer cannula on her tracheotomy, even if we removed everything including that, the hole would stay open there is thick scar tissue keeping it open."

"Will she miss a lot of school? How many procedures, then?" Mom cleared her throat, stood up and shifted her sweater around, then laid it next to the chair and sat back down.

"Are you okay? Can I get you a glass of water?" the doctor asked.

"Please, I'm sorry, I wasn't expecting—I don't know what I thought," Mom said, her voice fading to almost a whisper.

The doctor left the room.

Mom put her head in both hands, rubbed her scalp and cleared her throat a few more times. "Should she leave while we talk?" Mom asked, pointing at me when the doctor returned.

"No, I'd like her to know what to expect, no surprises. I know it's difficult. You'd like to shield her, but I find it's better to be open and include the patient in these discussions."

Mom sighed and nodded. "Okay—so lay it out for us."

"We'll put her to sleep, take out the tracheotomy, including the inner tube. Then, while she's asleep—so you won't feel this—" he said, looking in my direction and pausing. I smiled to let him know I was paying attention. "We'll sand her neck and scar tissue down to a bloody pulp. She'll stay in the hospital a few days, go home, and fully recover. Then we'll do it all over again; each time we do it we'll sand a little lighter."

The doctor took out a piece of paper and drew a straight line with a sharp c curve then a straight line again. "We can't have it heal like this. This is what would happen if we just did the procedure once: the skin would heal on the outside first, and the inside would have a little cup or dent in it that would be prime for infection. That's why we have to sand it down several times." He then drew a long straight line and made a skinny rectangle. "This is what we want it to heal like," he added.

"That's going to be quite a scar," Mom said, again clearing her throat. She took a sip of her water.

"Yes, when we're through, she'll have a nice wide, thick scar. That's what we want, so it's smooth on the inside."

Mom stood up. "We'll see you tomorrow?"

"Yes, we'll get some tests done tomorrow and schedule the first surgery."

Mom leaned over and grabbed her purse. I stood and followed her to the car.

"Let's go see Dad—he's going to be so fooled with our practical joke," Mom said in a perky, upbeat tone.

Bloody pulp. He wants to do it several times. I knew she didn't want to talk any more about the surgeries.

"Dad's going to think I'm such a brat, putting ice cream on his drawing" I said and laughed, pretending to forget about the surgeries. I wanted to forget about the bloody pulp and have some fun.

#

2013

"Phone is for you, it's Anna," my husband Bob told me. Anna was the sister of Scott's deceased wife, Constance's aunt. I gave Bob a pinched-frown look. I knew Anna very well, but it was odd for her to call me—in fact, I couldn't remember a time she ever had called.

"Hello?" I said with curiosity. I could hear Anna crying. *Constance? It's Constance—Oh God*, I thought, *maybe it's Scott and Constance. No, please no*. I stayed on the phone line, waiting.

Anna finally caught her breath and said, "I have bad news." *Oh God, no*, I thought again, *please, please no—make Scott okay, make Constance okay. Please don't let this bad news be really bad news. Maybe just a little bad, like an accident but they are okay*, I prayed. Finally, Anna finished, "It's Scott."

"Is he going to be okay?" I asked.

"No, Pam, he's gone, I'm sorry. I know this is awful for all of us."

"How?" I asked, not crying, shocked and wanting to die myself. I prayed for God to strike me dead, just let me die—or wake me up. *I'm done. Game over.*

"A head-on car accident. Just south of Camp Verde. Yesterday," Anna said. I had dinner with Scott the night before. Why hadn't I hugged him when we parted in the parking lot? Why hadn't I told him I loved him? I felt heartsick for Constance now fifteen. She hadn't had a mother for a long time, and she'd been so close to her dad. "Where is Constance?" I finally whispered.

"She's at her cousin Arthur's house," Anna answered.

Anna and I spoke of funeral plans and of Constance. Anna would take custody, but because Anna lived in Hawaii, Constance could stay with me and finish the school year. We had a bedroom for her. She'd be comfortable, maybe feel at home with us. I knew she was close with her aunts, uncles, cousins and grandma. I could take her to visit often because most lived nearby. I knew Bob would support this; he also loved both Scott and Constance.

#

Perfect weather for a car ride, I thought. I enjoyed playing on my cell phone as Bob drove the car headed to San Diego. Clouds had started to build as they do for Arizona monsoons. The report on my cell phone indicated a small fire just three acres outside of Yarnell. The fire was on property held by the Bureau of Land Management, and the report said that they were going to let the fire—caused by a lightning strike—burn while they continued to monitor it. The fire had started around dinner time on June 28th. That was the day before yesterday.

Another wildfire. About two weeks earlier we had the Doce wildfire just west of Prescott. Several hundred homes were evacuated. Those residents had to stay with friends, family, or at the Yavapai Community College gymnasium. Granite Mountain was charred black by that fire.

Wildfires are typical in Arizona. I hoped they wouldn't let this one burn too long. I got updates throughout the day, but it made me nervous—*just put it out!* I knew I didn't understand fire suppression and realized they had their reasons to let it burn. I was pleased when the update said they were finally fighting it. *Poor firefighters. They must be exhausted from just finishing the Doce fire.*

I continued to watch my cell phone. If the assessor's office needed to make maps for emergency services and the firefighters, we would be ready. I silently prayed that this one would be easier than the Doce fire. For that one, county staff had worked around the clock creating maps for emergency service. At least one of my employees had been evacuated from the fire area. Luckily no one was hurt, and all properties were saved.

We settled into a two-story Budget Motel in San Diego. Bob and I stood on the balcony enjoying the sea breeze after our long day's drive from Prescott. Mike, my oldest son, and his girlfriend

Jaime would be meeting us at the motel soon. We'd hang at the pool for a little while, then go to dinner. We planned to go to Sea World the next day together.

I continued to monitor the fire and tried not to worry. This fire seemed ordinary. I wondered what ranchers did with their livestock when wildfires broke out. Did they have to get on their horses, round up the cattle and locate them to another area? Or were cows smart enough to run away from fires? I supposed that the animals moved away from the smoke and the heat of a fire on their own.

As the day progressed, I received more updates on my phone. The fire had grown; they were fighting it hard now. *We probably would be making some maps*, I thought. I emailed the office to put them on alert.

Bob and I got into our bathing suits. I phoned Mike, who'd arrived and was getting settled in the next motel room. "Meet us at the hot tub," I said.

"Okay, just F-Y-I, I'm bringing beer down with me," he said with a good-humored laugh.

Duly warned. I wouldn't give him the Mom-look or any body language about my disapproval of his adult decisions. I wished he didn't drink so much, but I supported free agency—even if I secretly damned it. I worried about Mike. I chose not to drink at all and raised him in the Mormon Church that discouraged drinking. I'd hoped he'd decide not to drink and go on a mission, a two-year commitment that consists of teaching the gospel to people interested in learning about the Church and Jesus Christ. Neither of my boys chose to serve a mission. That had been disappointing.

I grabbed my phone and wrapped a white towel around my waist. It was dark, the night calm and warm. My husband, dressed in a blue bathing suit, and I walked down to the hot tub. Mike, my young son in his late twenties, dark hair and cinnamon-colored eyes, met us with his six-pack. He climbed into the tub.

"Jaime will be here in a minute," he said, looking directly at me as he popped his beer can open. I wanted to control him. My kids would be happier if they just lived life the way I wanted them to, but Mike had taught me years ago that if I nagged him, I would be sorry. He would stay away if I lectured. Having him in my life was more important than pushing him to do things my way, which had never worked anyhow.

My phone beeped as I sat on the concrete dangling my feet in the hot tub. I looked at the phone. Bob and Mike exchanged glances as if to say, "She's doing it again, refusing to ignore work."

The message on my phone said *19 firefighters dead in Yarnell fire*. My heart cramped, my mind was confused. *What? That's wrong! Nineteen? But it's a small fire!*

Jaime leaned over the railing above us at the motel and yelled down, "Mike, I just got a call, nineteen firefighters are dead in the Yarnell fire!"

"Who? Travis?" Mike asked, alarmed.

"Names aren't released yet," Jaime responded, breathing hard and gulping in air. My hands started to shake. My eyes teared up. I didn't know what to do or think.

Jaime disappeared back into the motel room. Mike, Bob and I stared at each other, stunned.

"It's got to be a mistake," I finally said, showing Mike my cell phone messages of the last two days. They reported: a *small fire, three acres, about eight acres, they're going to fight it*. Then, *nineteen firefighters, dead*.

Jaime leaned over the railing again, "The television reports it was nineteen Prescott Hotshot firefighters. Still, no names released."

We got out of the hot tub. Not in the mood for a vacation. Not in the mood to do anything but pray. We knew several members of the Prescott Hotshot crew. If it was indeed nineteen dead, that only left one member alive. It had to be a mistake. We went to our motel room and monitored the television reports. *Please not Travis*, I silently prayed. *Oh Heavenly Father, let's just make this some terrible mistake, and they all are okay.*

I soon received the answer—the reports were accurate, and Travis was named among our fallen heroes. Travis Turbyfill had been a friend of Mike's for years. I cried for Travis, his wife, his parents, and the other Hotshots and their families. I cried for Yarnell, for Yavapai County. I believed the whole world cried with me. I had experience with prayers, understood they were heard, but not always answered the way I wanted.

For an Arizona assessor, destruction by flood or fire is recognized in the same tax year it occurs. This was problematic because valuations had been completed a year before the fire occurred. Tax rates were already being set. Our office had to re-do seventeen hundred valuations, and do it as soon as possible so that the taxing jurisdictions could rely on the new valuations. Much depended on us, including government assistance, insurance settlements, budgets and tax rates. Our office pulled together, made maps, inspected properties and provided timely re-evaluations.

#

1969

I sat on the bed in my dark bedroom. I was eight years old. My back was against the wall, knees against my chest, holding myself. Alone. I reflected on the last several years, contemplating the upcoming surgeries. I wanted the tracheotomy gone, but I didn't want procedures that would include my neck being made into a bloody pulp—multiple times. *I'm done,* I thought with a feeling of hopelessness. I sat very still, silent. *I don't want anything, anymore. I want everything to end.*

"You'd miss your mom and your sister," came into my mind, but I had the impression that the idea hadn't come from me. My mood changed. I felt warm, loved and accepted.

Soon I sank back into my hopelessness. I would miss them, but I still wanted it to end. *It's too hard, I can't do it.* I wanted to no longer exist; I wanted to never have existed at all. I wanted the light that was me to be extinguished, or to never have been turned on. It felt like an all-consuming, overwhelming giving up. I didn't have the words for my complete despondence.

"What if I told you—you have a purpose, even if that purpose is just being here for your mom or your sister?" As I heard the thought, I again felt loved and understood, not judged.

I don't want more, I'm done. I knew that if I didn't exist Mom would be sad and my sister Bevy would miss me. But I just didn't care. I was completely and utterly done.

Then my dark room grew lighter and lighter. I looked to my right; the source of the light was a beautiful woman. She had long dark hair, slightly curled at the ends, stunning blue eyes and a very fair complexion. She wore a white flowing dress, and the light seemed to radiate from her, enough to remove any shadows from my bedroom. I wasn't startled. I felt calm and loved.

"Lay on your back, put your hands on your side—lay very still," she said.

I felt tired, my body heavy. I did as she asked and placed my hands to my sides. "What are you going to do?" I asked, curious but unafraid.

"I'm here to fix you," she said.

With that, I grew more tired and closed my eyes. I felt comfortable, relaxed, and still. In the next moment, I felt tinkering and movement on my neck.

Finally, she said, "Untie it."

I sat up, opened my eyes, and untied the straps on the back of the tracheotomy.

"Slip it out," she added.

The metal contraption, in bulk, slid smoothly out of my neck. I held it all, and the parts fit neatly together in one bundle in my right hand. I looked up at the woman of light, surprised; the permanent inner tubing wasn't supposed to come out, but it had easily slipped out. In fact, my neck felt liberated! Free from the weight, the bulkiness and heat that I'd lived with so long, I threw the offending thing as hard as I could. It thumped against the wall, slid down, hit the floor, rolled, and stopped.

"Lie back down and be still again," the lady of light said.

I closed my eyes and lay silent and still; it was easy because I felt heavy and relaxed. I felt a cool breeze on my neck and felt wispy movement there, nothing painful, but little adjustments.

"Finished," she said.

I wiped my hand across my neck, a crusty grittiness and a slimy wetness seemed attached to my throat, the wetness sluffed off and stuck to my hand. I wiped the yellowish muck onto my sheet.

I searched for the hole or an opening in my neck, but it was gone! I could only feel smooth wet skin. Feelings of relief flooded me.

"Thanks," I said, my eyes so heavy I could hardly keep them open. The lady smiled, and as her light faded, she disappeared. I lay down, rolled over on my tummy and went to sleep. The air, and the sheets of my bed, lightly touching the skin on my neck, felt wonderful.

#

"I'm not sure what happened," Mom said to the doctor, handing him the bundle of gunk I'd removed from my neck the night before. "I guess it fell out while she was sleeping," she added.

The doctor felt my neck with his thumb. "No, what's odd — what's impossible—is, it closed." He sounded distracted as if he were speaking to himself. "After sixteen weeks with a tracheotomy, the opening won't close on its own because scar tissue forms. As I told you, the opening needs to be surgically closed after that. In fact, your daughter's had this for much longer than sixteen weeks." He continued to gaze at my neck, puzzled.

Mom agreed, "The tracheotomy has been in for way more than a year."

"I saw the scar tissue yesterday," he said, still musing over what he had seen. "Even if the inner cannula were to fall out, the tracheotomy wouldn't seal. In addition to all that," he paused momentarily, then continued, "it's healed from the inside out. There's . . . no dent inside. It's a nice, thick, smooth pad there— that's impossible! No, my professional opinion is that we've just witnessed a miracle!"

The doctor called his nurse into the office. He told her to

look at my neck. After she left, another group of medical staff was instructed to view my neck. After a while a group of medical staff crowded into the area, all peering at my neck, discussing it animatedly with one another. In the end my mother and I were allowed to leave, no future bloody pulping procedures.

For years Mom, Grandma, aunts, uncles and other adults marveled and discussed my miraculous recovery. No one asked me for an explanation. Why would they? They were looking for a medical explanation. I kept the experience close and didn't share it. I didn't tell my mother about the angel for years, I didn't tell anyone. I didn't have the words to explain the experience, and I'd learned by this time that adults couldn't always understand things.

As a young adult I sat down and finally told my mother and Bev about the angel and the healing. I felt inadequate to fully articulate the experience, but they got the gist of it.

"When you were in the hospital after the attack the doctors told me to prepare myself because you weren't going to make it. I had a calm, peaceful feeling that assured me you would survive. Doctors and some family members said I was in denial but I knew I'd received a promise," Mom said.

Even today, all these years later, I don't know why some prayers are answered *yes* with a miracle to follow and others are answered *no*. I like to think that little girl was healed by an angel because God loved her and understood how much she needed to know He was there and cared.

6

TACTICS

2014

I FOUND MYSELF ONCE AGAIN walking up the concrete steps to the old Maricopa County Superior Court building. I'd been here a few years ago when we defended the Phoenix Cement lawsuit. Now I was back entering through the arched entry and carved double doors that I admired so much. I'd be in court all week representing the assessor's office in this Arizona Beef Association lawsuit.

The lawsuit was about the new twenty-seven-cent per acre tax increase phased in over the next seven years. We had Kate—the amazing brunette that I wanted to emulate—as our attorney. Jerry Fries, a youngish man with as much passion as he had intelligence, was the attorney representing the Attorney General's Office defending the Arizona Department of Revenue. The ABA had Moo-moo as their lawyer (name changed—and you can picture him any way you want).

Moo-moo, during his opening statement, said I wouldn't be needed to testify. That was a relief. Testifying is stressful. I sat and enjoyed watching Kate and Jerry work their magic. Moo-moo was pretty cool to watch, too, although every time he got up to speak he stood in front of me with a wedgie. He was overweight, and he tortured me all week by exposing this wedgie. I couldn't escape it. *Could it be some kind of strategy?* My sister Bev and several assessor staff members accompanied me to court each day. The wedgie was the big discussion on breaks.

At night Bev and I'd read the book *Feelings Buried Alive Never Die.* We had both received a copy of this book from Scott when he'd found out Beverly had breast cancer. The book had sentimental importance to both Bev and me now that Scott had passed away. He had loved this book and referred to it often. I had also brought scriptures with me that I'd received from my husband Bob for my 30th birthday. I had notes from the young women's group at church tucked inside. The scriptures, along with the book Scott gave me, brought me comfort—and I thought perhaps good luck.

Bev worried about my health because I wasn't sleeping, nor did I look well, so she came along for most of the week. We'd gone shopping in preparation for court and purchased makeup, dresses and high heels. The final day of the trial she headed home; she needed to get back to work.

It was my birthday, so I put one of my new dresses on and looked forward to getting back home to Bob after court. We'd celebrate the birth of me, which I always enjoyed.

I checked out of the Phoenix motel carrying my suitcase—full of my new dresses, high heels, scriptures and favorite book from Scott. I added my office keys so it would be easier to get through the metal detector at the court building. I drove to the courthouse for the final day of court, locked my car and headed to the imposing building. As I walked away from the car I hit the beeping remote on the key chain to assure the car was locked. It beeped several times.

Seated in court next to Kate, I watched as Moo-moo announced, to my surprise, that I'd be testifying that day! Kate objected, and Moo-moo went on to make claims such as, "I don't know why she's reluctant to get on the stand and just tell the truth."

My blood boiled. I wasn't reluctant, but I'd have liked a chance to review my deposition and the math behind the lease-studies. Judge Fink finally ruled I'd testify, but it would be after lunch, so

I'd have some time to confer with my attorney.

The day went fine and my testimony was okay, probably because I hadn't had a chance to stress over it. We finished the hearing and I headed off for home. Once home I discovered my suitcase had been stolen! *How could my suitcase be stolen when the car was locked and still locked when I got to it?*

I called the Prescott Police Department and made a police report. They told me that beeping the remote as I'd done was probably the problem. Apparently, this sound could have been captured by some creep's cell phone and used to unlock the car. Crap! My county keys were in that suitcase! My keys had a master that opened many doors to both the Prescott and Cottonwood county buildings. *Crap, crap, crap.*

The air felt hot; my insides felt sloshy. I had to call Jim Argyle, of the county facilities department, to report the theft of the keys. How would he respond? I assumed it would be with contempt, as if I'm ridiculous and incompetent—like the board of supervisors had treated me for the last year. Instead, he was kind.

Months later Judge Fink ruled on the court case. He ruled for us: state land leases are not arm's-length leases and should not be included wholesale in the lease-study. That was our position all along. Leases from one family member to another or any lease that did not represent a typical market deal should not be included in a lease-study. A lease-study should look only at market leases in the area. We won it, but the values were reduced to less than I had on the tax rolls and substantially more than the ABA was asking for. Both sides touted the decision as a victory. However, ABA later appealed the decision.

The Arizona Beef Association then lost their appeal—which was a huge victory for the other taxpayers of Yavapai County. ABA and Mattie had flexed their political muscles, gotten powerful friends to bully and threaten, but despite it all, the grazing values were updated and would continue to be updated according to the law with lease-studies. *At least for now,* I shuddered. *They're not done, they'll get me if they can,* I thought, picturing Dorothy in her little red shoes and the ugly green witch screaming in the wind *"I'll get you, my Pretty!"*

I wished I could click my little shoes like Dorothy and put everything back to the way it was before I ran for office. *Oh, to have Scott alive, be back working with him, not taking on the big bad witch.* It was nice being married to my prince charming, Bob, with his support, always in my corner to protect me. Now with Barney's powerful Republican position loss and ABA's lawsuit loss I felt like I was barely a step in front of the big bad witch Mattie, and the tornadoes she stirred up. I was sure she'd probably get me in the end, and I didn't think Bob could protect me.

By this time, we'd gone from three supervisors to five on the board. The new board of supervisors appeared to want the ABA to have everything they wanted. They started to make remarks that Kate was "too aggressive—and perhaps needed to be fired." *Really?* Fire an attorney for winning? Not only had Kate won the ABA lawsuit, she'd gotten increases on the Phoenix Cement lawsuit.

Around this time I no longer was invited to the supervisors' meetings when they discussed property assessment lawsuits, and I started to receive pressure to reduce the valuations of ranchland to ten dollars and ten cents per acre. The board of supervisors let me know that they might not punish me if I cut the grazing values back down. I couldn't do that—I had to follow the law and appraise these properties by doing lease-studies. I wasn't allowed to pull a number out of the air just to satisfy the board of supervisors. All properties had to be treated fairly, or it would shift the property tax burden from those getting favors to the ones not receiving special treatment. I'd tried to explain this to the board members, but they didn't seem to care, or perhaps they didn't believe me. They wanted what they wanted, and they were accustomed to getting their way.

#

1980

Mom and I drove through the night in my brand new blue 4-door Subaru. I'd obtained my real estate license and had excitedly bought the car. I knew it was perfect for a real estate agent, with its front wheel drive and electric windows. I loved the dashboard lights of bright orange and blue, reminding me of a cockpit on a plane. I'd gotten my real estate license at seventeen years old, before I'd even graduated high-school. Within the first month of having my license I fell into three listings and sold them all the same day, and my reputation grew as a go-getter. It was good luck more than skill. I bought the car at age nineteen. It was exciting to be one of the youngest realtors in Payson, AZ. Now I had a new car, fabulous clothes, and was making good money in commissions.

Mom drove the car as I navigated with the California map, the soft whooshing of the air-conditioner in the background breaking the silence. The cool air hit my bare legs and sandaled feet, so I pulled my legs up under me and loosened my seatbelt a little.

"You getting cold?" Mom asked as she fiddled with the air and flipped the knob over to heat.

"I'm a little cold but I'm afraid I'll start to doze off if it gets warm in here," I said. I leaned over and turned the knob back. The cool air was helping me stay awake. Mom had been driving for over fifteen hours, and it was now dark outside. Stars shimmered in the distance.

Being on this spontaneous road trip with Mom was fun. She and I headed to San Francisco from Arizona to be with Bev. I hoped her ten-month-old son Bobby would be okay. He'd been born with aortic stenosis, the same heart valve defect Gil Sieling had been born with. Bobby needed emergency open heart surgery. They'd be doing that in the morning at the San Francisco VA Medical Center. Mom and I headed out for San Francisco as soon as we got the news.

"It's weird doing this without Dad," Mom said, leaning in towards the steering wheel and scrunching her eyes. It started to drizzle rain, and the road was shiny, making it hard to see the lines on the road with the glare from the street lights against the wet pavement. The car bumped over some yellow circular speed bump barriers that partitioned the road from the shoulder.

I laughed. "Are you driving by Braille now?" I asked. "Actually, I'm proud of you that you'd be brave enough to head out to be with Bev without Dad." I leaned down, looked at the map, and tried to get some light on it from the sparkling new dashboard.

My adopted dad was certainly the patriarch of our home. Driving was his job. We leaned on him for things like this. But he couldn't get away with such short notice. He was busy building houses as a successful general contractor. Mom and I weren't going to wait for Dad to work things out. We'd be there for Bev, in time for little Bobby's surgery. My car was dependable, and Dad gave Mom some cash so we were set. I felt like a grown up on the trip with just Mom. This was a first. It was nice to have her to myself.

We had problems finding the hospital and pulled over to the side of the road to ask a woman for directions. She walked over to the car and very sweetly, in a deep voice, gave us directions. "That was not a woman," I said. "And he was wearing Charlie perfume. It used to be my favorite," I added as Mom pulled away from the sidewalk.

"I think it was a prostitute because we are in the Haight-Ashbury district, probably the worst place I could have pulled over."

Wow, a man, dressed like a woman who smelled better than me! Prostitute! How cool was that? I couldn't wait to tell Bev, and in about a half an hour I did.

#

2014

"But, it's a rock quarry. That should be a commercial classification," I said, leaning in. Muttley, the attorney who worked for Mike Parks (AKA Dick Dastardly), sat at my desk across from me.

"You know Rowle wants it classified as agricultural," Muttley said. He looked uncomfortable asking me once again to explain why I didn't want to change the classification.

This property was a seven hundred acre ranch with a commercial rock quarry on it. The gravel had been sold to the county for building a road. My office had changed a portion of the land's classification to commercial when we discovered the sale last year. Now, the property owner agreed to give gravel to the Yarnell Water Company free of charge, and she demanded that the entire seven hundred acres of property be classified as agricultural.

"If she gives away the gravel to Yarnell Water Company, her property taxes should be nothing on just that portion. Why isn't that good enough?" I asked.

"You're the assessor, you can classify it how you think is correct. But as you know Rowle wants it all classified as agricultural because the property owner won't give the gravel to Yarnell if it's not classified as agricultural," Muttley answered.

During the Yarnell fire, the water company's pipes had been destroyed by heavy fire trucks driving over the roads where the pipes were buried. After that, Supervisor Rowle Simmons put together a project for the water company that included free supplies, including gravel and pipes. These items would be donated to help them repair the damage. It was interesting that they also received some federal funds even though this was a private for-profit company.

I didn't pay much attention to the favors and deals given to this water company—only the property classification aspect which was my responsibility. When Rowle was involved, I got used to seeing backdoor secret favors and deals. He prided himself on "putting things together," as he put it. I'd heard him on KYCA, the local radio station, bragging how he'd done deals when he was mayor of Prescott. Now he was a supervisor on the county board and used his secret backdoor skills to give out favors.

"The truth is, she's sold a conservation easement right here," I said, pointing to the map of the property that outlined the conservation easement. "The rock quarry is right on the conservation easement. That's why she wants me to classify it as agricultural," I reminded Muttley. "This isn't agricultural!" I insisted as tears started to fall down my face. I wiped at them. They seemed to make Muttley uncomfortable. He shifted in his seat as I blew my nose.

I was so frustrated. This conversation was a daily thing, and I knew it would continue until I gave in. Rowle had stopped speaking to me. He was angry that I wasn't changing the classification as he wanted. Now he was working through Muttley.

This matter couldn't just be about taxes. I'd offered to value this portion at zero from the beginning. The problem was that I objected to calling it agricultural when it was being used for mining rock and gravel.

Earlier that week, I'd gone to another supervisor, Arlo Davis, about the political pressure I'd received from Rowle about this rock quarry property. Arlo had said it was unfortunate that Rowle was pressuring my office. Then he chuckled and admitted he'd gotten gravel at a discount from this very property because they had leftover materials after the road job.

I'd nearly choked, thinking, *Wouldn't that be a conflict of interest to purchase material at a discount when you're in charge of their contracts?*

"That reminds me," I'd said to Supervisor Arlo Davis, "When the county purchases materials for roads, could we put on the bid sheet that the company needs to produce a clearance from the assessor's office that they are current on their taxes? I'm seeing a lot of these contracts where they don't have a file with us. It's self-reporting, and they aren't paying taxes on their business property. It's not fair that taxpaying companies are sometimes passed over on these bids. It'd be simple to assure that only companies doing things correctly get contracts."

Arlo agreed; going forward we could have a stipulation like this in the bids, he assured me. That never happened.

Now Muttley was back encouraging me to classify this property as agricultural. Between Supervisor Simmon's insistence and that of Muttley, a deputy attorney, the pressure was intense for me to just give in and classify all this land as agricultural. He suggested having the property owner sign a contract agreeing not to sell any more aggregate; she could give it to the Yarnell Water Company but make no sales. If the assessor's office discovered more gravel was sold, he added, we could change it back to commercial.

With that concession, I agreed to change this portion of the property's classification back to agricultural, though I knew it shouldn't be changed until gravel excavation stopped and the property was put back into grazing. I knew the demands had to do with the conservation easement that reduced this property owner's income taxes, but I was tired of the conversation and having to defend my position once again. It was clear that daily conversations like this would continue until Rowle got his way.

#

1980

Bev looked tired. Mother and I joined her husband, Paul, his mother, and Dan, a Navy buddy of Paul's, and camped out at the hospital during my nephew's surgery. He looked so little at only ten months old. I prayed he'd be all right. Beverly took me aside and told me how helpful Dan, Paul's friend, was. She was impressed with how attentive he'd been with little Bobby.

As I sat in the waiting room, I secretly observed Dan when he wasn't looking. He was handsome in the same way my adoptive dad was handsome, with similar dark hair and eyes. His hair was short, a haircut common to the Navy guys. His confidence reminded me of a soldier. He had Bev's seal of approval and he loved my nephew. He was attractive, and I decided I'd like him to notice me. So I schemed. It wasn't hard to get his attention, but it wasn't the way I'd planned. In my fantasy, he'd notice my stealth grace, my amazing beauty and fall in love. Perhaps that did happen —but not at first. The reality happened more like this:

I said to Dan, "Mom wants to ride with Bev, so could you go to Bev's house with me in my car? I don't know the way to her house in Vallejo from here." Dan agreed with a friendly grin, and his intense eyes gave me a look that made my knees weak. You hear that in the movies and read about that in books, but in this case it was real. I gulped, pretended to be confident, and headed to the parking garage. He followed me.

About this time, I realized I didn't know where Mom and I had parked. Dan and I walked one level of the parking garage, but couldn't see the car. We went to another level and couldn't find the car. Every level of the parking garage looked like the level before.

I finally took off my high heels that made my legs look long and sexy. Now, limping with blisters, I searched for my car. We finally found it.

I guess Dan had fallen smitten with me by then. He laughed and seemed happy to be with me. As he laughed, I noticed and loved his dimples. We spent most of the waking hours together for the next week and a half. He would pick me up from Bev's house and we'd drive to the hospital in his El Camino, spending all day at the hospital. In the evenings we went to Chinatown, or to Fisherman's Wharf. On Saturday we went water-skiing.

The night before Mom and I headed home to Payson, Dan and I went to a drive-in movie. There Dan asked me to marry him and I quickly agreed. I thought I was engaged to be married to the love of my life. At that very young age, I fell in love with dimples.

We planned my move into Navy housing in Vallejo, near Bev. Life was perfect.

#

2014

"Did you know that Mattie is the President of the Verde Ditch Association as well as the president of the Arizona Beef Association?" the reporter asked, holding her notepad and pencil in the air. She'd come into my office unexpectedly.

"No," I answered, and stood up to shut the office door so we could talk privately. I liked Tami, a good reporter. She was shorter than I was, with long, brittle brown hair. I always sensed she wanted to be accepted by the leaders that she reported on, yet it seemed she never got the respect she deserved.

Tami stood by the green upholstered chair in front of my desk. "She's the President of the Verde Ditch Association, and she's pulling her special tricks on people in that capacity, too," Tami said.

I sat behind my desk and motioned for Tami to sit, too. "Hmm, I don't follow the Verde Ditch Association much—makes sense she'd be president; her ranch has water rights from the Verde

River."

"This won't be in the paper, but do you want to hear what Mattie's done now?" Tami asked, scooting up to the desk and leaning in.

"If you mean troublemaking, please do tell," I said with a laugh. I liked inside information. Later I'd pass it on to my sister. If Mattie was picking on someone other than me, all the better. I believed the lawsuit with the Arizona Beef Association had been her doing to drum up membership for ABA; she was an expert in exploiting fears. *Now, what's she doing for the ditch owners?*

"Well, the town of Clarkdale wanted to encourage tourism for their community. They came up with an event using the Verde River for rafting, kayaking, tubing. You'd pay money to use the river. The people putting on the event contacted Mattie and asked if her association could refrain from irrigation for a few days before, and the day of, the event because sometimes there are flow issues with the Verde River if the irrigation ditches drain the water out."

"Unfortunately for them, Mattie's the president," I said and giggled, knowing the story would get worse.

Tami laughed and continued her story. "Yep, so they asked Mattie if it was possible to let the Verde River flow freely for a few days so they could have a nice tubing event. Mattie agreed in the sweet typical Mattie fashion. So everybody planning the event believed the flow would be fine."

"She didn't do as she promised?" I asked. *Mattie agreed, but then didn't? Why doesn't that surprise me? It sounds exactly like Mattie to promise something she has no intention of doing.*

"Mattie waited until the morning of the event, opened the irrigation sluice gate full-fledged and let it rip, draining the Verde River almost one hundred percent—south from where Sycamore Canyon runoff trickles into the Verde. This made the river non-navigable in that area. People couldn't float! They had to get up, carry their tube or kayak over the dirt and hike to where the stream started up again."

"Uh, just puddles and dirt—no river?"

"Right."

"What happens to the fish that live in the river when it's all drained out into irrigation ditches or onto farmland?"

"They die! They can't get out and walk across the dirt. They literally drained into the dirt where Mattie diverted the water. Because people paid, they didn't want to carry their stuff, so volunteers had to grab the kayaks and inner tubes and carry them past the dried area to where the river started up again."

"She destroyed the event on purpose. Why does she do things like that?"

"Because she can. Did you know she killed some pet Labrador dogs?"

"I did. She's a nut."

Tami agreed. "Well, anything going on with you that should be reported?"

"No, it's been fairly calm here. Hope it stays that way. We won the Arizona Beef Association case and their appeal over their valuation updates and the lease-study, but they've filed new lawsuits each year on their valuations. In the end we'll win those, too."

"You'll never win in the end, they're terrorists," Tami said.

Does she really mean that or does she want me to drop my guard and say something quotable. I think she wants a headline. I already called Mattie a nut.

"It's always nice to visit with you," I said and walked Tami to the door, hoping I wouldn't see a headline the next day quoting my nutty remark.

#

1980

"Dad, I want to marry him," I said. Mother and I sat by the fireplace surrounded by flagstones. Our home was beautiful, a five acre estate in Payson, Arizona, with horse corrals, barns, chicken coops, a few cows and a guest house, where Grandma lived.

"What about college?" Dad asked, his eyes tearing up. I didn't want to disappoint him, but I was nineteen and in love. I'd be dropping out of college. Dad was my hero; he'd adopted us and loved us. Gil Sieling, my biological father, was out of prison, his parental rights were severed and I didn't think of Gil as my father.

"I'll be moving to Vallejo, California, living in military housing."

"You're too smart for this," Dad said in a whisper. "She just wants to be by her sister," he said to my mother. Mom nodded in agreement but said nothing.

Dad was partly right. Bev was married, and her husband Paul was in the Navy with my new fiancé Dan. They were on the same ship—the *U.S.S. Point Loma.* I'd live in military housing by my sister and nephew. It was my dream come true. But I loved Dan; that was true too. I loved his sweet talk, his attention. I loved his smile and especially his dimples.

"I can go to college in California," I said softly.

"You won't. Honestly, honey, you're too good for him. I don't want to be mean, but you are," Dad said, almost pleading. "Is he even a Mormon?"

I shook my head, Dan wasn't Mormon, but that didn't make me better than Dan, and I knew Dad didn't believe it did. My whole family, including Grandma and Bev's husband, had converted and we'd all been baptized together in the LDS church just five months earlier. I didn't want to disappoint Dad, but I couldn't bear to think of a life without Dan. It was perfect that my sister and my nephew would be in the same military housing. She'd married and moved away; I missed her. I saw the convenience of picking Dan to be my husband, the best friend of Bev's husband. It was perfect all around, as if it were meant to be.

Dad finally agreed. "Okay, but make me a promise that no matter what you'll keep up your real estate license. Even if you live in California, you can come back to Arizona and renew your classes and renew your license. Don't let that license go."

It seemed silly to me to keep a real estate license in Arizona when I wouldn't be living there. But I agreed. Dad had been proud that I'd gotten my real estate license so young.

"With a real estate license you can always manage apartments or motels. It just gives you options," Mom said.

I agreed. I walked over to Dad and gave him a hug. Then I hugged Mom. I was getting married! I was moving to live by Beverly—life was perfect. I knew they were disappointed, but they'd see Dan was a great guy. *They'll learn to love him too*, I thought. I was wrong, but I was young.

Dan and Pam Ford – August 15, 1980

#

2015

"Explain why you value the grazing properties the way you are valuing them, so I can explain it to the board of supervisors," Bill Drone, our county administrator said. His enormous body barely squeezed between the armrests of the chair in my office. He smiled and appeared friendly. I felt revulsion at his sweaty, balding enormous head, and I smelled something on him, maybe rubbing alcohol?

"Sure," I said as I pulled out the lease-study. "Let me make some copies of this for you; it's a statutory calculation, and it's easy math."

I left the office with the paperwork and rushed to the public bathroom, making it into the stall just in time to throw up. Something about the smell of rubbing alcohol triggered a distant memory of the hospital—maybe those pipe cleaners used to clean the medical apparatus. *Stop thinking of it,* I said to myself. *Think happy thoughts, think of grandbabies, laughter, cooing. Life is good.* I sat on the cool floor leaning against the toilet bowl. *What was I going to do? Bill's appearance and his smell makes me sick.* I sat for a few more minutes against the cold, smooth surface of the tiled wall. Finally feeling better, I went to the sinks, washed my face, leaned down and looked under the stalls for feet. I was relieved to discover no one appeared to be inside any of the stalls.

I quickly made the copies of the lease-study and calculation sheet, then returned to my office. Bill sat, still squeezed into the chair, a smirk on his face.

"Here you go." I handed him the copies. "You take the last five years of arm's length leases, average them, subtract the allowed expenses and divide the cap rate into it. The department of revenue provides the cap rate. It's that simple. The value ends up being about eighteen dollars an acre."

"You know the board of supervisors settled this last year for a value of ten dollars and ten cents an acre," he said, not even looking at the papers I had given him.

"Yes, I know," I whispered. My throat tightened making it difficult to breathe. It ached, I assumed from the stress of throwing up earlier. My right side vocal cord started to twitch and do its little dance. I took my hand and rubbed my throat, hoping Bill wouldn't see the twerking vocal cord.

"Okay, I'll give them this. Please let me know what you decide to value the grazing property at when you make your decision," he said. He looked dubious, unconvinced.

I looked out the window. It was windy outside. The parking lot light post was swaying lightly, the trees all in motion. In the lower right corner of my big window sat the treacherous brown recluse spider I'd spotted before, still working and building his web. It was already about three inches long and thin. Several leaves were snarled up in the web, but I didn't see any victims—yet.

"Bill, I just handed you those sheets of paper, including the arithmetic; the other is the lease-study. With both, you can see exactly the assessments we are sending out and how we decided on the values."

I turned my copy around and pointed to the eighteen dollar figure, the value of the grazing properties. I couldn't understand why Bill didn't seem to comprehend what I was saying.

"Ten dollars and ten cents an acre or even maybe as high as eleven dollars an acre is okay. Anything more than that and we'll have another round of lawsuits on our hands," he said vehemently.

I stood up, "Duly noted." I smiled, trying to appear sweet, and looked down at my desk, attempting not to see Bill squeeze out of his chair.

My stomach turned. *Don't breathe, don't breathe.* I noticed my trash can sitting beside the desk. Good, if I get sick I can use it. I sat back down and pulled the trash bin towards me. My head grew warm, my stomach cramped. Bill exited my office, apparently not noticing my discomfort.

After Bill left, the nausea lifted and I felt better. I lay my head on my desk. His smell had reminded me of medical procedures, the suck machine and pipe cleaners. But I was also tired of his visits to my office. They were aimed to intimidate me.

#

1982

After I'd been married a couple of years, we were transferred from Vallejo to San Diego. I managed the apartment complex we lived in, and in exchange we received free housing and a monthly stipend. This, in combination with Dan's income from the Navy, allowed us to live fairly well. Beverly had returned to Payson about a year earlier. So except for a few neighbors and church friends, I was alone in California with Dan. My friends were wonderful although I never confided anything personal to anyone.

In July of 1982, I was five months pregnant with my first child, and we were at a party with friends. Moments before this photo was taken, a very overweight woman walked up and said "So, I see Dan's running around taking photos of MaryAnne."

July 1982

I smiled and sat down on a concrete bench next to a picnic table. She sat next to me. "Yep, he likes to take pictures. We have stacks of photo albums," I answered.

"It's not good for the baby for you to diet when you're pregnant," the overweight woman said to me, and I heard giggling to the right of me. I turned to see two women. One whispered to the other but I couldn't hear what she said.

Who was this fat chick and what's her deal? I wondered. I folded my arms, resting them on my baby bump.

"I'm not dieting at all. The doctor said that he wants me to gain twenty-seven pounds total throughout the pregnancy and

I'm right on track to gain that," I answered. *I don't have to defend myself to this stranger,* I realized.

"That MaryAnne girl your husband's chasing around, taking pictures of, that's his girlfriend. She works on the *U.S.S. Point Loma* with us. They've been inseparable from the time we left port in Alameda until we docked in San Diego," the fat lady blurted out with a grin, seemingly happy to pour out her information and ruin my day.

The air around me seemed still. I reminded myself to breathe. *Stay calm, don't give her the satisfaction of responding.* I remained quiet, looking at her with a blank stare. The silence was awkward. Finally, she got up and walked away. *Life sucks,* I thought.

One of the two women to my right that I'd heard giggle, now spoke up. "She's five months pregnant."

"Who's five months pregnant?" I asked, wondering if she was talking to me or about me.

"Sarah, the gossip who just told on Dan cheating on you," giggle girl said. "You look fine at five months pregnant. Sarah's pregnant and someone told her you were as pregnant as her and hadn't gained near the weight. That's what set her off."

"So is Dan cheating with MaryAnne or did fat pregnant chick just make that up?" I asked.

"Oh, I'm not going there. That's none of my business," giggle girl answered.

I didn't confront Dan. He was my best friend, I believed he was faithful. Fat chick was probably jealous or a trouble maker.

Five Months Later

Two in the morning the phone rang in our apartment. I ran to grab it, hoping it wouldn't wake Mike, just 25-days-old.

"Get down here and pick me up," Dan yelled into the phone without explanation.

"Where are you?" I asked, astounded that he was yelling at me. He'd been such a jerk when he'd left with his friends. It was his birthday. I'd asked where he was going, but he replied I wasn't his mother in a nasty tone, and told me I had no right to know where he was going.

Angry at his tone of voice, I firmly said, "I'm not your mother. Call her. Where's the car? How am I supposed to come get you? You took the car, asshole."

I could hear a man's voice in the background saying, "You need to let her know there will be bail money needed, and you may not be released right away."

"I'm in jail, just get down here and get me."

I bundled the baby, went outside and walked to my favorite neighbor's apartment. When she answered the door, I told her about Dan and asked for a ride.

Right away she said, "Oh Pam, I saw him with Carol. He's been hanging with her."

Still standing in her doorway, my mind whirled. What could I do? I didn't want to go home to my parents, let my Dad know I'd failed, bring the baby home and burden them. I shivered from the breeze. My neighbor loaned me a sweater and gave me a ride.

When we got there, we couldn't get Dan out of jail; I needed a thousand dollars for bail, but the most money I could get my hands on was two hundred dollars from the bank machine at the jail called the "ugly teller." The next morning Dan was released on his own recognizance and he was angry at me because I'd left him in jail for the night.

Dan had been arrested for driving drunk and our car was damaged. Ironically our neighbor Carol's arm was broken. I never questioned out loud if there was a connection or not.

Once home, Dan cried, apologized, sweet talked and convinced me he'd be a better husband. I wanted to believe him —so I did.

There were more women, more bad days. I pretended to not see, tried to enjoy the times he was in a good mood. I worked harder at being a wife he'd want. I had my baby and focused on being a good mother. Sometimes Dan would be gentle and apologize. I missed my mom and my sister, and wished I was back in Arizona near them, but I was ashamed that I was failing at marriage. I didn't want them to know.

#

2015

I had to drive to a tax conference. My sister Bev said she thought it would be fun and offered to come with me. About three hours into the drive, we stopped at Blimpies, stretched our legs, got some lunch, and Bev smoked a cigarette.

As we settled into a booth with our food, Bev said, "Pam?" as if it were some sort of question.

I responded, "Bev?" as if I were asking her something, too. When I looked up, Bev wasn't smiling. Her bright green eyes looked serious.

"What?" I asked, a little startled.

"Pam, don't be upset, it's okay. I have something I gotta tell you. It's okay," she repeated. I was getting upset because in my experience when someone starts repeating *it is going to be okay*, it's a red flag that something's not okay. The last bite I had taken from the submarine sandwich stuck in my throat, and my throat felt tight. Finally, Bev said it—"I have breast cancer again."

I sat in silence. The bite felt like a lump or like it hadn't gone all the way down. I stood up, unable to speak, rushed into the public bathroom and lost what I'd eaten. I washed my face while a stranger washed her hands next to me. The stranger glanced at me but said nothing. *She probably thinks I have some kind of eating binge disorder,* I thought. *Oh well, I'll never see her again. Just hope I didn't spoil her appetite.*

I returned to the table and sat across from Bev who said, "It's really going to be okay. I have a mastectomy scheduled, and I won't have to do the chemo or radiation this time."

She continued to eat her lunch and didn't mention my abrupt departure.

"When is your surgery?"

"This Tuesday."

"The day after we get back?" I asked, surprised. I looked at my food, but I couldn't eat. I sipped my tea instead.

"Yep—thought I'd have some fun with you first."

"Shit, now I have to be fun? I thought that was your job," I said, wiping at tears and trying not to cry. Bev chuckled at the slightly naughty word—I knew she would.

"I promise, Pam, it's going to be okay."

" . . . and I swear, we're gonna have some fun."

"Deal," Bev said, then added, "As if a tax conference could be fun."

"Oh crap, you're right! You'll be bored. I'll have a good time, and you can watch." I understood circumstances were what they were, and I could do nothing about it. I didn't like it. It wasn't okay, but we'd enjoy the day as much as we could.

#

1983

Dan was released from the Navy with a "General Discharge." There'd been an incident with a married woman, and Dan had been injured. Dan didn't explain the specifics as to why it wasn't an honorable discharge. It suited me fine. I knew he had no honor, so I was glad to hear the government agreed. Still, when he gave me that look with his cinnamon brown eyes, and grinned like I was the most important thing in the world to him," I melted. I loved him and wanted him to love me. He'd tell me how sorry he was for his latest escapade. He'd cry and he'd tell me how much he loved me. I wanted to believe him.

Things were going to be better, I thought, because we were moving to Prescott, Arizona. My parents had purchased the Mission Inn Motel, located on Gurley Street in Prescott. Mom said I could work there as a desk clerk and night auditor, and I wouldn't need a babysitter. My parents would let us live in one of the units with a kitchenette. Although Dan had no experience, my parents said they'd hire him as a cook at the Salad Patch Restaurant that they owned. Bev waitressed there, so it was perfect. I could hardly wait to be with my entire family again. I knew it would be nice for Dan, too. Paul, Bev's husband, had gotten out of the Navy with an honorable discharge. He was living with Bev in Prescott working for my dad's construction company. It would be nice to have this re-set, we could start over and do things right.

#

2015

Because I'd been frustrated with the constant demands to give wealthy landowners favors that were not legal, I'd fought with Bill. I didn't like Bill, but I had promised myself and God I would try to be kinder.

Bill scrunched himself into the seat in front of my desk. I tried to distract myself from watching him by singing in my head, "*The itsy bitsy spider climbed up the water spout, down came the rain . . .*" Even though I had vowed to be kinder, Bill still reminded me of a spider. He always smelled like rubbing alcohol and sour dirty used pipe cleaners. He made me sick to my stomach.

"Bill, I'm glad you came by. I want to apologize. We haven't been getting along, and I would like to start over," I said, feeling embarrassed that I'd been so revolted by him at our last meeting— even if he hadn't noticed it.

Bill cleared his throat, ignored my apology, and then said, "I just wanted to let you know that in the budget we will be considering a request to transfer the cartographers from under your authority. They'll move to the board of supervisors."

I grabbed a paper clip, looked down at it, studied it, twisted it and said, "You can't do that. It's against the Arizona Constitution and the state statutes. It would essentially strip me, the duly elected assessor, of any ability to do the job I was elected to do."

I grabbed my trash can and moved it conveniently to the right of my chair, in case I got sick. I was growing hot.

Bill grinned a scary, smelly, spider grin and said, "Really? You think it would strip you of the ability to do your job? Hmm. Mike looked into the legality of it and assures me it's legal."

With that, he laughed a deep belly laugh. He then squeezed out of the chair and stood up.

"Just wanted to let you know—we wouldn't want to blindside you or anything."

Why doesn't it surprise me that Dick Dastardly would assure the smelly bulbous-headed spider that this scheme was okay? I thought.

"If the law—if the law and constitution—isn't of concern, is there anything that can be done to change the board's mind?" I asked, trying to sound reasonable.

He gazed at me seriously, seeming to consider the question, then said, "You need to think outside the box!" With that Bill left my office.

I sat at my desk and looked out my window. The spider web now had grown, overtaking the lower right corner of the window. I didn't see the spider, but when there was a web, I guessed the spider would be close. I suspected the scheme of Bulbous-Head and Dick Dastardly to take these employees from the assessor's office was political punishment for my refusal to lower the agricultural values as they'd wanted and for complaining about the theft of Pictometry. I'd been blindsided and needed to take action.

#

1983

"Hey, Dad, I got a job offer—I can be an appraiser. My teacher for my real estate license offered me the job today," I said, sitting at the desk in the front office of the Mission Inn Motel.

"That's great!" Dad said.

Everything was working out. I could help out at the motel and work as an appraiser, too. Dan could work as a cook until he found something better, and our little kitchenette was big enough for Dan, me, and the baby.

Later that month the office phone rang. "Can I put you on hold for just a minute?" I asked and finished checking in two guests and gave them their keys. "Sorry about that, how can I help you?"

"Is this Pam?"

"Yes, it is," I said with a smile. *Maybe it's about my new job*, I thought, feeling excited about being an appraiser.

"Uh, this is Helen. I work at the Salad Patch with your sister Bev."

"Hi there," I said, as I sat down at the office desk. I looked for a throat lozenge. I'd been talking at the front desk all day, and my throat was starting to hurt.

"Well, um," Helen said, sounding uncomfortable. I found my lozenge, opened it up and slipped it in my mouth. It was peppermint and felt soothing. "Bev said I should call you and tell you. I—I'm divorced and my husband was a cheat so I know how that feels. I hate guys like that."

Crap, crap, crap! This is about Dan, I realized.

"Your husband's been asking me out, tried to kiss me and tells me how unhappy he is," she said, talking fast and running her words together. "Bev said you aren't separated and she's sure you don't realize how sleazy he's being."

"I didn't realize that," I said, knowing Dan was indeed a sleazebag, but wishing Beverly hadn't discovered it. "Thanks for telling me. I know it had to be difficult for you." I sounded poised but felt I might vomit.

What could I do? Divorce him? Throw his butt out? I could hardly stay here in Prescott with him. I confronted Dan that evening and made it clear I was finished with him. He'd have to leave.

Father's Day was in a couple of days—June 19th—a Sunday. Dan had talked me into letting him stick around until after Father's Day. Then he'd move to Ontario, Oregon, and live with his dad until he was able to get on his feet. This way Dan could spend Father's Day with our son Mike. Dan had cried, begged and been exceedingly nice, but I remained firm. He'd been a despicable husband and I was finished.

That afternoon Bev invited us on an adventure. "You and Dan want to take a day trip with Paul and me?" Bev asked, looking down and shifting her weight from one foot to another. We stood in the front office of the Mission Inn Motel. I could smell eggs and bacon cooking in Mom's apartment next to the office.

"What's up? You look like you have a secret," I said.

"Gil Sieling lives in Camp Verde. Paul and I are going to take little Bobby (their son who was now a toddler) over there to see him—thought it'd be fun for you to go, too."

"Gil Sieling! You're going to go see him today? I said, feeling a little excited.

I'd been curious about my biological father. He'd been released from prison nine years before, in 1974. Since then, Bev and I'd found his phone number in the white pages. We started calling him in 1975 to hear his voice. Then we'd hang up without saying anything. Sometimes he'd say hello, then say "Pammy" or "Bevy." It made me feel giddy that he'd say my name and probably think of me the rest of the night. He'd taken my mom to court two times to force visitation. The first time he'd lost. The second time Mom had his parental rights severed. Then our new dad adopted us. Mom probably thought that would be the end of that. Now Bev and I were adults and curious. "Are we going to tell Mom?" I asked.

"I already called him, and I told Mom. She understands why we'd want to see him. She's not thrilled about it but you know her, she's understanding. Gil's excited to see me and meet little Bobby. We're leaving in an hour. You're coming with us, right?"

I agreed and headed for the kitchenette to invite Dan and to get Mike ready for the trip. Our kitchenette smelled of the wet diapers in the diaper hamper.

"No way are we going," Dan said. He was sitting on the couch. The television played in the background and the baby swing clicked in even intervals, moving baby Mike back and forth. He'd fallen asleep in the swing, his head tilted at what appeared to be an uncomfortable angle, resting against the metal bar that held the seat to the swing.

"You can go or not," I said "but make no mistake, Mike and I are going. I'm inviting you because you only have a few more days here. If you want to stay here by yourself, that's more than fine with me."

"You're crazy! Why would you go see him?" Dan asked, his voice raised. Mike was startled awake and started to cry. I went to him, stopped the swing and slid him out. Grabbing my diaper bag, I started to change Mike's diaper.

"I'm not arguing, go or stay. Your call," I said calmly as I placed a clean cloth diaper under Mike.

I took the baby washcloth and cleaned the baby's bottom, then pulled the diaper through his legs and fastened it with the safety pins. I looked at baby Mike's eyes, *are they changing colors?* He'd been born with blue eyes but they were changing—maybe to brown? He had lots of brown hair. *He's the cutest baby boy ever to be born,* I thought.

"Then I have to go because I need to keep you safe," Dan said.

"Okay, be nice today. It might be fun. You and Paul used to be best friends," I said.

I knew Dan would be nice because he still hoped I wouldn't make him leave or that I'd come with him to Oregon. He'd said he didn't want a divorce, he loved me, wanted his family to stay together. He was angry with Bev's husband, Paul, though. Bev had persuaded her husband to tell her everything he knew about Dan's many infidelities. Bev had reported back to me, so Dan had no room to fib his way out of his past behaviors.

#

2015

I made appointments with each supervisor to discuss the loss of mappers in my department. Maybe I could persuade three members of the board to support the constitution, the statutes, or me. *If not*—I wouldn't think about that now. If I failed in this, I essentially failed as the assessor because I could no longer do the job. The board of supervisors would be taking it over.

I took Natalie Odell, the chief cartographer, with me to the meeting with Rowle Simmons, one of the board members. He sat behind a massive wooden desk. Natalie and I both sat across from the desk in oversized leather seats.

Long ago, Rowle had dated my sister-in-law. To hear him tell it, he was devastated when she broke the relationship off. Much had happened since then. He had become the Prescott Mayor and lost re-election, possibly due to his very public DUI conviction. He later ran and won a seat on the board of supervisors. I supported his campaign. Once, I considered him a friend. I still enjoyed his sense of humor.

"Rowle, the assessor has the responsibility of identification, classification, and valuations of all properties in Yavapai County according to the constitution and statutes," I said, as I handed some print outs of the sections of the constitution and laws I was referring to. "We need to retain cartography in our department."

Rowle seemed uncomfortable. He looked down as I spoke. *Why won't he look up at me?* I wondered. He took his right index finger and held it in his left fist and rocked slightly from left to right.

Natalie Odell then interjected, "Yes, Rowle, 100% of the cartographer's work is performed for the assessor. I've heard rumors that the board believes we perform work for other departments, and that isn't so."

I wondered what Rowle thought of Natalie. She was in her early fifties, and, in my opinion, easily the most attractive woman for her age working for the county. She reminded me of a 60's era girl with her straight hair to her waist and bangs. She had an artistic way of dressing, too. Today she wore a skirt that fell to her calf, a sweater cinched at the waist, and a large silver and turquoise necklace.

"Now Natalie . . . " Rowle smiled but didn't look up, just this slight rocking back and forth. He was good looking for his age, but round, as men of means sometimes become. The rocking reminded me of a distinguished, bearded Humpty Dumpty. "Natalie, this is not what I'm hearing. I hear your work is for several agencies and could be more efficient if you were under the board."

"Rowle, I thought that might be what you heard, but it's just not the case. Other departments can rely on our work, but the work is done for the assessor so the assessor can fulfill her constitutional duties," Natalie said.

"Okay, great. Thanks for coming and clarifying," Rowle said, finally looking up and giving a sheepish smile. He stood, which signaled the meeting was over. Natalie and I left.

"I think we can count on Rowle's support, pretty sure he will help us," I said.

Natalie disagreed and shook her head. "I didn't like his body language. He seemed conflicted to me. I wouldn't count on Rowle."

I believed she was wrong. Rowle was basically a good guy. Bill might desire to grab power, but he would have to get at least three board members to go along with him. That wasn't going to be possible. I smiled. *This was going to be okay after all*, I thought.

#

1983

It was a beautiful day in Camp Verde on Relo Lane where Gil was building his house. He'd finished a very small apartment where he was living on weekends while he built the rest of the home. He and his wife Flo explained that they both lived and worked in California. Gil had resumed his career as a glazier, and I wasn't sure what Flo did. They would come to Arizona to work on the house as they could afford it.

Gil seemed so loving and happy to visit with us and meet our babies. Dan behaved like a perfect husband, attentive to the baby and to me.

Gil barbecued hamburgers and hot dogs, and Flo chatted and made things comfortable.

She took me aside at one point and said, "This is a wonderful Father's Day weekend for your dad. He's so happy. But it does hurt his feelings when you girls call him Gil. You should probably be calling him dad."

"I can't do that. It'd be disrespectful to my real dad," I said, trying to be honest and not hurtful to her.

"Your real dad? That doesn't make sense. I thought Gil was your real dad," Flo said, looking confused.

"My dad is Jerry Sturdevant. I may have been born as Pam Sieling, and Gil might be my biological father, but he's not my dad, and I won't call him that. I can guarantee Bev won't either . . . I think if you're both alcoholics you know to take one day at a time and not push . . . it's pretty gracious just being here," I said.

Bev and I weren't going to play into some fantasy of being a family or being daughters. Surely they could understand that maybe a relationship was possible but not one of father and daughters. I reached into my purse to try to find some candy or a lozenge. I'd done a lot of talking today and my throat was sore—which reminded me why I'd never call him dad, ever.

As we drove away, that night, I thought about myself as a little girl, playing with Gil, lying on the floor with him as he watched television, putting my head on his chest, listening to him breathe, loving him so much.

Bev spoke up, "Do you remember the time Gil was beating Mom up and you climbed under the kitchen table, put your fingers in your ears and sang that Sunday school song named *Do Lord Remember Me* at the top of your lungs? I followed you under there and copied you. You must have been about four years old, so I was about two; remember that?"

"Yes, I never wanted to see him hit Mom. I'm surprised you remember that."

Mixed feelings of guilt and happiness engulfed me. I was being disloyal to Mom by coming and visiting with Gil. I'd heard him slap her around more than once. But at the same time I was happy that I'd let Gil see baby Mike. Mike deserved to have anyone who'd love him be part of his life. I smiled with the realization that I'd never felt bittersweet before. It was an emotion both interesting and painful. I was glad I had Bev. She understood.

7

GAME PLAN

2015

NATALIE AND I HEADED UP the stairwell to Supervisor Tom Thurman's office. She could answer his questions regarding what the cartographers do and why it was essential for them to remain in the assessor's office.

Tom Thurman was the supervisor I liked best. He had attended Prescott High School with my husband, so I'd gone to many school reunions with him. Oddly enough, Supervisor Thurman looked like Gil Sieling. They had similar features: blonde hair, blue eyes, both tall. Thurman wasn't crazy like Gil, not an alcoholic like Gil, but he had the best parts of Gil, the easy smile, the quick laugh, and a liberal non-judgmental attitude. I often wondered why I wasn't afraid of Tom. I typically kept my distance from anyone that reminded me of Gil. Tom was easy to talk to, fun to joke with, an all-around nice guy. He tried to please everyone. In politics that means you stand for nothing and fall for everything, so I wished he would stand up against things that were wrong and get rid of bulbous-headed Bill and Dick Dastardly. In my opinion both were utterly corrupt. How could the board of supervisors not see it?

Natalie and I took our seats across from Supervisor Thurman, who was sitting at his desk. His office was adjacent to Rowle's. It was the same size and the same layout. While Rowle's was decorated with the constitution, award plaques and flags, Tom's had a simple desk, some books and a couple of chairs.

"Tom, we're here to discuss this plan to take some of the assessor's assigned duties and put them under the board of supervisors," I said, starting the conversation.

Tom interlocked his hands behind his head and leaned back in his chair. He smiled with kindness and said, "Pam, this is political retribution."

My face probably fell in surprise. I already knew this decision had been for political punishment. Bulbous-headed Bill had made it clear, as had Dick Dastardly. Both had indicated if I didn't value the agricultural grazing land at ten dollars and ten cents an acre there would be consequences. Barney, the GOP guy, had made it clear to me, too. But I never thought that Supervisor Thurman, or the rest of the board members, were aware of the threats— the pressure I was under to value select properties less than the statutory calculations required.

I looked over at Natalie to make sure she had heard what Supervisor Thurman had said. I was surprised Tom would say it in front of a witness. Natalie's face was pale, her mouth drawn and serious.

"Political retribution?" I asked, rummaging through my purse for a throat lozenge.

Tom sat up and made a hitch-hiker symbol and motioned over his shoulder, pointing towards either Supervisor Brown's or Supervisor Davis's office. I wasn't sure which supervisor he was indicating. Then he took his index finger and looked to the west directly in front of him towards Rowle's office.

Tom whispered, "Your grazing values. You've ticked off a lot of people, and you're being punished."

"Can I count on you to support me? Will you do the right thing?" I asked, my throat closing.

I could barely breathe, though the menthol in the lozenge was helping. Was he warning me? Or was he just trying to explain politics and let me know why my enemies thought I deserved this.

Tom shrugged, "You've made some powerful people mad."

"I need these employees to do the job I was elected to do," I said in a dull voice. I believed once Tom thought this through he would support me. That's why he'd been honest with me. He knew the change was wrong. He'd step up.

I had to convince at least one more board member, maybe two. If I could get three board members to support me in keeping all of my staff intact, I could continue to do the job I was elected to do. If not, those that I made mad, that wanted a select few wealthy people to be given favors, would win, and the supervisors would grant themselves the power to supervise the employees who located and identified properties within the county—but what could I do about it if the board decided to go against the state's constitution and take over their supervision?

#

1983

I moved to Ontario, Oregon, with Dan. After three years of marriage, it was too early to give up. I loved him. He was fun, could be thoughtful and he said such sweet things to me—made me feel like his princess. I went to the church bookstore and sometimes the library to get books on how to love unconditionally, on how to be a fascinating woman, and anything I could find to help me be a better wife and a nicer person. My efforts at unconditional love for Dan seemed to be working. I stopped nagging. I decided to love the things about him that were lovable and ignore the things I didn't like.

We lived with Dan's dad, his stepmother and stepsisters. Dan and I slept on an air mattress in the den and Mike was nearby in a playpen. Dan worked with his dad selling used cars.

Like me, Dan had a big family with aunts, uncles, cousins and grandparents; they all lived nearby. His parents, Don and Gina, were fun, loved to go to country bars. Sometimes his sister, Beth, would babysit for us, and Dan and I would go along. Sometimes we danced. Other times we'd go to the home of Dan's Aunt Marilyn and play poker. We'd take Mike with us and he slept as we played cards.

One night, Beth, Dan's fourteen-year-old stepsister, agreed to babysit so Dan could take me out to dinner. I dressed in my jean skirt, a country looking blue flowered shirt with white lace around the bodice, and fringed white leather dance boots. As we climbed into the car, I could tell Dan had put aftershave on and he smelled good, like peppermint. I snuggled up to him and he held my hand. I felt safe and happy.

As we were seated in the booth at the restaurant, I noticed Dan's hand shaking. "Is something wrong?" I asked, feeling a little concerned.

"We'll talk about it later," he said. The waiter handed us the menus, and I turned my attention to the dinner options. As I looked up, Dan's hands were still visibly shaking.

The diner served great home cooking. It wasn't fancy; it had concrete floors and vinyl booth seats with Formica-topped tables. A juke box sat at the west wall, with a counter and stools that lined the north wall.

"I'll have chicken-fried steak, mashed potatoes and corn," I said to Dan, ignoring his shaking. *I'm getting so good at relaxing and not prying.*

I enjoyed dinner, although Dan didn't talk much. He seemed preoccupied. I worried, *Is it his health, or is there an issue with his dad? I could get a job managing an apartment and we could move if his parents were tired of us living with them. I wish he'd just tell me what was bothering him. Maybe he knows; no, he couldn't know yet. I'm not showing at all.*

After dinner Dan drove to Interstate 84 and traveled east for about a mile. We pulled into the Ontario rest stop, and he parked the car where we could see the lights. I scooted over and sat close to him, enjoying the scent of his peppermint aftershave. He draped his arms around me and again I felt peaceful and contented. In Oregon, I missed my mom and sister, but it felt good to be an adult on my own with my husband.

"I have to talk to you," Dan finally said. It sounded serious and he seemed sad. I scooted over so I could see his face as he spoke.

"I'm in love," he added seriously. *Oh, he's seen the changes in me! I've succeeded! He loves me—what I yearned for.* I felt joy that I hadn't felt in years. I remembered how handsome he'd been on our wedding day in his Navy uniform. I smiled and scooted closer to him, lay my head on his shoulder and looked out to the lights.

"I love you, too, so much," I said, admiring the view of the lights and thinking, W*hat a perfect night.*

"You've misunderstood," Dan said. "I'm in love with someone else. I want a divorce." Dan's words came in a rush.

I pushed as far away from him as I could. I got far enough away that he couldn't touch me, pressing myself against the cold steel passenger door. Saying nothing. I just looked at him, trying to make out his face. I pressed the heels of my hands to my eyes until I could see sparks.

"I want you to be happy for me. That's what you want—me to be happy. Why can't you just be happy for me?" he asked. "This is a good thing. There's nothing wrong, this isn't bad, it's good."

These statements made no sense to me and I didn't have the words to react. *Well, now's not the time to tell him I'm pregnant. Could I have messed up my life any worse?*

Dan continued to talk. I picked up it was Wendy, the girl in the band, that he loved. He said something about giving me a car and I could leave tomorrow. It was a blur. I continued to hold my hands against my eyes, seeing the sparks and wishing I had the power to disappear.

#

2015

The day after talking with Supervisor Simmons and Thurman, I packed my briefcase to go speak with Supevisor Jack Smith. He was the final vote I needed from a board member to assure I could keep my staff.

Natalie, the chief cartographer, who advocated that this department needed to stay with the assessor's office, peeked into my office, "Got a minute?" she asked.

"Sure, just getting ready for our meeting with Jack this afternoon," I said.

"I don't think I should go."

"You did great in Rowle's meeting. We have Rowle's vote. I'm sure we'll have Tom's vote, too. We just need one more! I think we can get Jack's and Craig's so that's four, one to spare in case." I put the job descriptions in my briefcase for the meeting.

Natalie sat in the chair and looked at me. Today her long, straight blonde hair was tucked behind her ears and fell naturally to her waist. She wore a green skirt with a black blouse, cinched with a big belt. Her silver and turquoise necklace added to her striking appearance. I couldn't tell from her face if she was in a serious mood or sad about something. Her face was drawn, her lips pursed.

"Is something wrong? You don't have to go. I can go without you. What's the matter?" I was concerned that Natalie might have something personal she needed to attend to. I knew her horse, Gus, had been very ill. She loved that horse. I quickly prayed that the horse was okay.

"I don't think I should go with you to see Jack. You shouldn't count on Rowle's vote either. I have it on good authority that you don't have his vote. I can't tell you who told me, but don't count on him." I wasn't sure why Natalie didn't want to go see Jack with me, or why she believed Rowle's vote should affect her going to see Jack.

"Okay, I can go see Jack without you," I said, wishing she would tell me exactly why she didn't think I had Rowle's vote. I remembered his weird body language, and Tom's statement about political retribution. But I had faith Rowle would do the right thing. He might go along with Bill for a minute or two, and fantasize about how I should be punished, but at the end of the day, would he really vote to violate the Arizona Constitution? He studied the constitution, respected it, ran his campaign touting that he adhered to it. Rowle might punish me by leaking the Gil Sieling articles with Barney, the GOP guy, but Rowle would support the constitution, if not me. I still counted Rowle in the probable support column.

Natalie moved around in her chair appearing uncomfortable. "I was surprised with Tom's statement that taking my department from your authority was some kind of retribution," she said.

"I was surprised he admitted it, and in front of you, too," I replied.

"Pam, I don't want their shady changes. I like you, and I want to have my department stay under you. You've been a great leader, and I respect you. But if the board moves us, I can't burn bridges—I would have to work with them. I can't afford for my department to be destroyed. I just can't go with you to see Jack. I can't lobby anymore for us to stay with the assessor's office." Natalie's voice started to shake.

"Okay, that's fine. You have to live with their vote, I get—"

"Pam, Rowle came to see me!"

"What? When?" I put my briefcase down and sat in the chair.

"After our meetings yesterday, Rowle marched into our cartography department. Said he wanted to talk. We slipped into the conference room, and he told me I had hitched my horse to the wrong wagon, that I needed to stop going to board members explaining why we needed to stay under the assessor. He then put his hand on my arm and, like a father, said, *'This meeting never happened.'* I felt threatened. You don't have his vote."

I sat, trying to assimilate the information. This was a surprise. I had admired Rowle. Now I knew that Tom had been correct when he pointed in Rowle's direction and claimed it was political punishment. I had thought Bill, the county administrator, was behind the political pressure, but apparently Bill had the support of Rowle and others.

"Thanks for telling me. It's important I know what I am dealing with."

Natalie stood up and walked over to me. We hugged. I loved her; she was as smart and kind as she was pretty. I might lose this, and if I did—no, I couldn't think of it now. If I lost this, I would lose the ability to do the job. That just couldn't happen. "I will try to keep you out of this going forward," I told her.

Later that afternoon, I waited outside Jack Smith's office. He was the youngest of our board of supervisors. Smith was forward thinking, supported technology and efficient government. He was a brunette with brown eyes and good looks that would help him go far in politics. I suspected his sights were on higher office—perhaps Congress one day. When Jack ran for board of supervisors, I supported him, believed in him.

My heart pounded loud enough that I could hear it. *Breathe Pam, take deep calming breaths.*

Jack's assistant escorted me into his spacious office, decorated like Rowle's with the constitution, flags, plaques—meant to be impressive.

"Jack, there is a scheme to take five of my employees—cartographers, who are basically mappers—from under my purview and place them under the board of supervisors. Do you know about this plan?"

"No," Jack said and leaned forward, giving me his full attention.

"I have to have these mappers! I can't perform my job as the assessor without them."

"Well, it makes no sense to me that there's a proposal to take them from you."

"Okay, listen—here's the interesting part. Supervisor Tom Thurman said that it's political retribution! I'm being punished because of my refusal to value the agricultural grazing lands at a lower number than it should be. Jack, I've had similar threats of punishment from Bill, the county administrator!"

"Supervisor Tom Thurman said that it was retribution?" Jack said, crinkling his nose in distaste.

"Yes, ask him. This is punishment because I'm refusing to play along and give favors. Please, Jack, I need to count on your support; I can't do the job without your support." Tears filled my eyes. *Calm down Pam, talk slower and breathe,* I said to myself, *be professional and don't cry.*

"Of course I support you; it doesn't make sense to take mappers away from the assessor; you do the assessor parcel numbers don't you, using these mappers?"

"Exactly!" I said. "I can't identify the properties without mappers. I have to have them to create the assessor parcel numbers."

"You can count on my vote," Jack said and stood. I wanted to hug him. I stood too, understanding the meeting was over. The relief felt good, and my heart stopped cramping. That was at least two votes—his and Supervisor Thurman's. Now I had to get Supervisor Simmons or Brown, and I was golden. I sighed out all the anxiety and left Supervisor Smith's office.

As I turned the corner, I noticed bulbous-headed Bill sitting in the lobby. "Supervisor Smith will see you now," Jack's administrative assistant called out. Bill stood up, nodded his bulbous head in my direction, smiled his spider smile and walked by without a word.

Too bad for you Bill. Jack won't support your power grab punishment scheme. He's too good for you, I thought. Unfortunately, I was in for a surprise.

#

1983

I told Mom and Bev I was there for a visit. Didn't tell them I'd been kicked out of the marriage. They didn't ask many questions and that made it easier. I worked at the Mission Inn, and stayed in the kitchenette that had been my home with Dan. Then I found the instructor that had offered me the appraisal position to see if it might still be available. He agreed to hire me. I'd start my new job the following week.

I answered the phone on the desk in the motel front office as I was creating a check-in and check-out sheet for the maids to fill out. Dad wanted it done by tonight.

"Hi, can we talk?" I heard Dan say on the other end.

"Sure," I answered as I placed the paper in the roller of the typewriter.

"Are you coming home? I bought you a surprise and I'm really missing you," he said with his charming voice. I felt nauseous about the situation, or maybe it was just morning sickness.

"I have to tell you something," I said, sucking my breath in. "I'm pregnant."

"That's great! It's going to be wonderful. I'm in counseling, and you're going to be so proud. I'm doing very well. I realize what's important now; it's you and Mike and maybe our new little daughter or son. I don't know what my problem was, but with counseling I'll learn. I need you here. This is where you belong." It sounded like he was crying. I wasn't surprised to hear him cry. That was typical when he was in apology mode.

Would this time be different? What else can I do? I wanted someone to share the excitement of the first movement or the progression of my belly growth, someone to go to the doctor's office with me. Someone to love the baby as much as me. Plus, little Mike deserved to be close to his dad. *Maybe Dan would even start going to church with me if I went back.*

#

2015

I shut my office door, got comfortable in my chair and dialed my sister's cell number. Bev was home, recovering from her mastectomy. I wanted to bring her dinner, see what sounded good to her. The phone rang several times before she answered.

"Hello," she said, sounding tired.

"Wow, you answered! I've missed you. Lots to catch up on. Are you up for some gossip?" I shut my office door and took a seat behind my desk.

"Yep, they gave me some good drugs, so if I start to snore it's probably 'cuz you're boring, or the gossip isn't up to your usual standards."

I caught Bev up on Bill and his plan to abscond with my employees, which would make it impossible for me to do my job as assessor. I reminded her that Bill had an enormous head and reminded me of a spider and told her about the conversations with both Supervisors Thurman and Smith. I detailed Supervisor

Simmon's clandestine meeting with Natalie, the chief cartographer. I talked of Constance, Scott's daughter, how she was doing with the loss of her Dad, and what it was like having Scott's teenager living with me. Bev laughed; we gossiped. Mostly Bev listened.

"Supervisor Brown will help you. Have you talked to him yet?" she asked.

"No, he hasn't returned any of my phone calls." I opened my top desk drawer and rummaged for a lozenge. Finding one I opened it up and plopped it in my mouth. I needed a good voice for this conversation.

"He'll support you. He promised Mom and me if he got elected he'd help you. Remember? It was at the meet and greet I gave for him during his election?" Bev said. I continued to suck on the lozenge and rubbed my neck as my left vocal cord started to twitch.

When Craig Brown had run for the seat on the board of supervisiors, he was disliked by the ranchers, by the elite, and by most of the power brokers. There were five men all running for the same seat. Georgene, the candidate and her supporters from my first election, all supported Craig. They said he had the correct stance on water issues and road problems. He was their man for their rural area. Because of my love for Georgene, I openly supported Craig. I spoke highly of him to all my supporters. I asked Bev and Mom to help him along with everyone who lived in his district including my kids, my cousins, nieces, and nephews. Craig had made promises to me that he would help me; he would stand with me against undue political pressure—favors for some at the expense of others.

I considered Craig a friend. Since his election my husband and I had gone out with Craig and his wife, Sandy. I went to lunch with Craig on several occasions. Craig and Sandy sent Christmas cards. When my husband had back surgery, they sent a get well card. Craig never forgot to ask how my sister was doing each time he saw me. I figured I had Craig's support, but I would feel better once he told me I had his vote.

"I remember," I assured my sister. "With Craig, I'll have three votes—Tom, Jack, and Craig. I'll be okay. Stupid Bulbous Bill—can you believe Rowle's weird double agent stuff?"

"Rowle Poly, Humpty Dumpty, tipsy dipsy, double trouble," Bev sang, referring to Rowle's looks, his DUI, and my issues with him.

"You're silly when you're buzzed," I said, laughing.

#

1983

Dan's call left me drained and needing advice. I walked over to Grandma's apartment in the Mission Inn Motel. I was glad to have her nearby. I gazed at the striking blue sky with a few white wispy clouds. *I want to go back to Dan, but maybe I shouldn't.* I knew if I asked Dad he'd say that I should know better than that and it was time to start making smart decisions. *That's why I'm gonna ask Grandma,* I thought and smiled to myself. I couldn't fool myself, though. I knew I would go back to Dan. I just wanted someone to back me up.

"Grandma, I'm pregnant," I said, sitting at Grandma's dinner table. A purple carnival glass pitcher and goblets sat on display in the center of the table.

"He cheats, doesn't he?" Grandma asked, looking at me, no judgment on her face. I didn't feel embarrassed or that I needed to hide the truth. I knew Grandma would understand and guide me wisely, or support me with any decision I made.

"What do you want to do?" she asked.

"I want to go back to him, but he kicked me out, said he was in love with someone else. Now he wants me back," I blurted out, then added, "It's not that he cheats sometimes; he's constantly on the hunt for someone. It's not just a few times. It's been numerous and constant. Pretty much the whole time we've been married. Said he's in counseling now and he realizes it's some mental problem. Do you think counseling would help him?" I took a sip of the iced tea Grandma sat in front of me. The cold liquid felt good on my throat.

"I wouldn't want to be pregnant without a husband by my side, but I think you could do it if you wanted. You have family and a support system that would be here for you," Grandma said. "A man who's a cheat like that probably will continue to be unfaithful, and it might just be a matter of time 'til you're kicked out again. I think you're too good for him, but I'm also a woman so I understand the whole matter of staying because of the children." I loved that Grandma never tried to manipulate. She listened and gave her honest opinion, if you asked for it. I also knew that no matter what my decision was, she'd defend it, if anyone ever questioned it.

#

2015

I sat at my kitchen table and dialed Craig's cell number. No answer. I waited an hour, dialed again, no answer. Then I waited a half hour and dialed again. I'd call every half hour until he answered. It was Saturday, and our budget hearing to discuss the county administrator's scheme to abscond with some of my essential duties was Monday. If they took these employees and the duties they performed, that meant the board of supervisors would then be in charge of the employees who determined who the property owners of the county were, the addresses where they received their notices, where the properties were located and all features that contributed to value such as topography issues. I had to know I could count on Craig. He wasn't answering. *Did that mean something?*

I rinsed the dishes, preparing them for the dishwasher. *Could I rely on Craig? Craig wouldn't go along with political punishment for me. Craig was honest, had integrity. He used to be a cop in California, and he understood how the wrong decision would violate the confidence the citizens had in him.* Half an hour passed, I dialed Craig's number.

When he answered the phone, he sounded annoyed. I explained I needed his support, told him how valuable those employees were for the assessor's office.

"Frankly, Craig, I feel blindsided because I know that

Supervisors Simmons and Davis support this insanity, and I don't know why. If I knew their position, I could provide a counter position Monday."

"Don't ever say I'm doing anything to blindside you!" Craig yelled into the phone. I was caught off guard, had not expected this reaction. I sat down, surprised by his outburst.

I tried to backtrack, soften what I'd said. "Craig, I can't prepare if I—"

"This change will be more efficient! The board has every right to take these employees along with their responsibilities and put them wherever the hell we want. I don't know who you think you are," Craig went on, still yelling.

I wasn't going to have Craig's support after all. He was angry, he was defensive, and he yelled for about half an hour. What he said made little sense to me. He yelled about how the budget was the board's responsibility, and I was being problematic by not cooperating.

Not cooperating? I literally could not do the job as the assessor if I were not able to identify properties. That was an essential responsibility for the elected assessor! I couldn't rely on another department to do it for me. Craig talked over me, and though I tried, I wasn't able to get another word in until he finished his rant. This was the first of several shocking surprises I was in for.

I listened until he ran out of steam. Then I asked, "Is there anything I can do to keep these employees?"

The Geographical Information System, known as GIS, was a department under the board of supervisors that created maps and put them together on the county website, managing and updating them as needed. These maps came from several county departments.

Craig explained, "GIS needs resources; they have more mapping than they can do. Your mappers are under-utilized so they can pick up the slack for our GIS." This was a false statement; my mappers were working hard and full time.

Development was up. More subdivisions were being created, and this all impacted our office. We had fewer people than ever, and more work. But I realized that arguing my mappers were not under-utilized wasn't going to be persuasive. I needed to come up with something else. *Think out of the box*, I said to myself, remembering Bill's words to me. *The board shouldn't take work assigned to the assessor by state statute and the Constitution and assign it to themselves! The board of supervisors seemed to think they could take the employees I had for identifying and mapping properties the assessor's office was responsible for and assign these staff members additional tasks.*

"Craig, I'm gonna figure out more resources for the county's GIS, so maybe we can cut my budget and keep my staff. Would you support some alternative solution if I come up with one?"

"Yep—if you can figure out something that really does all that, I would support it."

I thanked him and hung up. When I found my purse, I grabbed a lozenge. My neck throbbed. I must have strained my damaged vocal cord by trying to speak up. Darn it—when would I learn not to push my voice?

So, only two votes for me—Tom and Jack—and three against me: Rowle, Arlo and Craig. I went to the refrigerator and grabbed some ice cubes, wrapped them in a wash rag and lay on the couch with the cloth on my neck. My left vocal cord was jumping. It settled down after about an hour of rest and time to think.

I realized I was caught up in shady politics, and this surprised me. Craig had made promises to help me when he ran for office. Now he was willing to take away the resources that I needed to do my job. This plan would cripple my office. There weren't enough of my mappers to continue to perform their duties and take on additional responsibilities. If they were instructed to do things incorrectly for me, or not at all, I'd have no recourse if these staff members didn't report to me. This wasn't Bulbous Bill's plan on his own, as I'd initially thought. According to Supervisor Tom Thurman, this scheme was retribution for the agricultural grazing values. I remembered the times I'd seen Boe and Mattie in the county building meeting with the supervisors. At first, I hadn't thought Craig would be willing to participate in this political retribution. Now I could see he was very willing. *Had he ever been a friend?*

#

1984 -- 7 Months Later After I Returned To Dan

It was snowing in Oregon. I sat in my dark living room nursing Nicky, now a month old. With his blonde hair and blue eyes he was a perfect newborn, never fussed. Keep him dry and fed and he was happy. Little Mike, with dark hair and cinnamon eyes, slept peacefully in his bedroom. Now sixteen months old, Mike was an active toddler. It was quiet in the apartment. I watched out the windows as snow accumulated. It looked light outside with the moon glow reflecting off the snow. I looked at our furniture, it was beach motif with bamboo curtains, coconut monkeys hanging on the wall and sitting on the tables; glass and brass coffee table. It was nice to be in our own place. We were managing this apartment complex and received our apartment for free, along with $2.35 an hour pay. Dan worked as the maintenance man and I worked as the manager. Fortunately, the apartment needed minimum maintenance. I'd sold my saddle for a thousand dollars, and Dan used the money to start a bicycle shop where he worked most days.

Our marriage had been bad since I returned. Dan usually spoke unkindly to me. He'd grab me, throw me against the wall or twist my arm when I'd question him about anything. I tried to be low key during my pregnancy. I didn't want to set him off, afraid I might lose the baby if he threw me against the wall too hard. He'd often say, "If you don't like it, leave. But you're not taking my son!"

Dan had let me know that he'd never missed me; he'd really only missed Mike. I could stay and he'd take care of me, because I was the mother of his sons, but I needed to be grateful, count my blessings and settle down or I could "get the hell out." I knew he'd never let me take the boys if I left. Sometimes he was nice, but after a tirade he no longer apologized or took any responsibility. There was no more sweet talk.

I burped Nicky as I looked at the snow falling. When I'd decided to move back, my heart had filled like a balloon with hope that Dan had changed or that counseling would help. I wanted to have a happy marriage and a nice little family. Now the hope was gone and my heart deflated. I'd leave—not sure when, but I wasn't going to stick around much longer. I'd find a way to escape.

I pulled my wedding album from the end table and patted Nicky's back, soothing him to sleep. Balancing the album on my lap, I looked at Dan, so handsome in his Navy uniform, and me, so young and naive, in my white wedding dress and veil. *I wish I could go back and whisper the truth to that me*, I thought, looking at my younger self, so thrilled to be marrying Dan and believing my fantasy future lay ahead.

Mom, Bev and my grandma had left a week earlier. They'd met little Nicky and visited with Mike and me. I remembered what Mom said when she held Nicky for the first time, "He smiled at me! I swear he smiled at me." It'd been so good to see them.

Dan had treated them rudely. He didn't even pretend to be nice to me in front of them. He constantly complained about their visit. I hadn't shared with them how bad Dan had been to me, but it was impossible to hide it because Dan wasn't pretending that he liked them or me. He'd walk through the house, say nothing to any of us, plop down on the couch, turn on the television and completely ignore us.

Mom begged me to leave with them. If there had been room in the car, I might have gone.

The day they left, I said, "Mom, I'm going to leave, I can't stay. But not today. I promise I'll fly out when I get some money."

"We'll figure it out. I'll make room in the car," Mom said and started to tear up. "Or I can give you money so you can leave."

"I promise I'll leave soon. I don't want to take any more money from you. I'll figure it out," I said.

I waved as they drove away. Then I went into the house, lay down on the bed and cried.

As I looked at the wedding album, I reflected how I'd almost lost it along with Mike's baby book. While I was still pregnant, Dan and his dad had left me in Oregon with Mike for about a week. They went to Prescott, to gather our things from the storage shed.

After they got back, it seemed like we were missing some things, although they assured me they'd gotten everything.

Months later, Bev received a phone call from the storage shed manager. The manager said she saw a letter from me among the articles in the storage shed, and noticed Bev's address in Prescott Valley was not far from the storage place. She had looked up Bev's telephone number in the phone book. The woman told Bev that there'd been all sorts of stuff left in the shed, all female items, like clothes, books, letters, perfume, makeup, photos. They were going to sell the articles, but when she saw the baby book she knew something was wrong. A mother would never leave the book behind. Bev ran up to the storage shed, paid the overdue storage fees and retrieved my baby book, wedding album and the rest of my belongings. Dan continued to deny leaving anything behind and refused to listen to how Beverly had gotten the items.

Tonight, Dan and his twelve-year-old half-brother, Sam, were at one of the neighbor's apartments playing cards. I was surprised that they were out so late. When I last checked it was two in the morning. Sam had asked his Dad if he could spend the night with us.

I liked Sam, a cute kid. I wondered if Nicky would look like him when he was twelve. They both had the light blond hair that Mom called towheaded. I thought that was funny. They both had very light blue eyes, too, and I wondered if Nicky got that from my side of the family? Gil Sieling, my biological father, had those pale blue eyes.

Nicky was asleep. I got up from the couch and placed him in his bassinet.

At that moment, Sam came noisily into the living room through the kitchen door. "Hey Sam, you're finally home," I said with a smile, glad to see him back.

Sam's eyes were wide and he was breathless. "Where's my brother?" he asked.

"I thought he was with you. How'd you get separated?" I asked, starting to feel suspicious at what Dan was up to.

Sam sat down on the couch, not answering my question. He

asked one of his own. "Could he be at his girlfriend's?"

My head dropped forward; my hands started to shake. "Girlfriend's? What? Tell me!" Sam started to cry, his lips quivering. I sat down next to him and placed my arms across his shoulders. "Tell me what happened; I won't get mad at you or Dan," I said with a promise.

"Dan said I could spend the night at Russ's," Russ was our elderly neighbor. Russ had taken an interest in Sam, buying him comic books and telling us that Sam reminded him of his grandson. "When I went to bed, I stripped to my underwear," Sam added. I felt a cold breeze and the hairs on my arms stood up. "Russ crawled into bed with me . . . I want my brother, or my dad," Sam finished.

I knew what Sam was telling me. "This is not your fault. It's Dan's or mine—not yours," I said, then I stood up and ran to the kitchen door. I looked out the window and could see our car sitting in the parking space, the snow still falling. The snow on the ground appeared smooth and undisturbed. Wherever Dan was, he had to be in this apartment complex. He hadn't driven anywhere.

"I don't know a girlfriend. Do you know of a girlfriend, who she is or what apartment she lives in?" I asked Sam.

He shook his head, placed his hands over his face and continued to cry. I sat down next to him while he leaned into me and we rocked back and forth. I comforted him like my mother would do for me when I was upset.

"It'll be okay, you're fine, you'll be okay," I kept whispering as I rocked back and forth with him in my arms.

About an hour passed before I heard the kitchen door open. Dan came in quietly, trying to sneak in. He saw us when he walked into the living room. "Where were you?" I asked, my voice calm and steady. The rage I felt inside was not registered in my voice.

"What are you doing here?" Dan said in a gruff tone directed at Sam. I stood and walked to him. I was ready to hurt him. Dan didn't know how close he came to being attacked.

"Dan, where were you?" I asked again in a calm, evenly paced voice. I didn't want Sam to witness the domestic violence I was fantasizing about inflicting on Dan.

Dan looked from right to left. He looked down, and then he finally looked at me. "I don't know. I think I drank too much," he said and stumbled, pretending to be drunk.

"Sam, sweetie, you can sleep in Mikey's room; there's a bed in there. We'll talk about this tomorrow with your Dad," I said, walking Sam into the bedroom.

I left Dan where he stood. *I'll deal with him later.*

"I don't want my Dad to know," Sam said in a pleading voice.

"Okay sweetie, we'll deal with this tomorrow, but know this is not your fault. This is Dan's fault. It's up to us adults to keep you safe. It's on Dan, not you sweetie."

Sam lay down fully clothed. I laid next to him, whispering that he was a good boy, and I was proud of him. I repeated this over and over until I heard deep, even breathing.

I couldn't sleep. This was my fault. I couldn't ignore Dan's behavior anymore—my children weren't safe. I knew I had to leave with my boys, and it would be soon.

Looking back at this molestation event brings up my greatest regret: four years later Sam committed suicide. I wished I'd never returned to Dan. I could have had the pregnancy and baby Nick with my loving family around. If I'd done this I would have avoided this chapter of my life. Good intentions and high hopes weren't enough to save this marriage.

#

2015

It was Saturday. The assessor's office was closed, empty and dark. I didn't like it quiet. I missed the usual hubbub of the office. I flipped on my radio, then printed out the organizational chart and the budget and began studying it.

How could I cut my budget back enough that the board could divert funds and hire another mapper for themselves? I sat staring at the organizational chart. I *couldn't cut back on education or on supplies. I had to have every one of my appraisers—in fact, we were short there. I couldn't meet my statutory requirement of inspecting properties once every four years as it was. Cutting back there was not an option. Customer service was assigned other duties—historical homes, exemptions—so nowhere to cut there.*

Cartography was not under-utilized, even if that was the narrative Bill was espousing. Workflow for parcel splits, combinations and subdivisions had all increased. It would be easy if I could eliminate one cartographer's position and give the board the savings to hire one mapper, but I couldn't.

I realized both the cartography and title departments had their own supervisors with only four employees each. The other departments, such as customer service and appraisal, had at least ten employees per supervisor. If I could eliminate either the title or the cartography supervisor, there would be plenty of savings to hire another mapper for the county. My chest fluttered, and I smiled.

I went to the metal filing cabinet that stood outside my office and grabbed the employee files for both supervisors and returned to my office.

On my computer I downloaded the job descriptions for the title and cartography supervisors. The pay schedules for both positions were the same grade and range. The title supervisor's position did not include cadastral mapping requirements, while the cartographer's job description did, as well as title interpretation work. So the cartographer supervisor could supervise both departments, but the title supervisor could be eliminated.

That was good news, and bad news. As the elected assessor I could eliminate the title position and expand the cartographer's job description to include more duties without the board of supervisors' permission because my budget would be decreasing. If this reorganization plan had resulted in an increase to the budget, I would have needed their permission—because budgets and financing the county fell under their constitutional purview.

The difficult part was that the current title supervisor was Lynette—the county administrator's wife. The change was definitely a nuclear option. I had never seen a spider go nuclear, but I figured I was about to see what that would look like.

I typed up the reorganization plan and started a press release regarding my cutback idea and the savings to the citizens. This press release wouldn't mention the employee or position. It just would tout the savings.

I called Supervisor Craig Brown. When he answered, I explained, "I'm creating a reorganization plan for my office and eliminating a position, with a plan to save the citizens about $70,000 a year. You could reallocate those funds to your general funds and hire a mapper of your own. Is that something you could support?"

"Yes, ma'am," Craig said, enthusiastically.

"Here's the tricky part, Craig—the position I'm eliminating belongs to Bill's wife, so that might be an issue,"

"It doesn't matter who is related to who," he shouted. "If it's a good idea, I would support it!"

He was in a foul mood, obviously. I hadn't experienced his yelling before, and now it came twice in one day.

"Okay, then I'm going to move forward on this plan and present it Monday at the budget hearing because, as I told you, I have to keep the cartographers under the umbrella of the assessor's office."

"Sounds like a plan."

With that we hung up and I felt happy beyond anything I'd enjoyed for a long time. Bill had tried to do a jihad on my office. Now there was no way he could take the cartographers if I had them in the title department with only one supervisor. I smiled.

I leaned back in my chair and grinned. I could see the plants outside my window, the parking lot and the street. Something was missing. The parking lot was empty; it was usually full of cars and movement, *but that wasn't it. What was it?*

The spider web was gone! Facilities must have cleaned the windows. Relief swept over me, and the flutter in my stomach had gone with the spider's web.

#

1984

I heard a thud as the mail hit the floor. The mailman had just dropped a pile of mail through the letter slot in the kitchen door. I ran to the kitchen, bent over and gathered it up.

Dan, on a recliner in the living room, watched television like he always did, day after day. The noise from the chatter was constant. Our son Mike sat on his lap. Dan hadn't left the apartment since the incident with Sam last week. I didn't know, nor did I really care, how he'd kept his bike shop closed this long.

It felt like we were playing a cat and mouse game. Dan probably believed I wanted to leave him, and he was going to make sure if I left I couldn't take Mike. We both knew I'd never leave my boys. Dan seemed depressed.

I looked through the mail and found a letter from the utility company and a letter addressed to Dan's dad, Don Ford. It was clearly addressed to Don but delivered to us. This happened occasionally; it was a small town and the mail carrier would see the name *Don*, mistake it for *Dan*, and deliver it to our apartment. There was also a letter from the I.R.S. *Is this our income tax refund?*

I quietly slipped the silverware drawer open and hid the unopened letter from IRS under the plastic utensil container. I walked into the living room, dropped the remaining mail on the coffee table, and sat down on the couch near Dan's recliner.

"The snow needs to be removed from the sidewalks and parking lot—someone might slip," I said. My voice sounded even and dull. I didn't want to start a fight. Dan's mood was unpredictable lately.

"I'm not doing the shoveling. I don't get paid enough around here for that. I'm not John's slave," Dan said, referring to the property owner. He looked at me with a glare—daring me to say more.

"I don't understand your attitude. I was always taught that you do more than you're paid to do. If you do less, it's stealing. I'd be honored to be a maid as long as I was working hard and earning my paycheck. That's more honorable than getting paid to manage a motel and slacking off. We agreed to do the job, and taking care of the snow on the walkways and in the parking lot is part of our job."

"Oh, that's right. You're better than me with your honor and all that crap. I forgot," Dan said with a smirk. He seemed to be in the mood for a fight—but I wasn't. I smiled, trying to look calm and non-confrontational. I wasn't going to play into an argument and get slammed into a wall or thrown to the floor.

A plan was forming in my mind; I didn't need to beg or fight to get out of this marriage. I could think my way out. I was no longer a turtle, hiding in my shell, thinking nothing could really hurt me as long as I stayed there. Now I fully understood hiding didn't prevent bad things from happening; it just prevented me from protecting others and maybe even made me responsible for some of it. No more sick turtle games for me.

I wasn't ready, though. I felt like a fly trapped in a spider's web, watching as others approached the web, got caught up in it and were eaten right in front of me. I watched and did nothing to help. But I knew I'd escape this web with my sons before they were victims like Sam had been. I wasn't sure exactly how we'd escape, but a plan was forming and I felt calm and happy. I was planning a solution.

"I'm going to the store to get some groceries," I said matter-of-factly.

"You can't take Mike. He's staying here with me," Dan said. With his shaggy, uncombed, shoulder-length hair, beard and mustache, he looked quite different from the clean shaven Navy man I'd married. Today his eyes looked wild. I was revolted by his demeanor.

"That's fine, makes it easier—but why?" I asked. I stood up and cranked the lever on the baby swing several times. Nicky was sleeping in the swing and I didn't want it to wind down completely. I waited for Dan to answer the question.

"You're not leaving the house with Mike," Dan said. He looked at me as if that explained things, but I sat waiting for more. There was an awkward silence despite the noise coming from the television. Then he added, "I think you plan to leave me. I don't want you to, but if you do you won't be taking Mike."

There it was, he finally articulated the unspoken game we were playing: I wanted to leave with the boys and he wouldn't let that happen.

"I'm going to go get groceries, not leave you. But what's the deal? I can leave you, but not with Mike? If I were going to leave you, wouldn't it be better for the boys to be with me, their mother? They're awful young to not be with me." Here it was, the conversation I'd avoided. I wanted to hear why he thought it was okay for me to leave, but he'd deny me the boys—or at least Mike.

Dan started to cry. Tears ran down his cheeks. "I don't want you to go. I want you to stay. But you don't love me. Mike loves me no matter what I do. You—you only love me when you think I'm good enough to love. Now you hate me. Fine!" He wiped his tears away, then continued, "You can go if you want, but you won't be taking Mike."

Little Mike lay asleep on Dan's lap, content and happy. My heart softened a little. I didn't like this guy, but oddly I loved him. *I hate the heart twisting, cramping feeling in my chest,* I thought.

"I'm not leaving you. Just going to go get some groceries . . . Say, didn't your mom leave you with your dad when she left? She just took your older sister Jackie and little sister Kim. Right? Was it because your dad insisted she could go, but not with you?"

"No, she left me because she didn't want me. It was easier for her to just take the girls," Dan said and started to cry again, a noisy, gulping cry with tears streaming down. These tears did nothing to change my resolve to get away from him, escape his games. I was surprised his tears disgusted me so.

"Do you wish she'd fought for you—taken you with her?" I asked, trying to understand. I pulled my purse up from the floor, put it on my lap and rummaged for some gum or a lozenge. My throat was aching, felt dry, crispy and sticky, as if it wanted to close. I took my hand and rubbed the right side of my neck, trying to soothe it so it would stop twitching.

"She didn't want me. I wanted to live with her later. I called and asked her if I could—but she said no, it wouldn't work out."

"How about I make homemade soup and rolls, and we can invite your Aunt Marilyn, your dad and Gina over tonight for dinner?"

"Really?" Dan said, wiping his eyes, the tears finally stopping.

"Sure, I can get the groceries for that. I have plenty of time. They always have us over. Want to call and see if they can come?"

"Okay," Dan said. He looked a little suspicious but kind of happy. "You still can't take Mike with you to the store," he added.

"That's better anyhow. Can I leave Nick, too? That way it'll be faster for me."

"Oh, that's fine, but don't be long. I want to take a shower."

#

2015

I had worked the entire weekend on my reorganization plan and on the new organizational chart.

I dreaded giving the news to Lynette. I'd do it first thing Monday morning, before the budget meeting. I would rather her husband Bill, the county administrator, be caught off guard in the budget hearing without advance notice, but I couldn't let her find out her job as title supervisor was being eliminated through the grapevine. I liked Lynette. She was my age and had flaming red curly hair. Her vocabulary had been an issue from time to time because she'd been in the Marines and carried herself like one—with speech to match.

Most of her vulgarity and her temperament had been ignored by her supervisors and me because of her marriage to the county administrator. Also, it had been fairly clear that information about the assessor's office went upstairs to the board through her. When Lynette saw something one way, so did her husband. This made her difficult to manage.

On the other hand, Lynette had given me some of the cutest shoes I owned. She was one of the most thoughtful people I knew, often hiding surprises in my office or pulling jokes on me. She never forgot a birthday, Boss's Day or any occasion when she could give a card. Often she would cook wonderful treats for the office meetings. In many ways Lynette was one of my favorite people. I thought her husband was a problem, but I liked Lynette. This made what I had decided to do such a challenge.

#

1984

The bank smelled of cookies. It was coming from a platter of freshly baked cookies to the left of the teller cubicles.

"I'd like to make a deposit," I said, walking up to the first available teller. A young blonde smiled at me. I had signed my name and Dan's name on the back of the IRS refund check that I handed her. My insides felt like jelly, and my stomach reminded me of the times I'd been on a roller coaster, traveling full speed.

The check was for $1,756. It was fun because I knew how much Dan wanted that refund check. He had no clue I'd taken it. Stealing the check was something my precocious sister would do, not me. But I had!

I hated the person I'd become with Dan since I'd returned pregnant with Nick. I'd felt so broken down, weak and lost—just a shell of the person I'd once been. *How had I let this happen?*

The bank teller gave me a friendly smile. She explained that I could make a deposit, but the money wouldn't be available for at least a month—"It had to clear."

She gave me two signature cards and the paperwork to open a savings account. I took everything and hurried to the parking lot. I sat in my car, put Dan's signature on his signature card and filled out the paperwork—two forgeries in ten minutes. I smiled, proud of myself and a little surprised that I'd be this daring. There was no turning back now.

Dan would not be amused when he found out. I ran the paperwork and check back into the bank. The teller didn't seem surprised to see me return so quickly, nor did she question anything. It was obvious that I forged Dan's signature.

I rushed to the market, grabbed the needed supplies for the

soup and rolls and returned home. Dan had already taken a shower and looked a lot better. His eyes seemed less wild and he was in a good mood.

"You took longer than I expected," he said, more as a comment than an accusation.

"Yep, I saw Sherrie in the store and we yacked for a while." Dan didn't seem to think much of it. Lying to him was pretty easy, I realized.

We had a nice dinner with Dan's dad, Don, Gina, and Aunt Marilyn. No one brought up Sam. It seemed to me they were a bit mad at Sam for getting Dan in trouble with me and all the drama it had caused, rather than angry with Dan for putting Sam in a position to be molested. I thought it was an odd reaction. Instead of discussing Sam's situation, we spoke about Dan's stepsister, Beth, and her upcoming wedding and the excitement around wedding plans.

#

2015

"Lynette, could you come visit with me a minute?" I said, standing at her desk in her cubicle. I tried to keep my voice light so her co-workers wouldn't be alarmed. *I hate this.*

"Sure," she said with a warm smile. My stomach cramped with anxiety.

Lynette sat down to the side of my desk and started to talk about an upside-down cake she was going to make for the upcoming assessors' meeting. I waited awkwardly for an opening to let her know her job was going to be eliminated. She kept talking, and I had to interrupt because the budget meetings were coming up in an hour, and I needed to get my paperwork turned into the human resource department before that.

I held my hand up. Lynette stopped her upside-down cake conversation. "Is something wrong?" she asked.

I nodded, my eyes tearing up. "I'm reorganizing the office. I have to eliminate your job and offer the savings to the board of supervisors so they can hire their own mapper and not take ours,"

I said, wiping my tears from my face. Lynette was fighting back her tears, too.

"Do I have a choice? Can I be demoted, bump someone else out of a job? I need five more years. That was our plan, to go another term with you."

I hesitated. "Okay, we'll soon have a level III appraisal position open. We could re-write that job and transfer you to that position. I don't know what it would look like, but you'd still have a job. Think about this over the weekend. Monday we'll meet and you can tell me how the new job could look and how it would offer value to the office. I need to run, because I have to present this reorganization to the board for the budget requests. I wanted you to know before your husband—"

"Can I tell him?" Lynette asked. She looked like she'd shrunk, small and vulnerable. I'd never seen her look so helpless. My breath caught. If Lynette figured out how to re-write the Appraiser III position, and offer value to the assessor's office, she'd still have a job. It was on her to figure out.

"Yes, you can tell your husband. Please wait to discuss this with office staff, though. I'll send out a memo with the reorganization plan after the budget session."

8

EXECUTION

1984

I'D WIPED DOWN EACH COIN-OPERATED washing machine to the scent of Pine-Sol. A soothing dryer rumble and the rhythmic clicking sound of Nicky's baby swing provided the background. I smiled. The clean machines sparkled and made me feel productive. Nicky smiled back unexpectedly and then made cooing and ah-ing sounds—his first babble. I leaned over and clapped my hands, proud of my baby's new skill. I tried to get him to do it again, but Nick just smiled back at me.

Little Mike sat on the floor, his attention focused on a toy car. Dan had headed to apartment eight, responding to a toilet clog issue. I scooped out the quarters from the coin box meter cases on each machine and started to sweep the floor. Working in the laundry room was my favorite time each morning.

"Hey, there you are," John, the owner of the apartment complex, said in a bright friendly tone as he leaned in through the laundry doorway. I could see his pre-teen daughter behind him. She gave a little wave and a sheepish grin.

"Hi, there," I responded and propped the broom against the wall.

"Can Alice hang with you?" John asked. "I have some guys

coming to work on the boiler system today, and I want to discuss the project with them."

"Sure," I answered, happy for the help. Alice loved to play with Nick and Mike. I noticed a gift-wrapped package in Alice's hand and lifted my eyebrows, hoping it was for Nick.

"Oh, here you go," Alice said, moving quickly and handing me the gift. I tore the yellow lamb-printed printed gift wrap to expose a little yellow onesie sleeper with snaps down the front.

"Thanks!" I said. I hugged Alice and rushed to John to give him a hug, too. There hadn't been a baby shower for Nick. That'd made me sad. He was so precious; I wanted everyone to celebrate what a blessing Nick was, and I was grateful to John and Alice for their thoughtfulness.

John left, and Alice sat on the floor to play with Mike. "Can I hold Nick?" she asked.

"Sure, let's go to the apartment; then you can hold him." I got Nick out of the swing and grabbed the diaper bag. Nick cooed and smiled at Alice. "Can you carry the swing?" I asked her and she nodded. "Come on, Mike," I said. We made our way slowly towards my apartment, loaded down with the kids and equipment.

Just before getting to my door I heard yelling. Most of the words were muffled, but I was able to make out, "You're a pompous ass!" It sounded like Dan's voice. We went inside the apartment and unloaded everything.

"You can sit down and I'll hand you Nick," I said, wondering what was going on with Dan.

Alice looked awkwardly down at her hands and then answered, "I'll be right back. First I want to see if Dad's almost finished." I nodded, knowing she was really just curious about the yelling. She rushed out.

I laid a receiving blanket out on the floor, smoothed it out, then carefully placed Nick in the middle on his belly.

The front door slammed with a thud and Dan stomped through the apartment.

"Well, I let John know exactly what we think of him!" Dan

shouted. "Oh, and we're fired." He slumped into his favorite recliner. "So we have to move before next month."

I knew better than to laugh. This was perfect. I'd worried about leaving John high and dry, knowing I couldn't tell him I was leaving—now I didn't need to. "Why are we fired?" I asked in my most serious voice, pretending to be distressed.

"Stupid Karen's kid flushed a toy down the toilet. I took the toilet off the base, and when I flipped it over to look at it, the water came rushing out of the siphon area—made a mess on the floor. I grabbed towels, soaked up the water, fixed the toilet and left. But Karen complained to John about the mess I left behind. What was I supposed to do? Whole thing was her kid's fault anyway."

"Couldn't you have flipped the toilet over the bathtub?" I asked. *Where had he been if he wasn't working on the toilet?* He'd left Karen's apartment long enough for her to find John and complain, but he hadn't come home.

"Stop!" Dan yelled. "You think you're so smart. I hate that. I didn't expect the water to come out! I thought it was out of the toilet, but there still was some in that trap siphon thing." He lit a cigarette.

"You smoke now?" I asked, stunned. *I really don't know this guy at all.*

"Sometimes. So now we have to move, no job, no money— good thing that IRS tax refund is coming. It should hold us over."

"Let's sell everything, our furniture and all our household stuff," I suggested. "Cash it all out, then when we get another job and settled, we'll just slowly replace everything." Dan nodded in agreement so I continued, "Was it you I heard yelling?"

"Yep, I let John know exactly what we think of him. Called him every name I could think of." Dan's chest puffed up with pride. "Oh, one more thing, the best thing I forgot to tell you," he said, stopping in mid-sentence for effect and looking at me.

"What?" I finally asked, seeing he wasn't going to continue until I asked. "You're such a goof," I laughed. I got up from the chair, picked up Mike and stood with him in my arms, waiting for Dan to continue.

"Apartment fifteen—you know Terry and Jan? They're the new managers, effective now!" With that Dan started to cry—huge ugly sobs, snot dripping down his face.

I walked into the kids' bedroom and placed Mike down in his crib. I pulled Nick out of his swing, fixed him a bottle and laid him down in his crib, too. When I came out, Dan was already watching television.

"I'm going to apartment fifteen—find out what all of this means and what we should do as far as my paperwork and stuff," I said and gathering up the logbooks, the cash from the laundry room, and keys for the laundry machines and apartments.

Dan didn't respond. He appeared not to hear me and continued to watch television. I stood for a minute, looking at him, waiting for some kind of acknowledgment. He continued to watch television. The silence from him was awkward, I finally gave up and left.

I pulled my jacket tightly around me as I walked through the apartment complex looking for John. It was May and the snow had melted, but it was still cold and cloudy.

Eventually, I found two guys working on the heaters and old boiler system. They indicated that John and Alice had left. They didn't think they were coming back today. I saw several neighbors hanging outside their front doors and felt a little self-conscious. *Do they already know Dan and I were fired? News travels fast around here.* I cupped my hands around my mouth and nose and blew; my breath warmed my hands. It was getting colder.

I walked over to Terry and Jan's apartment, sucked in my breath and knocked.

"Hi, do you want to sit down and go over things now?" I asked Terry when he answered his apartment door. I still could see several neighbors standing or sitting outside their apartments, pretending not to watch, but now I was sure they were paying attention to the drama.

"Come on in," Terry said. "I'm sorry about all this. I just was asking John if he had any other jobs. I didn't mean to take your jobs—didn't mean to do that at all." He crossed his arms across his chest.

"It is what it is," I said. "So should I talk to Jan about the accounts—the records I send to John each month, keys, storage units, laundry room? Or do you want me to discuss it with you and give you the stuff? Or is now even a good time for you to do this?" I suddenly felt tired.

"Talk to Jan about it. I've gotta run. Anyhow, she'll be doing all that. I need to get the tools from Dan."

"All my stuff is in the storage shed. I'll give Jan the keys and show her where everything is," I said, putting my hand on my hips and looking around. I needed to sit down; I suddenly felt hot and dizzy.

"Jan, Pam's here," Terry called out. "Go on into the living room; she'll be out in a minute," Terry told me and left.

I went to their couch, sat down, put my head down by my knees and tried to breathe. *What's wrong with me? Everything is working out in a way that helps me leave. God, please give me courage—I can do this, I can get away with my kids.* I was always casual when I spoke to God, because I had a close relationship with Him. I prayed in my heart to him constantly. I'd been counseled by an LDS church leader that I needed to be more respectful when I prayed—use old English words such as *thee, thou, thy, Heavenly Father,* words that indicated I was showing respect to God. Out loud I complied; I didn't want to appear disrespectful. But my silent prayers remained casual. I loved God, felt close to Him and knew without a doubt He was aware of me and loved me. I believed He understood I respected him. After a moment, I felt better and sat up.

Finally, Jan came into the living room carrying a laundry basket. I was shocked to see she had a big black eye, swollen almost shut. "I'm sorry about this, taking your job and all," she said and sat down by me on the couch.

"Is now a good time to go through what I've done so far and what typically is done for the complex?"

"I feel bad about taking your jobs," she said again. She looked so sad.

"Dan didn't deserve this job," I said. "It's a good job. John's a good boss. You guys will do better. Really, it's fine. I'm not upset at all." I put my arm around her shoulder and gave her a hug. *Should I say anything about the eye or let it go?* I took in a breath. "I'm leaving Dan, I don't want this job anymore. It works for me that you got it. I'm happy for you. Please don't tell anyone. I want it to be my special surprise." I laughed, trying to lighten her mood.

"I'm going to leave Terry tomorrow."

"Wow, you got me beat! I'm not leaving Dan for about a month . . . did Terry, do that?" I asked pointing at her face.

She nodded. "I was in the shower. I'd left dishes on the kitchen counter. He came in and dragged me to the kitchen naked! Then he poured soda on me from a liter bottle that he found in the refrigerator. It was cold and so humiliating! My daughter hid under the kitchen table. He beat me with the soda bottle, and I think he kicked me in the eye, not sure if it was the bottle or his foot . . . I heard Dan beats you too; that's the rumor anyhow."

"No, not like that," I said, rummaging in my purse. I needed a lozenge or some hard candy. My throat was starting to throb.

"I guess you know Dan's got a girlfriend that lives in the complex?" Jan said, as she pulled her laundry basket towards her and started to fold the laundry.

"I suspected," I answered.

"The rumors are that Dan actually is juggling two different girlfriends—both live in these apartments. They say he beats you up and won't ever let you leave with your kids."

The rumors had some truth to them. "So, how are you getting away?" I asked, looking around, wondering if we should be speaking so openly with Jan's little daughter in the house.

"I called a wife abuse hotline," she said, then lowered her voice. "They're going to make arrangements for me, and I'll be leaving with them tomorrow. They'll help me with a protection order, my divorce, counseling, and even a job." Jan leaned back into the couch. She covered her eyes with the palms of her hands and rocked back and forth for a minute. I waited. She uncovered her face and looked at me. "Do you want to come, too? I can call them for you."

"No, he doesn't beat me. When I'm ready, I'll need a ride to the airport. If I could get help like that, it would be perfect."

"I'm sure they'd do that; call them when you're ready," she said. "About the paperwork, money and keys—you can leave all that with me. I'll call John when you leave and let him know I have it. I'll check it all over, and if it all balances I'll let John know. When I leave tomorrow Terry will be responsible. If he doesn't give all the money to John, it'll be on him."

Jan stood. I hugged her, hoping she'd get out of here before Terry had a chance to abuse her anymore.

#

2015

The board of supervisors meeting room was a large open room with about fifty chairs in straight rows. On an upper tier, called a dais, were ten chairs with metal name plates identifying each board member, the clerk of the board, the county administrator, and Dick Dastardly, whose title was now the assistant county administrator/deputy county attorney. For this budget hearing, tables with the supervisors' paper name plates were set up on the floor with chairs behind them. This meant the five supervisors sat level with the audience, not elevated above on the dais as they typically did. The various department heads sat in the audience waiting their turn to make their budget presentations. The tables had large notebooks for each board member illustrating the budget requests of each department. The reporter for our local newspaper sat to the left of the audience at her own table.

Ralph Harley, the Yavapai County Director of Management Information Services, presented his budget, then answered questions. He gave a five minute presentation on the efficiency of taking the mappers from the assessor's office and putting them under him in the Geographical Information Service department that he managed. I raised my hand, asking to speak.

"This is not open to the public. You can't speak," Chairman Craig Brown said in a gruff voice. I was alarmed. He seemed angry.

"Natalie Odell, can you answer some questions for us?" he added.

Natalie, the supervisor of our mapping department, stood up. "Actually, I have a PowerPoint, if I may," she said. The supervisors all nodded and Natalie gave a convincing presentation on what the cartographers—also called cadastral mappers—do and why they must be under the jurisdiction of the assessor's office.

"I take offense to your mission statement," Supervisor Arlo Davis said. "It's too slanted to the assessor's office. Your department works for the county, not the assessor."

He's wrong, I thought, but I knew I didn't have his support. I raised my hand again, thinking: *It's not fair to have Natalie defending or lobbying for me.*

"This isn't public speaking time; you don't get to talk," Chairman Craig Brown said again.

"I want to speak as the county assessor, not as a member of the public," I said without his permission. Chairman Brown grunted, and I wasn't sure if it was approval for me to speak or if it was refusal. I spoke as quickly and loudly as I could. "I have an office reorganization that will result in a savings of $70,000 to the assessor's budget. I'm going to speak more about that tomorrow in my budget presentation, but I wanted to quickly lay this out here today, because you can re-distribute this savings to the MIS department and hire a mapper for them, rather than take the mapping department from the assessor's office."

"Why is this the first time I'm hearing this?" Chairman Brown asked.

"It's not. I called you and told you about this plan last weekend. This is not the first you're hearing about it," I said. *Why was he lying? How could it possibly go well for him to lie? My cell phone could prove the call I made to him.* I looked at the reporter who was taking notes.

Chairman Brown's mouth opened and shut a couple of times but nothing came out. Finally he said, "We'll discuss this further tomorrow morning during your budget presentation."

As I started to leave the room, Tami Maurie, the local reporter, asked me, "Is it true you're eliminating the job of the county administrator's wife?"

I nodded and left the room. *How does Tami already know? Did bulbous-headed Bill say something to her?*

In my office I finished the press release. It touted the $70,000 savings but did not mention that the job being eliminated was that of the administrator's wife. I sent the press release to all my media contacts. *Now they can't take my mappers! Bulbous-headed Bill's gonna be ticked, but these are desperate times . . ..*

#

1984

Jan left our apartment and her husband. Terry came over to my apartment in a rage. He asked if I knew where his wife went. I denied knowing anything.

Two weeks later I saw them together, holding hands as they walked through the parking lot to their car. I never questioned her on why she'd returned. She had free agency to choose for herself, and I certainly wasn't the person to judge.

The next few weeks, I patiently waited for the refund check to clear the bank. I wrestled with my conscience. The money we managed to obtain from selling our furniture and big items was barely enough to pay our bills. I knew if I left with the entire refund check Dan would be in dire financial straits.

I began debating and rationalizing my decision. *He deserves to be left with no money, he's an ogre, and he can go live under a bridge where he belongs.* His sweet talking skills, friendship with my brother-in-law and the fact that he lived close to my sister had been enough to persuade me that he was the one I wanted to spend the rest of my life with. This was my fault. It was a terrible decision to marry Dan, but I was the one who'd made it. I deserved the ogre I picked but I needed to make better decisions for my boys. Stealing the whole check was wrong—even if it was from a monster. I went back and forth from feeling clever and good about my theft to feeling that I was a slug and deserved to be hit by a bus.

It'd been more than a month since the refund check was

deposited. I made an appointment with WIC—Women, Infants and Children—for Monday, June 4th, and hoped I'd have the money from the check by then. If not, I'd have to rethink my plan. The WIC appointment card was prominently displayed on the refrigerator. I'd nonchalantly mentioned it to Dan. If we qualified they'd give us coupons for free formula, juice, cheese, peanut butter. This would help us financially, I explained. It was a pretense, an excuse to leave. I wasn't going to attend the meeting, but I knew this was a way I could leave the house with the kids.

A few days before, on Friday, June 1st, I went to the bank. I discovered the check had finally cleared, and pulled out $1,700, leaving a $56 balance. I carefully tucked the money into my makeup bag and placed it in my purse. Adrenaline pumped through me, making me feel jittery and excited. Finally my plan was going to be put to the test.

I returned to the apartment complex and walked to Jan's apartment. "Is Terry here?" I asked when Jan answered the door. I noticed a fat bruise on her left cheek and it appeared swollen.

"No," she answered and opened the door wide, motioning me to come in to the kitchen.

"Can I use your phone?" I asked, pulling out some cash from my purse. "I need to make some calls, and one is long distance but I have cash." Jan nodded and motioned to the phone. It smelled good in her house, like homemade cookies.

"I'll give you some privacy. Terry will be back in about an hour," Jan said and left the kitchen. She went to the living room and flipped the television on. I was pretty sure she didn't want to know who I was calling or what my call was about. I called the women's shelter, talked to a volunteer and she agreed to meet me on Monday, June 4th, nine a.m. at the WIC office and give me a ride to the Boise Airport.

Then I called my mother, who was excited and agreed to pick me up from the Little Rock airport. Mom, Dad, Bev and her husband all lived in Harrison, Arkansas, now—just about two hours outside of Little Rock. Dad's birthday was June 5th, so this would be a nice surprise for him. Dad had been polite to me since

I married Dan, but our relationship had been strained.

After I finished my phone calls, Jan brought me a plate of peanut butter cookies. They were warm and tasted wonderful. I'd miss her. We said some pleasantries and I left, not giving her any details on my plan. I was sure she pretty much knew and she'd keep it to herself.

I drove our white AMC Javelin to the store and purchased some groceries and a Father's Day gift for Dan—a mug that said "Greatest Dad." I purchased a card for him, too; it said "Dad, you're someone to look up to no matter how tall I grow." I went out to the car, signed Mike and Nick's names to the card, and hid the mug and card in the glove compartment. Monday I'd leave these items on the seat of the car for Dan to find. This was me being spiteful. I hated Dan and wanted him to hurt. To insure he'd miss me I'd been especially nice to him all month.

Next, I went to the bank where we owed $700 on our car. *That's not half of the money I took,* but *it's close enough to ease my conscience.* I paid the car off.

Now I had to wait, just two more days. Just two more days of not getting caught and I'd be home free.

#

2015

"Hello, this is Paul Endicotte of KYCA. Do you have time to visit?" the reporter asked over the phone. Paul had interviewed me in the past and was always fair.

"Sure, just a minute. Let me close my office door." I leaned out my door and spoke to my assistant, Lorrie. "I'm being interviewed by KYCA. Don't let anyone interrupt." I shut the office door and returned to speak to Paul.

"Ok, I'm going to record this," Paul said. This was familiar; we'd done it many times for various reasons: we'd discussed Notice of Values, the real estate market, even budget items. Now I supposed we would discuss my reorganization plan to save taxpayers money—as I'd explained in my earlier press release.

Instead, I heard, "As our County Assessor, you're being investigated for nepotism. Can you tell us about that?"

It felt like a knife had just been plunged into my windpipe. *What? Nepotism! Crap! Smelly bulbous-headed Bill—did he send an accusation to the press? Paying me back for eliminating his wife's job. Relax, you're okay. Just tell the truth.* I tried to breathe.

In a few seconds my throat felt open, I took a breath and asked, "Nepotism? Is the investigation about my daughter Ashley?" I knew it was about Ashley, but this was an interview and the audience would need to know what the investigation was about.

"Yes," Paul answered.

"I never hired my daughter, and any nepotism investigation will show that. My daughter's husband is in the military. Whenever he's deployed, Ashley comes for a visit and volunteers at the office. At one point the administration in the assessor's office asked if they could hire my daughter for a temporary job. I said it was fine as long as it was okay with human resources."

"It's been said you're planning to eliminate the position of the county administrator's wife because you're upset with this nepotism investigation against you and you're getting even," Paul said.

"No, the investigation will show that human resources approved the hiring and that I was not the person who hired her. The county administrator's wife's position is being eliminated to save money and allow the board of supervisors to shift that savings to their GIS department rather than take the cadastral mappers from the assessor's office."

The phone showed another incoming call from *The Daily Courier*, a local newspaper. I ignored it.

"Is there anything else you'd like to say?" Paul asked.

"I'd never break the law. The investigation will prove this," I answered.

My stomach cramped and twisted. I was tired of this game. *Bill was dangerous; what would he do next?* I knew I'd crossed him when I refused to value the agricultural properties the way he'd insisted. Then I'd thwarted his retribution. Now he'd brought my daughter into this mess. *He wants to make it look like I broke the law.* I swallowed hard.

"Okay, thanks. I've stopped the recording," Paul said, sounding sincere. "I always like working with you. You've been open and kind, and I wish you the best."

"Thanks. When will this play?" I asked, noticing my hands were trembling, my throat feeling like it was closing up again. I rummaged for a lozenge in my desk and looked at my poster that read: *The highest courage is to dare to be yourself in the face of adversity. Choosing right over wrong, ethics over convenience, and truth over popularity...these are the choices that measure your life. Travel the path of integrity without looking back, for there is never a wrong time to do the right thing.* My husband had given me this poster for Christmas so many years ago. At the time I hadn't realized how much these words would keep me on track. People tomorrow would hear on the radio that I might not have integrity, that mattered so much to me. I wiped at my tears. *Don't cry. Bill wins if you cry. Don't let him win. You know the truth. He can't take integrity from you.*

"This afternoon," Paul answered and hung up.

I sucked on the lozenge and said a quick prayer. Then I dialed the cell phone for my husband's cousin, Vicki. She had experience with human resources and public relations. We had discussed these issues in the past. *I love her, she'll give me some points I can make to the media.*

"There's an accusation to the media that I broke the law with nepotism. I think Bill's sent a press release out or something. He seems to be saying that the elimination of Lynette's job is connected to my anger with this nepotism investigation." I talked quickly and choked back tears.

"What an ass."

I felt instantly better. "I need to call *The Daily Courier*; they're trying to reach me, and I already spoke to the radio. I just wanted to get your take—real quick—about Bill's spin that my reorganization plan is in response to this nepotism investigation against me."

"Well, that's just silly! Let me get this straight. He's trying to say that because there's an investigation about a temporary, minimum wage job your daughter held—and H.R. had approved—you got mad at Bill and eliminated a seventy thousand a year, full time position, for his wife? Sounds more reasonable to believe Bill started the nepotism investigation against you because of your reorganization plan. Especially given the timing of the investigation. If there was a problem with your daughter being hired, human resources would not have allowed it in the first place, so that investigation's not going anywhere."

"Exactly—that's exactly it! I suspect Bill's behind the whole nepotism investigation and leaking the information to the media because he's mad about his wife's job. I don't have evidence but it makes sense to me." I grabbed another lozenge from my desk and plopped it in my mouth.

"It'll work out, people will see through it. Just tell the truth, and if they say something farfetched, point it out," Vicki said before we ended the conversation.

I felt better. Vicki seemed confident that citizens would see through the manure Bill was throwing. *Please, let me be articulate,* I prayed. I rubbed my neck; my throat was tired. I needed to stop talking soon or the vocal cords would start jumping and dancing.

I picked up the phone and dialed *The Daily Courier*'s number on my caller ID. "Hi Tami, did you try to call me?"

"Yes, I'm following up on a nepotism investigation. Do you have any comments?" Tami said in a professional cold tone.

Newspaper reporters were easier to talk to than radio news reporters, because they like quotes rather than sound bites. "Tami, it's silly to think I'm doing the reorganization in response to this nepotism investigation."

"You're right. That'd be stupid," she answered. Tami was smart. *She'll see this for what it is.*

"The investigation will find there's no merit to this accusation," I said, giving her the quote she wanted.

"You understand why I have to report this?" Tami said, lowering her voice and sounding more personable, like the Tami

I'd joked with and visited with many times.

My hands grew cold and still trembled. Placing them on my neck felt good. My neck was warm to the touch and my vocal cords were beginning to twitch. I'd take a pain pill when I got home, and hoped the vocal cords would settle down by tomorrow morning. Speaking for any length of time was fatiguing, but speaking under stress, like I was today, was worse. My throat felt as dry as crackers, and I thought I could taste blood.

#

1984

It'd been almost a year since I'd reconnected on Father's Day with Gil Sieling. Since then Gil had called every Sunday at two p.m. sharp. At first I hadn't seen the pattern and sometimes would miss the phone call. When Dan answered the calls from Gil, Dan would hang up on him. Once I realized that Gil was calling every Sunday at two p.m., and that Dan was hanging up on him, I tried to be the one answering the phone. The phone calls were short, and I didn't usually have much to say, but I appreciated the effort Gil was making. I didn't think it was right for Dan to be rude.

Today was a little different. The phone rang at two p.m. I rushed to answer it—"Hello?"

"Hi, how's your week going?" Gil asked. I sat in the chair next to the phone to get comfortable for a conversation.

"Hang up the phone!" Dan screamed in my direction. "You're not going to talk to that son of a bitch."

I tried to ignore him and put my hand over the receiver, hoping Gil couldn't hear Dan. This was none of Dan's business, and he needed to leave me alone.

Dan got up from his recliner and turned the television up loud. I moved the telephone as far away as I could. Once the cord was stretched as far as it would reach, I placed it on the kitchen table and pulled the receiver as far as the spiral cord would allow. This got me all the way to the kitchen back door. I scooted the chair over.

Now I could hear Gil again. "It was a good week. How was yours?" I said, almost wanting to laugh. It was so comical, with the television blaring and me pretending not to hear it.

Dan got up from his recliner, stormed into the kitchen and pushed the telephone hook down. He held it there, disconnecting the phone call. "No more of this crap! You're not going to carry on with him anymore. It's done! This is crazy," he screamed.

"Carry on? Who's carrying on? Me with Gil, or you with Melissa or is it Rhonda? Or, Mr. Stud Monster, is it both of them, you ass!" *Oh crap did I just yell that out loud?* Instantly my throat revolted. It didn't like to talk, let alone make an attempt to yell. My right vocal cord immediately started to twitch, and I felt a sharp pain running all the way from the top of the right side of my clavicle up to my jugular area. I placed my hand on the offended area hoping to calm it down.

In one giant step Dan managed to get close to me. I wanted him out of my space and slapped him with the phone receiver, not trying to hurt him—or maybe I wanted to hurt him. I was blind with anger and not sure what I wanted. Then I lashed out to keep him away from me. When he got closer I tore into him like a crazy animal. I used my nails, my feet, and the telephone receiver.

He grabbed me by the triceps—one in each of his hands, turned me around and wrapped his arms around my arms, restraining me from any attempts to hit him. He then dragged me towards the living room. First, I tried to go limp and refused to move, making my body heavy and difficult to move. Then I lashed and yanked, attempting to get away.

"You're so stupid," he shouted. "You want to carry on with someone who tried to kill you! Stupid, stupid. Well, it ends now. You're not talking to him again."

"Who do you think you are? You think that because I married you, you became my master?" I whispered because my voice had become horse and raspy. "I can talk to whoever I want to, whenever I want." I struggled against Dan's bear hug like Houdini against a straightjacket. Dan just squeezed harder and pulled and yanked until he got me all the way to our bedroom.

The room was bare. No furnishings left; it had all been sold. A pile of clothes sat in the corner, and a sleeping bag with a couple of pillows were in another corner. Dan got me to the room and tossed me down like a bag of garbage. As I fell, I hit the right side of my back and my head against the wall with some loud thunks. I wondered if Rhonda could hear the commotion from next door.

"You're not going to talk to him again. You're going to listen to me! When you married me I promised to protect you and that's what I'm going to do," Dan said, standing over me.

I laughed. "That's ironic. My protector just threw me against the wall!" My head and rib cage still burned from the impact. I stayed on the floor, afraid if I stood up I'd get yanked or thrown again. I could hear little Mike crying in the next room.

"Look, you're a piece of crap. The only reason I even keep you around is because of the kids. If you want to stay you're going to promise not to talk to him again."

I could just promise and it would end. I didn't even really care if I ever spoke to Gil again or not, but I didn't want to be told I wasn't allowed to speak to him. I was tired of being meek. I said, "You're not even a Mama's boy! You're a Mama-wanna-be boy— pretending to be a big, tough, stud monster! You're not the boss of me and I'll talk to who I want to!" I wanted to scream it out, but it came out in a horse whisper. Nonetheless, Dan heard me just fine.

"Well, at least my parents thought I was good enough to live. Yours didn't even think you were worth that much! That's how worthless you are," he yelled.

That made me laugh. He'd gone too far. His words didn't hurt, and I was done arguing. I knew my harsh words had landed exactly where I'd intended. His verbal vomit had missed me completely.

He stomped out of the room. A few minutes later I heard the door slam. He'd left the house. Mike came into the bedroom and cuddled with me. He handed me his stuffed bunny and started to sing "Little Bunny Foo Foo." I laughed and sang with him: "I don't want to see you hopping through the forest, picking up the field mice, bopping them on the head." Mike laughed with me.

My throat ached, so I got an ice-pack. Tomorrow we'd be gone and this nightmare would be over.

I made a bottle for Nick, turned the television station to cartoons for little Mike and sat on the recliner in the living room to feed Nick. I held the ice pack against my neck by holding my head at an odd angle and scrunching my shoulder up. The cold was soothing to my tender vocal cord, but I found it more and more difficult to breathe as time went on. My neck was swelling and it felt like my throat was closing.

Dan finally returned after being gone for about an hour. It looked like he'd been crying. I hoped it was from the physical pain of being whacked in the head by the telephone receiver rather than the mental anguish I'd caused with my verbal attack. I'd meant every word I said, but wished I'd kept it to myself.

"I'm going to make dinner, you hungry?" Dan asked in a friendly manner as he leaned into the living room.

"I'm not," I answered. "I want to jump in the shower if you'll keep an eye on the kids." My voice sounded huskier and deeper than usual, and it took a lot of effort to speak—with a fair amount of pain.

Dan nodded and walked into the kitchen.

I laid Nick down in his crib, grabbed a light summer dress from my closet and went into the bathroom. Once I disrobed I examined myself in the bathroom mirror. Red speckles decorated the left side of my back. They would turn into bruises in the next couple of days. Red bands encircled both of my upper arms, and the right side of my clavicle bone was red and swollen. *Was I squeezed so tight I popped something?* I gingerly touched it; *Ouch!* It was tender. I showered and put my sundress on. The arm band of bruises, and the clavicle area, swollen and red, were now exposed.

Back in the living room, Dan was sitting in the recliner. The house smelled good.

"I made some spaghetti; can I make you a plate?" he asked, standing up and motioning that I could take the seat. Only a recliner and television were in the living room; we'd sold our couch. I shook my head and sat on the floor, leaning against the wall.

"How about some sherbet?" he asked.

That sounded good. I nodded and started to stand back up.

"No, sit—I'll get it for you."

He handed me the bowl of sherbet, then sat on the recliner and tapped his lap, motioning me to sit on it. Instead I scooted over to the recliner and sat at his feet, leaning back on his legs. He ran his hand through my hair, almost petting me like a favorite pet.

"I'm sorry," he said.

I nodded as I continued to eat my sherbet. It tasted cold and felt good on my throat, but swallowing was difficult. Dan then started with his flattery—kind loving words telling me how special I was. How lucky he was to have me. He said he'd broken it off with Melissa—didn't know why he did the things he did. He told me how I didn't deserve this. He denied Rhonda was his girlfriend.

I put my empty bowl on the floor and lay my head on his lap. Dan continued to talk, whispering and complimenting me. My body was sore, my spirit broken, but my heart soared. I loved Dan. I loved it when he was like this.

I was still going to leave tomorrow. I'd divorce him—but I loved him.

Finally, at two in the morning, I spoke up, "I'm tired. I'm going to sleep now."

"No, stay up with me."

I shook my head. "I have a WIC appointment tomorrow. I need some sleep." My throat sounded raspy, and the effort to speak was exhausting. I hoped my throat would be better tomorrow.

"Want me to go with you to WIC?" Dan asked.

Crap, that would sure mess things up.

"Sure, that'd be a big help," I said.

"If you need me, I'll come with you. If not I'll go to the post office instead. I want to check on that IRS refund check. We really should have gotten it by now."

That made me smile.

#

May 2015

"Hi, do you have a minute to talk?" asked Paul Endicotte, on the other end of the telephone. He was the KYCA radio reporter that I liked so much.

"Sure, let me close my door," I answered and put the office phone down on my desk. I peeked out my office door and said to Lorrie, "Don't let anyone interrupt me," then shut it with a louder thump than I intended.

"Okay, I'm all yours," I said, sitting back at my desk.

"Just a second—I'm setting up the recording," Paul said.

My heart started thumping. I pulled up the press release on my computer as I waited—the press release about eliminating Lynette's title supervisor position and saving the county $70,000. I hoped the interview was on this and not the nepotism investigation the board had forwarded against me.

"All right, here we go, " he began. "I understand the board of supervisors has scheduled a special executive session where they're going to discuss eliminating ten of your employees—your title department and your mapping department. What's your thought on that?"

The room started to spin; it felt like I left my body and could watch myself talking on the phone. I sat quietly, not moving, unable to process the information or articulate any response.

"Are you there?" Paul finally asked.

"Yes, sorry, I—I, this is new to me, the first I heard of an executive session, of them wanting to take the title department, too. Can we start again?"

"Sure, you can answer when ready. I can edit it and it will be fine or I'll start again."

"Let's start over."

"Sure. It's my understanding that the board of supervisors has scheduled a special executive session for Monday, May 4th, to discuss taking ten of your employees—both your title and mapping departments. What's your thoughts?" Paul asked again.

I started to cry, tears ran down my face. My hands shook. "It's hard to explain. They're doing it for political retribution because I updated the agricultural values," I said, blurting out exactly what I thought through my tears.

"Tell me a little more about updating the agricultural values."

"The values were seven dollars and fifty-six cents an acre for at least thirty years. I updated them a couple of years ago to twenty-five dollars an acre. This has resulted in lawsuits. Earlier I was told by the board to value these properties at ten dollars and ten cents an acre or maybe even eleven dollars an acre. Any more than that and I would be punished. Instead I updated these values according to the law, based on a lease-study. This is my punishment," I said, with more conviction and fewer tears.

"Okay, thanks—this will probably play tonight. Good luck. I'll see you Monday," with that the call ended. *A special executive session to take the title department, too, seems like both retaliation and nepotism at it's finest. What other explanation was there to take the title department away from me? I wondered.*

#

1985

About a year had passed since I escaped Dan with my boys. He called, begged me to return. He drove our car all the way from Oregon to Arkansas and begged some more. He sweet talked and made promises. But I was done. I stood strong and refused to reconcile with him.

Mom and I returned back to Arizona and began to work at Century 21—Northwest Branch—a large real-estate office in the Maryvale area of northwest Phoenix. Mom and me; together we were the perfect sales team. She and my adoptive dad were separated and contemplating divorce. I hoped it didn't have anything to do with my returning home with the boys, but I selfishly enjoyed having her to myself.

I sat at my little desk and tried to make my voice casual as I said, "I'm going to let Dan come get the boys and take them to Oregon for his grandma's birthday."

"How long will they be gone?" Mom asked. She appeared calm, but I knew she didn't like the idea.

"Just two weeks."

Tanya, a coworker who teamed with her husband Bob, came over and pulled a chair up to join the conversation. This was unusual for Tanya, who worked on the other side of the office. She was friendly, but typically kept to herself. Mom and I worked on the smoker's side of the office; it was rambunctious, loud and smoky. Tanya and her husband worked in the more reserved non-smoking section. I admired them. They had recently closed a commercial transaction and purchased a car phone. The phone was in a big clunky box, but it allowed them to make phone calls in the field. Bob and Tanya were the only people I knew who had a car phone.

"Don't let your boys go. Not until you have a divorce and have been granted custody," Tanya said, looking at me then switching her gaze to Mom. "I made that mistake and it cost me thousands of dollars in attorney fees. My husband hid with my daughter, and when I finally found them and went to court for the divorce, the judge awarded him custody of her! You wouldn't believe it. There were even porno pictures of my little girl! The judge said it was art and who was I to accuse such . . ." with that Tanya began to cry.

I looked down at the ground then at my mom. Who knew? Tanya always seemed so quiet and dignified. *I guess everyone has a story,* I thought.

"Dan's not like that. He wouldn't—" I said, but Tanya cut me off mid-sentence.

"I never thought my ex-husband would, either. Please, please don't. You'll be sorry," Tanya said, her voice rising.

Gary and other co-workers stopped their tasks to look in our direction. Tanya composed herself, stood, pulled at her dress as if to straighten imaginary wrinkles, smiled weakly and appeared to turn back into her former reserved self.

"I need to get back to work, but I wanted to warn you what could happen if you let the kids go before you're divorced and have custody," she added in a softer tone.

"I think you should give it more thought," Mom said to me as Tanya walked away.

#

2015

I drove my Jeep to the presentation. On the way my cell phone rang. It displayed Tami Maurie from the *Daily Courier*. *I wonder if the radio already played my interview.* "Hello," I said.

"Hi Pam, I see the board of supervisors is discussing taking two departments from you and placing them under their control. Do you think this is to save the job of the county administrator's wife's?"

"No, of course it isn't," I said sarcastically. It was clearly a move to save Lynette's job and so blatant! My respect for Tami grew; she was smart and could see the supervisors' plan for exactly what it was.

"I can't print it, if you don't say it."

"Okay, Tami—the move to take the title department from the assessor's control and place it under the direct control of the board of supervisors is clearly a response to my plan to reorganize the office and eliminate the administrator's wife's position. That way they can save her job—at a cost of $70,000 a year to the taxpayers." Still driving, I continued, "I need to add that the assessor's office must have employees that determine title and mapping. There is no legal or valid reason for the board of supervisors to take these responsibilities from the assessor and give it to themselves. The original plan to take the mappers from the assessor's office was in retaliation for my decision to update agricultural values. It's unfortunate that these board members are willing to break the law for special interests rather than stand up for the taxpayers."

I pulled my Jeep into the parking lot and parked. I looked at my watch and had two minutes to get to my presentation. "Tami, I have to go. Do you have enough, or can I call you back after my speech?"

"I think I got it, but if you think of more you want to say call me after your speech. I'll probably work until nine tonight and this will be in the paper tomorrow."

"Front page, you think?"

"I imagine."

With that I ran into the classroom and gave the class my typical one hour presentation and a bonus fifteen minutes. As I taught the aspiring real estate agents how property taxes worked in the state of Arizona, the story had unfolded of the board's plan to remove several key employees and why. My depression lifted and my blood began to boil. As a voter, and as a taxpayer, this was insulting to me and also to my students. Their outrage lifted me up and made me realize they also were the victims in this. *I work for them and I won't go down without a fight.*

I had no idea what my next move would be, but if the board did this, I vowed there would be political blood on the mat. I had no doubt it would be the board's. My political career could end, but I wasn't going to allow them to give favors, to make backroom deals for special interest groups without being exposed.

Over the weekend my mood swung from depression and fits of despair to outrage and anger. I felt lost, seeing no way out of the mess. Lynette must not have told her husband that I had promised her she would still have a job in the assessor's office, if she would rewrite the level III appraiser position with a job description that fit her skill set and offered value to the assessor's office. Her job just wouldn't be the title supervisor position anymore. That must be why he was so desperate to get her position protected under the board of supervisors. I wouldn't be able to perform the job I was elected to do if they took the title and cartography department from me, and I had no plan for a response. I knew I would need to react somehow. *Please help me,* I prayed. The scripture—*Be still and know that I am God*—came to mind. I felt afraid of what Monday would bring, but I also felt at peace.

#

1985

It had been more than a year since I'd left Dan. He'd called and asked if he could take the boys for a visit back to Oregon for his grandma's birthday party. After giving it some thought I decided

I'd let Dan take the boys for the visit, but I'd type something up—a contract that stated this was a visit only. We both would agree in writing I could keep custody, and he'd just take the boys for a visit, returning the boys by such and such date. That'd make Mom and Tanya more comfortable. I didn't have the money to file for divorce and ask for custody, and I wasn't in a hurry to divorce Dan anyhow.

Dan arrived in Maryvale and came to the house to pick up the boys. He looked good, his hair cut short and combed nice. "Come in for a minute," I said, looking down, not wanting to make eye contact with Dan's deep brown eyes. I'd paid special attention to my makeup and outfit, assuring I'd look my best. He walked past me into the house and took a seat on the living room couch. The boys were taking their naps—unaware they'd soon be on a trip with their Dad.

"I typed this up and want you to sign it to make sure there's no misunderstanding. I'm keeping custody of the boys, just letting them go with you for your grandma's birthday party and a visit," I said. I felt unsteady and queasy. What would I do if he refused or argued?

Dan grinned, showing his dimple, and his brown eyes caught mine. He seemed comfortable and full of confidence. He leaned forward as he sat on the sofa. "I've missed you." He then tapped the couch next to him, motioning me to sit down. He held out his hand for the typed agreement and took it and the pen I offered. Then he scribbled *I love you,* and signed *Dan Ford.* He handed it back to me, brushing my right arm with a familiarity that made me jittery. I looked away, uncomfortable with the prolonged eye contact. He continued to watch me, displaying an interest that made me feel both happy and uncomfortable.

"Why did you do that? You should've just signed it," I said, attempting to chastise him.

He laughed. "You're silly. I wouldn't hurt you. I love you. It's just a visit. I know they need their mother. Really, they need their whole family. But if this is what you want, then I'll just take them for a visit and return them—safe and sound."

With that I leaned against him and sighed loudly. What I wanted was for him to love me and only me. Was that possible? Had he learned his lesson? He put his arms around me and I melted *I do love him,* I realized. He kissed me, then he had his way with me. That's all it took—a flirty look, a kind word and there I was, melting and willing to do anything for him. After we finished, I thought we'd make plans: he'd move to Arizona or I'd go to Oregon with him and the boys. Instead, we made small talk until the boys woke up.

Dan and I put the boys with their suitcases into the car. He kissed me goodbye and the boys waved goodbye as they pulled out of the driveway. I retreated to my bedroom, lay on the bed and cried until I fell asleep.

When I woke up I went to the store and bought some Necco candies. I went to the nursing home where Grandma now lived. She wasn't alert anymore, and I missed our visits and her wisdom. I ate my candy in silence, sitting by her bedside. I felt both love for her and the love she had for me. I patted her arm knowing that on some level she was aware I was there with her. I believed if she could, she'd be encouraging me, saying, *"In the end it'll be okay, if it isn't okay, it isn't the end."*

#

2015

I decided to wear my red jacket and black and white chunky necklace. *Let them do the job the way they want it done. Let them give the favors they want to give. Who cares?* I tried to believe those words.

I looked in the mirror and smiled. I looked confident and professional. But my eyes were red from crying. I went to my bathroom cabinet drawer, grabbed some Visine, leaned my head back and squirted it, missing my eye slightly so some liquid ran down my face, messing up the makeup I'd just applied. At least a little made it into my eyes.

I reapplied my makeup and laughed at myself. *You thought you could take on the good ole boys and win? You're really a joke.*

Why don't you quit? You're a good appraiser, but you suck at politics.
I smiled in the mirror again. This time a person who appeared confident and happy looked back at me.

"You about ready?" Bob, my husband, said as he walked into the bedroom. He looked handsome in his light blue shirt and dress pants. Seeing him helped ease the cramping, squeezing-into-a prune trick, my heart had been doing all morning; here was my hero. He'd taken off work to be with me today, at the special session of the board of supervisors, where they planned to take over enough of my department to make me irrelevant as the assessor. Bob would be by my side as he usually was during the worst moments of my life. He'd been with me when I learned Scott, my mentor and best friend, had died. He'd been there the first time we'd learned Bev had cancer. And now he'd be there when my professional career was ripped from my control.

"Do I look like an assessor?" I asked, twirling around and letting out a laugh because I knew I looked great despite how I felt. I also believed that if I made light of the situation Bob wouldn't feel so bad for me.

Bob smiled and said "You are the assessor and you look great. Those bigots can't take either away from you." He walked over and gave me a hug. It felt so good to be embraced in his gorilla arms. "Let's go. Roger and Vicki will meet us there."

I loved Roger and Vickie, Bob's cousins, and was glad they'd be there to support me. They would witness for themselves the legal and constitutional violations the board was about to commit. It was still hard to believe that the board members I once respected might be willing to do this—out in the open for all to see. *How can this possibly go well for them? Breaking the law, violating the Constitution! Surely this will come back to haunt them if they go through with it.*

#

May 1985

The phone rang on my desk. I ran from Gary's desk to my own to grab it. "Hello," I said, out of breath from the short jaunt.

"Hey, it's me—we need to talk," I heard Dan say. His tone sounded like there might be a problem—a stark contrast to the orange blossom smell of the fresh spring air. I loved the spring and was in a happy mood, but sensed this was about to change.

I fished in my desk for a lozenge to waste time. Finding none, I finally replied, "What's up?"

"It's time you filed for divorce. It's been more than a year. What's the holdup?" he asked. I didn't want to hear that.

"I thought last time we . . . visited, you said you loved me, in fact I believe you wrote that down," I said, trying to sound sarcastic.

"It's time. It's been long enough. It's time we moved on with our lives."

"Okay, I'll file next week," I said with a sigh. Now I hated that it was spring and smelled like orange blossoms. I wished for clouds and thunder.

"Great, so when you file you can ask for custody if you want, but no child support."

"I haven't asked for a dime from you for the whole time I've been gone. I don't want anything from you. But even if I ask for nothing, the judge won't agree. He'll compute it based on your income, because it's for the boys, not me."

"Whatever. You don't get to talk to the boys until I have a divorce request with no child support in it. Oh, Nick's been asking for you. He's sick and asking for you, but you don't get to talk to him until I have that," he said, sounding cruel.

"Let me talk to him right now!" I said, raising my voice as loud as I could. Co-workers suspended work to look in my direction.

"Nuh uh," Dan said with a singsong tune, enjoying the cat and mouse game I couldn't win.

"But you're still returning them on Monday like you promised?" I whispered, my throat hurting from the attempt to scream. I was also trying to prevent Tanya from overhearing.

"No, I changed my mind."

The world slowed down, I could hear the birds chirping happily outside. I could see my co-workers pretending to concentrate on work at their desks while eavesdropping on my conversation. I saw Tanya stand up and look in my direction.

"You son of a bitch, you asshole liar—you gave your word! You signed a contract! You will burn in hell you—" I yelled with all the fury and hatred I had in me. The phone went dead.

I heard a customer sitting at the front desk say, "Wow, real estate is really hard."

I laughed an angry, sarcastic laugh. As always I was the butt of my own joke. Now I tried to figure out what I'd do next and how I would tell Mom and my sister Bev—or Tanya and the rest of my co-workers. I rubbed my throat, my stupid vocal cords were already twitching and complaining from my phone rant with Dan. My face was hot, my throat was burning. I stomped to the car and headed home. Once there I laid down with a rag, wrapped around ice cubes, gingerly placed on my throat. I hated Dan, I hated my stupid vocal cords, and I hated me—I realized it was time to start making the right decision for my boys and me.

9

DISGRACE

2015

WE ASSEMBLED IN THE GALLERY of the board of supervisors' meeting room at the county building on Fair Street in Prescott. It had uncomfortable vinyl and metal chairs in six neat rows, already full of spectators by the time I arrived. The dais extended across the eastern wall, creating desk areas and holding several computers for the board members. Chairs elevated above the gallery sat behind this structure and awaited the five supervisors. The county administrator, Bill, who looked like the bulbous, sweaty, smelly spider that I'd grown to despise, sat behind the wooden structure, playfully visiting with the clerk of the board, Katharine Marchand, an attractive brunette. Mike Parks (Dick Dastardly) also sat there. He appeared to be amusing himself by reading the paper. Behind Bill stood the flags of Arizona and United States. It occurred to me that the very thing these flags represented might be violated in this meeting, yet we'd stand in a few minutes and everyone would pledge our allegiance to the Constitution, the rule of law, open meetings, freedom, and serving the people.

I waved at Vicki King and Roger Pearsall, Bob's cousins, who sat two rows in front of us. Tami Maurie, the reporter for the *Daily Courier*, sat by the west wall at a table marked "reporter." Paul Endicotte, a reporter for the local radio station KYCA, sat in the front row to the east of me, preparing to record the meeting.

I scanned the room and saw it was full of friends. How kind! Many people felt compelled to come in support of me, or in support of our assessor's office, knowing it might be a bad day for both the office and me. I wrestled with my thoughts. My heart double-thumped against my chest. *Please, please, Heavenly Father, soften their hearts, make them not do this.* I prayed about the board and their upcoming vote. Then I remembered free agency, and I knew God would let them do what they would. He wouldn't interfere. *Please lead me, guide me, walk beside me.* I sang in my mind the primary song we'd taught our children, Mike, Nick, Heather and Ashley, so many years ago.

The meeting started, and I sighed when we said the pledge of allegiance; it seemed so hypocritical.

During the call to the public session, Bill Williams, a citizen from Prescott Valley, stated to the board of supervisors: "I think you should proceed with caution. It might be an open meeting violation if you do as proposed in an executive session. The affected employees, the public and our assessor should have a right to hear your conversations in an open meeting. A closed, secret, executive meeting to make this decision seems inappropriate."

Soon after that, the board adjourned into their executive session behind closed doors.

The citizens who gathered for the board meeting sat quietly and visited while the board was adjourned into executive session.

"I talked to Supervisor Jack Smith over the weekend. He understands how much the assessor's office needs mapping to accomplish your job. I think he'll vote against taking us," Natalie Odell, the pretty blonde chief mapper, said to me with a weak smile. "So that's one vote for us," she added.

"Bob, my husband, spoke to Tom Thurman on Saturday. You know they went to high school together?"

Natalie said, "Did Bob convince Tom to vote against this?"

"I think Tom will vote against their plan and support us. I think he has integrity. He told Bob he'd tried to warn me what would happen if I didn't do as they'd demanded over the agricultural—

land baron—valuation thing," I said.

"He admitted that to Bob? Remember, he told you this was political retribution right in front of me," Natalie said, her blue eyes wide.

"Yep, but that's just two votes to keep our office together. I doubt we'll get Rowle or Craig; I just don't know."

"I called Craig this weekend, too," she said. "He said he'd meet with me before the meeting this morning; then he had his assistant cancel. He wouldn't look me in the eye earlier. I think he's going through with this."

I pulled my purse onto my lap, rummaged through it, and found a lozenge. My throat was already throbbing. I'd talked on the phone all weekend to my friends in an attempt to get political pressure put on the board to change their mind, but I had no idea if it had any effect.

Roger, my husband's cousin, a handsome silver-haired man, turned in his seat and joined our conversation. "I've known Rowle for years. I spoke with him before the meeting, told him if he did this to your office, I might just do a documentary and expose all the corruption of this board of supervisors and this county." Roger had the talent and ability to do a documentary. He was well connected in the industry, had worked for ABC, Disney and Lucas Films. He'd owned Timberline Productions. Now retired, he could take on a project like this if he chose.

"Wow, maybe we'll have Rowle's vote after all," I said, my stomach feeling like I was in an elevator.

It seemed to take forever, but finally the board members came out and mingled in the lobby. It was announced that the meeting would resume in five minutes. I saw Jack Smith, the youngest board member, say something to Natalie Odell, the chief mapper, and then Jack left the building.

I worked my way over to Natalie, who was still standing in the lobby. "Well?" I asked.

"He said he had to go to Phoenix but he'd phone in his vote," Natalie said with a broad smile. "He seemed like he was supportive. I think we have his vote."

"Whew, it'll be nice to have this behind us—not knowing is hard!"

"We'll know one way or the other in about a minute," Natalie said as we walked back into the supervisors' meeting room. Everyone in the audience took their seats and waited until most of the board members came in and sat behind the dais and their respective nameplates.

"Here we go, we're back on the record," I heard Bill, the bulbous-headed spider, say. He continued speaking, but my heart was thumping so hard I couldn't hear anything more. I tried to focus, breathe slower, afraid that my husband and neighboring seatmates would be distracted with my loud heartbeats.

The clerk of the board got on the phone and connected with Jack Smith on his way to Phoenix. Chairman Craig Brown announced the item to remove the title and mapping positions from the assessor and place them under the board of supervisors and called for the vote. My heart slapped hard against my chest. *Was this a heart attack?* I had to smile, as I imagined how falling to the ground dead with a heart attack would play out; maybe headlines the next day would read: "Board of Supervisors decisions kill Assessor Pearsall."

Tom voted "Yes." *He's willing to go through with this!* I was surprised; and knowing math as I did, I realized it was over, I'd lost. Jack's voice on the phone said "Yes." I almost laughed. Jack had fooled me. He'd fooled Natalie, too. It made no sense. Why pretend to us that he wouldn't support robbing me of staff? *They probably promised him something in return for his vote.* Then Craig voted "Yes." Rowle seemed uncomfortable as he looked down and voted "Yes."

When Rowle voted, I saw Roger point his finger at Rowle, indicating *you're a self-serving good ole boy and I see it.* I heard a gasp behind me and turned in my seat to see Barbara Fox-Thomas standing in the back. She was Rowle's administrative assistant. *Is she surprised by Rowle's vote?* Barbara rushed over to Roger, bent over and said something. I couldn't hear, but saw them leave the room.

Later, I discovered that Barbara Fox-Thomas had accused Roger of pointing his gun finger at Rowle! She would report witnessing this gun finger pointed at Rowle to Craig Brown, and Craig would act irrationally in the parking lot; but at the time, I knew none of this.

Arlo Davis, the last board member to vote, looked at me with his cinnamon brown eyes. He gave me his flirty boyish grin—the kind of grin that makes girls swoon and their knees buckle—and then he voted "Yes." His eyebrows lifted as if to say, "There's nothing you can do about it." Then his eyes grew wider in a sad empathetic look, and he shrugged his shoulders as if to add that he was sorry. Then he grinned, letting me know he was actually pleased with himself. The meeting adjourned. Arlo's grin made me furious—I was seething inside.

My husband squeezed my hand, citizens buzzed around. I sat for a minute processing; every one of them had voted to take the mappers from me and made it impossible for me to function professionally as the assessor. Every one of them voted against the constitution and against state statute. I did not see that coming.

Tami Maurie, the reporter, walked over. My husband hugged me and left the board room to join his cousins.

"What are your thoughts on the action of the board today?" Tami asked me.

"I'm disappointed. I think the timing makes it absolutely clear that this board's action was to save the job of Lynette, the county administrator's wife. It's just too coincidental. I'm afraid that property owners could be assessed incorrect property taxes because the appraisers won't be able to double check the work of the title clerks." *There's your quote, should look pretty good in the paper,* I thought. I'd practiced it in my mind last night when I couldn't sleep.

"Were you expecting this when you came up with your reorganization plan?"

I shook my head. "I never in my wildest imagination thought they'd take the title department away from an assessor, and they still haven't explained why."

"Okay, I'm going to go talk to some of the board members—

thanks," Tami said, and rushed off.

I walked into the office lobby, outside the boardroom, where several county employees gathered at the double sliding doors, peering outside. I wanted to see what they were looking at as Paul Endicotte, the reporter for the local radio station, walked up.

"Ready to talk with me?" he asked.

I nodded and walked out the double doors. Paul followed and we stood left of the doors outside. He started his recorder. Paul asked what my thoughts were on the actions of the board. Before I could answer there was a commotion to the right of us. Paul and I stopped and looked towards the shouting.

Craig Brown, chairman of the board of supervisors, was shouting in the parking lot, "Do you have a gun? Do you have a gun?"

Roger replied, "What are you talking about, a gun? I don't have a gun!"

"Get out of here. Those sirens are coming for you; that's the cops," Craig screamed, his eyes bulging.

Roger and Vicki appeared to have been walking in the direction of their car when the shouting had broken out. I could see my husband and several others standing by the county building. Craig stood between Roger, Vicki and the citizens in the parking lot. Inside, still looking out the doorway, were a gaggle of county employees. Paul Endicotte aimed his recorder towards the ruckus, and I reached for my phone to try to video tape how crazily Craig was behaving.

"What do you mean he has to get off this property? This is our property! We own this. You work for us," Dennis Kapner, a local citizen standing by the building, called out.

Craig turned his glaring bulging eyes from Roger's direction to Dennis. "You get out of here, too," Craig screamed, puffing out his chest and taking a step towards Dennis.

"What did I do? What did he do?" Dennis asked, his voice raised. Nancy, Dennis' wife, sat in a wheelchair, her eyes growing wide—probably surprised to see an elected official treating her husband so disrespectfully, or maybe she was frightened by the outburst. Craig looked so intimidating that the hairs on the back of my neck stood out and goosebumps appeared on my arms. I was afraid that Craig might attack Dennis or Roger; he was certainly acting unstable.

"You threatened me, and he threatened me, too," Craig said, still shouting. I looked at Paul Endicotte. I was stunned to see Craig so out of control that he would outright lie and bully these people right in front of a reporter.

#

1985

"I need money and a ride to Oregon," I said into the phone with a sigh. Sitting on the couch, I looked at my glass of iced tea on the end table, the ice cubes clear, water droplets on the outside of the glass. I knew I should've told Dan no when he asked if the boys could go to Oregon for his grandma's birthday party and a visit. Now here I was trying to figure out my next move, again.

"I have to work, but I'll have Flo give you a ride. She has our credit cards, and she can use them for gas, food and motel rooms," Gil, my biological father answered.

I was relieved at his response. I'd assumed he'd do whatever I asked, but it felt good to have the confirmation. I hadn't spoken to Gil since our Sunday call and the blow up with Dan over it; this was more than a year ago. I felt a tinge of guilt that I'd turned to Gil because I wanted something, but I was desperate and figured he'd be willing to help. I hadn't forgotten our history—I didn't totally trust him.

I had decided not to ask Jerry, the man who'd raised me, adopted me, and was my hero in so many ways, for help. I was tired of letting him down and wanted him to be proud of me, and not find out about any more of my failures.

"I'm not sure how long it'll take, where exactly they are in Oregon, or how we're going to get them back," I said. "I'll figure it all out once I'm there. Thanks so much."

"I'm sure you will," Gil said. We had a nice conversation, catching up. Flo, Gil's wife, called me a few hours later. She was in California but let me know she'd be in Arizona by morning, and we could take off any time after that. I hadn't earned any commissions for a while so I didn't have much money, it was nice to know that money for gas, motels and food would be covered.

Now my only problem was finding where the kids were and getting them away without Dan stopping me.

Flo showed up as promised. We drove mostly in silence from Phoenix straight through to Oregon, a fifteen-hour drive. Flo tried her best to keep it from being awkward, since we had never had much time together before this. She spoke of her alcoholism, about the Alcoholic Anonymous program where she'd met Gil. They'd dated after he was released from prison, broke up, got back together and eventually married.

When Flo talked, I tried to listen. Mostly, though, I thought of what I would do when I got to Ontario, the steps I'd take to find the boys, how I'd get them away from Dan. I wasn't great company. I thought through what I did know. I'd stayed in touch with Jan, our neighbor, who had taken over the apartment manager's position after Dan and I'd been fired. She'd told me Dan had moved in with Rhonda two days after I'd left him. This was surprising because Dan had admitted the affair with Melissa but denied anything with Rhonda, our next door neighbor.

I reflected on the phone call I had with Rhonda yesterday after my call with Jan.

"Hey, Rhonda, this is Pam, I need to speak with Dan," I'd said, trying to get to the point but not be rude and say, *Hey Rhonda let me talk to my husband, you slut.* I'm nice to the tramps my husband lives with.

She cried, said he'd left her for someone else. She told me she knew he was like that with me, but never thought he'd do that to her. *Really?* Melissa was tall and thin, but Rhonda was big, real big, yet she was pretty, with dark hair and chestnut eyes.

I pretended to empathize as she cried, but I didn't really care that she felt hurt by my husband's betrayal of her. Overall, she was nice to me on the phone and tried to be helpful. She gave me an address of an apartment complex where she thought Dan's new girlfriend lived, but she didn't have an apartment number. Perhaps Dan was living there with his new girlfriend. It was a lead. I felt like a detective.

Flo and I arrived in town, got a motel and slept. She was exhausted. She'd driven eight hours from California to Arizona, then we'd traveled another fifteen hours to Oregon; I'd helped drive, but Flo hadn't slept. When she woke up she suggested I dye my hair the same color as hers, so if Dan did see us in her car he'd not easily recognize me. I thought that was a cool idea. We got some hair dye and I did it—my hair now the same reddish brown color as Flo's. Then she cut my hair to match hers. I thought it was weird, but didn't care. From afar Dan wouldn't recognize me, and if it fulfilled some fantasy of Flo's that I looked like her daughter, what did that hurt? My appearance had drastically changed, and that's what mattered.

We went to see an attorney. He confirmed what Tanya had said: as a married couple we both had equal rights to the boys. But he added that if I went to court, and I didn't have physical custody of the boys, it was unlikely the court would take them from Dan and give them back to me—especially when I lived in Arizona, and there was no sign that the boys were being abused. The attorney hinted I should just grab the boys when Dan was at work.

That night Flo and I went to a restaurant for dinner. To my surprise, Don and Gina, Dan's dad and stepmother, walked in and sat two booths over from us, but my disguise worked. We paid and slipped out unnoticed. It was fun; I felt like we were the undercover *Get Smart* spies I'd watched as a child with my Uncle Les.

The next morning we went to the apartment complex where Dan's new girlfriend lived. We spotted the apartment playground. It was simple with a swing, a slide and a sandbox. The apartment complex and grounds were older but well maintained, neat and clean. I spotted my son, Mike, playing all alone in the playground. How independent he'd grown in these few months, only three years old but unattended by any adult. It would be simple enough for me to snatch him. But I needed both my baby Nick and Mike; I had to be patient.

#

2015

The office was as impressive as it was intimidating, with its legal books on the shelves lining the southern wall and an over-sized oak desk in front of me. I looked at intricately carved moldings and wooden floors. The room smelled of cigars reminiscent of old legal institutions.

I sat in a large leather chair. My attention focused on Troy Fabio, the private sector attorney. He was very different from Dick Dastardly, the deputy county attorney who'd betrayed me. Troy Fabio was tall, and stood ramrod straight. He was the type of guy who wore puka shells when he wasn't wearing a suit and tie. He believed deeply in right, wrong, fair play, and the principles on which this country was founded. By contrast, Dick was a water carrier for a corrupt and bullying political system; he'd betrayed his duty to me as an elected official and seemed incapable of discarding his self-interest and acting according to his oath of candor and integrity.

"They charged me with nepotism," I said, looking down at my hands folded in my lap.

"It's not a big deal; this is a misdemeanor. Tipping a cow or running a stop sign is a bigger deal. Heck, a dog at large is more of an offense," Fabio said. He sounded fatherly, and I felt at ease.

"It could be a big deal," I said. *Even if this was a misdemeanor, it could end my career.* "It's political; they're trying to make me look like I don't have integrity. It may hurt my chances to be re-elected. That's why they're doing it." I swallowed.

It was so stupid! I hadn't hired my daughter, Ashley, for a part-time position and the county board knew darn well I hadn't. Also, the county, if this was legitimate, should provide an attorney for me. They hadn't because they were behind the accusations.

"I'm a criminal attorney. I don't—I haven't really done

misdemeanors. This is minor. I think they'd have to show intent. Just seems petty. I'm not involved in local politics," Fabio said as he read the charge.

I sat quietly, letting him read through the charges filed and the deputy's records on the issue. The record showed the deputy's notes on the interview with me, my office manager, and my assistant—including the telephone conversation with my daughter, Ashley. All clearly indicated Ash had volunteered on and off for years at the assessor's office when she was in town visiting me. It showed that Ashley had noted 'Mom—assessor' on the job application when asked if she had a relative in the assessor's office. The deputy's records further indicated the human resource department had approved the action form, even though they were aware of the relationship. If there was a law against having my daughter work for the assessor's office, the mistake appeared to have been made by human resources. I hadn't hired Ashley nor was I in a position to process the action forms. I silently prayed that Fabio would see it the same way and take this case pro bono. *How could I pay for an attorney? The fine would be $1,500!* Attorney fees would be way more than that to get to court.

"I'm willing to help you. I won't charge you anything. But you have to understand I'm not familiar with the county government process nor have I done misdemeanors. I'm not comfortable with this yet. Need to do some research to determine what this charge is and get familiar with the case." Fabio looked up. I was grinning. I believed him to be my knight in white shining armor.

I couldn't plead guilty; I hadn't hired Ashley. *The board of supervisors and the sheriff are acting like a bunch of bullies,* I thought. *They'd forwarded an anonymous complaint to another county for investigation. Really?*

I'd complained years ago to Muttley that I suspected laws were being broken by the county regarding business personal property and the tax rolls, collections and abatements. It wasn't an anonymous complaint, I had used my name and provided documentation. Failing to follow the statutes had cost taxpayers and taxing jurisdictions millions of dollars in lost revenue and tax shifts, but my complaint had been ignored. And yet, Ashley working for the county and earning her minimal wages hadn't impacted the taxpayers or hurt anyone—and I hadn't hired her! The truth was, I was being punished for changes I'd made to the agricultural values, the reorganization of my office and for the business personal property complaint. As a result, my problems were escalating and my enemies were increasing.

This charge against me was based on an anonymous complaint. It had made the front page of the local papers. I recalled headlines such as *We're Looking into It; We Think She Might Have Done It; We're Charging Her Because She Probably Did It.* They all appeared with my campaign photo, the one of me smiling happily. Local radio stations announced similar statements at the top of each hour.

Fabio spoke of his love of the Constitution and his desire to stand up against evil corrupt forces. Relieved that he'd stand up for me, I listened, enthralled by his intelligence, his humility, and his good looks.

#

1985

Mike played all by himself for about an hour in the playground. Then a brunette woman in shorts came, scooped him up and walked away out of our sight.

We continued to sit in Flo's car all day and watched, ducking down when anyone passed close to the car. We went to a Burger King, grabbed lunch, came back and parked in different areas of the lot or down the street trying to be inconspicuous—our eyes always on the playground.

That afternoon, Mike returned to the playground alone. I watched him play for about half an hour and then saw him leave by himself. I wanted to go hug him, love him up; I'd missed him so much. I got out of the car and hid behind a tree to get closer.

The apartment complex was quiet, no one around. I watched my son walk to apartment number nine, go in and shut the door. He looked good. I wondered if he missed me, or if he even noticed

I hadn't been around. Then I saw my husband, dressed in jeans and carrying a motorcycle helmet. *Do we own a motorcycle now?* Facing in my direction, he walked towards apartment number nine. I took several steps back, trying not to step on anything that would make noise and catch his attention.

My heart started to thump and my breath increased. *Be quiet,* I ordered my breath and heart, afraid Dan might hear even that. Once out of his sight I ran as quickly as I could to Flo's car. "Apartment number nine—that's where they are right now," I said. "I think he's got a motorcycle," I added. We drove around the parking lot and spotted a motorcycle. "Maybe that's his."

"So what should we do?" Flo asked.

"I think we go to the motel for tonight. In the morning we come back here early and watch Dan's motorcycle. When he leaves we'll have time to get the boys. It will take him awhile to get to work. She can't reach him until he gets there to tell him there's a problem." I tried to calm my heart again. "We go in quick as soon as he leaves. You grab one baby. I'll grab the other. Leave the front car doors unlocked so we can jump in with the boys and lock the doors. Then we'll head to Arizona as quick as we can. We'll be out of town before he can even get back to her apartment."

Flo started the car and we headed for the motel. "I wonder if we should call the police," she said. "We could ask them if they could send a policemen for a standby. She's only the babysitter and you're the mother; she has no right to keep them from you."

"That's a good idea! She might call the police and report a kidnapping, and your idea would prevent that."

I could hardly sleep. I imagined scenarios of Dan leaving on his motorcycle, of Flo and me barging into the apartment, of Dan returning because he forgot something—perhaps to kiss his new girlfriend goodbye—of Dan catching us. Maybe he'd murder Flo and me in front of the kids. These scenes played over and over in my dreams as I tried to sleep.

Dawn finally arrived. Flo and I loaded the trunk of the car with our suitcases. I called the local police department from the motel room and requested a standby. Explaining there might be an issue, so it would be better if they could come and prevent any problems. These were my kids, I told them. I had their birth certificates and could prove they were mine. They'd be with a babysitter who might feel uncomfortable giving me my children. I was going to take them with her cooperation or without. She might get hurt if she resisted. The person I spoke to refused to send anyone. They would come if there was a problem, but not just to prevent a problem.

I was going to get my kids back. What if Dan catches me, I wondered. What would he do? Dan wasn't one to be defied. I didn't have any idea how dangerous he might be. It would be bad enough to get physically hurt, but it would be worse for the kids to see their Dad hurt me.

Flo and I checked out of the motel before dawn, then headed to the apartment complex. We pulled up on the street outside of the complex. It had a good view of the motorcycle that sat in the same place as the day before. We waited, ducked down so no one would notice us. I hoped we just looked like a parked car.

As it got lighter and lighter outside, we sat silently as we watched and waited. People came out, people left, but not Dan.

Finally, after two hours, there he was. He walked to the motorcycle, flipped his leg over the seat, put his helmet on, started the motor and pulled out of the parking lot, driving right past our car.

Flo turned on the ignition and drove into the parking lot as close to the building as she could get. "Doors unlocked," she said. "We'll knock nicely. When she opens the door I'm going to shove the door all the way open and barge in and grab a kid." She paused and gave me a strange look "What if there are more than two kids? What if she has her own child? I don't know what your kids look like except I know they're little! What if she has one about the same age?" Flo asked, bringing up something I hadn't considered. I had no answer.

As we stood at the apartment door, Flo and I looked at each other and hesitated. I knocked politely. An attractive female about my age opened the door. She had dark hair and was small from the waist up; larger from the hips down. Actually, her body was fine —not great, but fine. However, from this day forward I'd refer to her as "Thunder Thighs" because calling her that seemed to bother Dan.

"Hello?" she said, as Flo shoved the door wide open and I barged in. There were three little boys sitting on the floor in front of a television set watching cartoons. My sons, Mike and Nick, looked up and both squealed "Mom!" They ran towards me, arms outstretched. I bent over and grabbed both boys, hugging them tightly, while Flo played defense keeping Thunder Thighs away from me.

I ran as fast as I could to the car—both boys in tow—got in the front passenger seat, and locked my side of the car, the boys safely in my lap. Flo flew into the driver's seat and shut and locked her side of the car. Thunder Thighs was just steps behind us.

"Let's call Dan," she said, pleading, "I can't let you take the boys!" She yelled and grabbed Flo's car door handle, trying to open it. She then held onto the antenna as if she could hold the car still.

Flo started the car. "Listen, bitch," she shouted, "just give me an excuse to run your ass over. I swear to God I'll do it, and then I'll let Pam kick your ass before we leave with her boys!"

I was sorry the boys were exposed to language like that—but I decided I loved Flo at that moment. Thunder Thighs let go of the car, took a step back, and continued to plead as we drove away.

Gil Sieling, Nick and Mike Ford, the day I arrived back
in Phoenix, Arizona, from my Oregon adventure with Flo Sieling.

#

1986

One year, and nine months after I left my husband, Mom babysat the boys while I went out with friends from the office. "It's my twenty-fifth birthday," I said to W. Steven Martin, a local radio show disc jockey. This was a person I did not know or recognize. I made this statement in a husky flirty way—flirty to a man I'd never met before. I was about to learn my lesson. I proclaimed my birthday to him inside Toolies, a western bar. The country music band in the corner played "Making Up For Lost Time."

My friends and I were out to celebrate the birth of me, and I was about to prove I could two-step with the best of them. I was on the prowl for a boyfriend, or at least a date.

As I walked towards our table, I noticed the person I'd so brazenly been flirting with on the grandstand with the band. "That's right, you come on up—yes—you..." W. Steven Martin said into the microphone, pointing in my direction.

I looked around. He was talking to me, but I pretended not to understand. I knew it was because of my proud, flirty behavior announcing my birthday. Two cute guys, dressed in cowboy boots and big belt buckles, grabbed me and dragged me to the stage. They lifted me up to W. Steven Martin—against my will. I wiggled and giggled. Once on stage, looking out to the audience, I could hardly make out individual faces due to the bright lights. With both hands I covered my face wishing I could make myself disappear—I could hear the audience laugh.

"I, uh, I heard from a little birdie that it's your birthday today. Is that true?" Martin asked in a singsong voice.

My face felt hot, my heart thumped so hard and fast I could hardly speak. I removed my hands from my face and nodded, saying nothing.

"How old are you? I heard something about you turning twenty-five. Is that true?" Again he asked this in a lilted voice, playfully torturing me like a cat with its favorite mouse. This was not how I'd planned my banter with him to go. In my mind he was going to be amused by my playful perkiness and attracted to my awesomeness. In reality, he was probably married and not interested in me, romantically. He was, however, apparently very interested in me as a comedy act. Again I nodded. "Well, let's sing you a little song," and the band started to play *"Happy Birthday."* The crowd and Martin sang to me. After the song I was allowed to leave the stage.

I joined my friends at their table. Still hunting for the next new love of my life, I noticed a guy at our table. I'd seen him before. He was a friend of a friend. "Want to dance?" I asked.

"My girlfriend's in the bathroom," he said.

"We better hurry before she comes out," I said with a laugh, knowing he wasn't the type of guy to dance with someone while his date was out of the room. What I didn't know was that the girl in the bathroom wasn't going to keep this guy's interest very long. I'd just met my future husband.

#

2015

I sat at my desk, holding my throbbing head in my hands. It felt as if a thumb was being jammed into my right eye, and a fork had been shoved into my temple. The constant thuds that echoed through the office weren't helping. The ground shook in concert with each thump.

Lorrie, my assistant, rushed into my office. She looked upset. "Amanda's complained they're tearing the conference room down, the wall literally next to her desk! She's afraid it might fall on her!"

I scooted my chair away from my desk and leaned back. I wasn't the director of Amanda's department anymore, the board was, so there was nothing I could do about her complaint. I stood up and sighed, "Let's go see what she's talking about." I tried to appear confident and not let my frustration show. *I need a conference room. They're tearing it down?*

Lorrie and I walked through a maze of cubicles. In the rear of the office were the vacated booths where the administrator's wife and her staff had worked; they'd been moved—after leaving food, crumbs, trash and empty wrappers in their area. It smelled like a dirty refrigerator. I crinkled my nose in disgust, looked at Lorrie and raised my eyebrows.

"I'm sorry," I said to the man who worked for facilities, pointing to the filth. He was busy picking up the garbage.

"This is nothing; you should've seen how the health department left their area when they moved WIC," the guy said, speaking over the loud thuds coming from the next room. His manner seemed friendly.

She did this on purpose. I took pictures with my phone. *I'll show Bev,* I thought. I thanked the guy for cleaning up and promised to make him some homemade root beer for his efforts. It was our tradition: facilities did a project for me and I'd make homemade root beer for them. It wasn't their fault they were deconstructing the assessor's office.

Lorrie and I continued to the rear of the assessor's office, out the back door and through the corridor into what had previously been the mapping department. The noise got louder as we approached. The thuds grew into bangs; the floor shuddered with each explosive rumble.

After I opened the door to this area I stood in amazement, surprised by the chaos. Amanda sat at her desk attempting to work, but the extreme noise made it impossible to think. Smell of drywall dust and the fog of it hung thick in the air. *That's got to be bad for their breathing.* A thin sheet of plastic hung from the ceiling adjacent to the four desks that lined the wall. I peeked into what had once been my conference room. The conference table, chairs, computer, projector and screen had all been removed.

Dean, the supervisor of the facilities team, saw me. He motioned for the work to stop and walked over to us. "I'm storing your conference table and stuff. We won't get rid of it until we see what happens." His voice sounded apologetic. He knew this wasn't over. It pleased me to realize there were others in the county who knew this move wasn't fair. The assessor's office needed the conference room to discuss confidential financial information with property owners, or to discuss issues with staff members.

It was going to be difficult to operate without one. No other department of our size in the county lacked a conference room. No other assessor's office in the state lacked a conference room. My head hurt too much to be angry.

"So the conference wall is coming down?" I asked, trying to ignore my pounding headache, but finding that impossible.

Dean nodded. "We're opening this all up," he said, as he pointed towards the conference walls and the map office. "Cubicles are going to come in. It'll be a tight squeeze—fifteen people where five were before." I looked at the plastic and then back at Dean. "That's to try to keep the drywall dust down," he added.

"Seems so loud for the staff and . . . Is this safe, I mean couldn't the wall fall on one of them?" I pointed to the staff members up against the wall that was about to be demolished. They had only the thin plastic sheet to protect them.

He shrugged. "There isn't anywhere to put them." He gestured to the affected staff. "The board of supervisors ordered this demolition and made it top priority to reconfigure this area. This isn't perfect, but under the time constraints and circumstances, it's the best I can do." He looked down at the floor. "It's my job," he added with a whisper.

Lorrie and I walked back to my office. "Call human resources, tell them of Amanda's concerns and the noise complaints. Get it documented by following up with an email," I said, sitting at my desk rummaging for a lozenge. "I can't believe they're doing this—demolishing our conference room, tearing down a wall as employees sit next to it! If a wall falls on someone—" Now my throat ached. Thin white drywall dust covered my desk. I placed my head in my hands, hurting too much to drive home.

#

1991

I had dated and married Bob, who was mature enough to understand I needed more than cute dimples and sweet talk in a husband. Bob was a man of integrity. He was handsome with a great build, At twenty-five years old I finally realized good looks and big muscles were only a bonus. His honor and integrity made him a man worthy enough to share the boys and my life with.

Dan, my ex-husband, hid to avoid his child support obligations. As a result, his parental rights were severed, and Bob adopted the kids. Over the years we added two daughters to our family. I missed Grandma since she had passed away a few years earlier. I often reflected on the times she had told me *"In the end it'll be okay, if it isn't okay, it isn't the end."* I now knew she was right. We could close the book of my life right here, because everything was better than okay—it was perfect. I appreciated the light so much now because I had lived through the dark. It wasn't the end, though, it was only the middle, but the middle was good. Husband, children, love and excitement—a perfect mix.

"Why aren't you going?" Bev asked on the phone.

I sat on the bar stool at my blue breakfast bar. The phone hung on a yellow wall, with wallpaper border of little houses trimming the ceiling. My three-year-old daughter, Ashley, played quietly at my feet with her blocks, stacking them as high as she could.

"No, I don't want to go. It's December. I'll be busy preparing for Christmas," I answered. "You're not going, are you? Seriously, we have a lot to do, like Christmas shopping." I needed to talk her out of going.

"No, I'm going. He needs me to go and we can shop there. It'll be fun, please come with me," Bev said.

Heather, my four-year-old daughter, walked into the dining area where Ashley sat stacking her blocks. Heather kicked at the blocks and they tumbled down, creating a crisis for Ashley. Pushing, shoving and crying ensued, and I let Bev know I'd have to call her back after I dealt with the sibling emergency.

I sent Heather to a thinking chair to ponder about how she treated others. Heather promised she'd think about her behavior. I set the oven timer for four minutes, then comforted Ashley while I thought about this trip.

I was torn; I didn't want to go, but I didn't want Bev to go alone. She'd have more fun if I were there. Gil Sieling, was having open heart surgery in Texas where they specialized in open heart procedures. He wanted Bev and me with him. He'd need someone to take care of him when he was released from the hospital to return home in Arizona. It was a fairly intense surgery—the aortic and mitral valves both needed to be replaced. He'd pay for our airline tickets, and we could drive his car. He'd pay for the motel.

I knew that if I wanted to go Bob would be supportive. Bev had four children of her own, and she was going to figure it out and go. If Bev could manage it, I had no excuse not to. *I hate Christmas time, and to be in Texas with Gil nearby . . . in December?* My hands started to tremble, and I found it difficult to breathe. I just didn't want to go.

"Mom, can I get up now?" Heather called out, breaking my thoughts. "How old are you?" I asked, playing out our typical skit.

"Four," Heather replied.

"You have to sit and think for four minutes. You know the timer will go off when you're done. I'm starting your time over." I went to the stove and re-set the timer for four more minutes. "If you ask again, I'll reset it again," I called out. I could hear her crying in the next room.

I didn't want to go to Texas, be away from the kids and Bob for at least two weeks. Every December I had so much to do—shopping, baking, decorating—and puking because I hated Christmas while pretending I liked it.

How could I fit it all in if I were in Texas? I didn't want to let Bev down. She said we'd have regrets if Gil died and we hadn't been there for him. I liked Gil all right, and I didn't want him to die, but I was not sure he should be a priority. I'd had a mixed relationship with him since he'd attacked me when I was a child.

Years after we'd taken my boys from Oregon, Flo and Gil had divorced and I'd lost touch with him. I'd kept in touch with Flo. In fact, Flo had been invited to my wedding; Gil hadn't been invited nor did he know where I lived. Bev, however, stayed in contact with both Flo and Gil. She didn't play the 'silent treatment—unless I want something' game like I did. I'd get in a mood and break contact with Gil for a few years, then Bev would invite me to a place where he'd be, and I'd think he was okay for a while.

The timer chimed. "You can get up now," I said and walked to the living room where Heather sat in a rocking chair. "Did you think about how you treated your little sister?" I asked in my most serious voice.

"Nope," Heather answered and giggled.

"Oh you!" I said and tickled her. She was such a cute cherub with her shiny brown hair. In the sun it shone like spun gold. "Go tell Sissy you're sorry—and be sorry! Don't do that again. It's mean," I added. Heather hugged me and danced away, probably to find some blocks to kick over.

#

2015

I looked through my purse and found a throat lozenge, unwrapped it and placed it in my mouth as I waited in the impressive but intimidating office with its law books and over-sized oak desk. The room still smelled of cigars.

I sat on a stool in front of a high table against the western wall of Troy Fabio's office and waited patiently for my attorney to discuss what he'd summoned me for, the charge of nepotism. It made me cringe. I wanted people to know I was the kind of person who walked in the marked crosswalks; I entered where it said "enter;" I didn't cuss, unless it was to entertain my sister; I never watched R-rated movies; I didn't drink; I tried to keep my life pure and live with integrity. It was important to me to maintain a sterling reputation.

"A couple things I want to go over," said Fabio, who looked like a Greek God. He rummaged through his briefcase, took out two files and placed them on the table in front of me. "First, I received this anonymous file. Look it over and see if it makes sense to you."

He slid the file towards me, then pulled the other stool over and sat on it. He started to read some documents in a second file.

The file contained a contract between Yavapai County and Improvement District Services, LLC. It included notes regarding the board of supervisors' clerk of the board, Katharine Marchand.

After I'd finished reading, I looked up at Troy and grinned, fully entertained.

"That's cool," I said.

"Okay, I'm not very familiar with the inner workings of county government and the players, I didn't really understand if this was important or what it was. It was slipped through my mail slot with no name on it. I discovered it on Monday."

I nodded, still grinning. The primary document had nothing to do with the nepotism charge against me. It looked like Katharine Marchand, the current clerk of the board of supervisors, might be behind this anonymous delivery to Troy's office. I couldn't imagine she'd go out of her way to help me. *Had she?* I continued to look at Troy with a grin on my face, but I wasn't sure what he wanted from me.

"I don't understand what this is supposed to mean to us. Do you know what it's about?" he asked.

"Well, this is a contract between the Improvement District Services, LLC—we call it IDS—and Yavapai County. It doesn't have anything to do with the nepotism charge against me." I held out the contract. "I think the point of this file is the lack of integrity of the board of supervisors. Melody Davis, wife of one of their members, has ownership in the IDS company, so when the county entered into this agreement it's a conflict of interest. As a side note, Melody Davis used to be an employee of the county, but she and another employee left and started IDS. Then they contracted with the county for the same services they used to do as employees of the county. Kind of cozy, huh? I bet it's more expensive doing it that way."

"So Mike Parks, the deputy county attorney, didn't do anything about this conflict of interest thing with the board?" Troy shook his head in disgust. "Mike's such a dork."

Dork? I'd always thought of Mike Parks as Dick Dastardly tying me to the railroad tracks and laughing because the train was coming. *Dork? Really? I guess to a Greek God perhaps Mike Parks would seem to be a dork.*

I sat thinking about the dork remark while my attorney read

the incriminating contract. I'd noticed Mike Park's dark hair and evil grin, but as I contemplated the suspenders he wore, it dawned on me Troy had a point. *Dorky.* I laughed. *He was a dork, a scary dork, a Dick Dastardly Nerd Dork!* I'd have to tell Bev later.

Troy looked up from the contract. "What else?" he asked.

"It says Katharine Marchand had her daughter work for the recorder's office when she was the recorder for the county. I guess the point is they didn't forward *that* for an investigation like they did for me—so maybe someone's hinting at selective prosecution?"

"Well, they shouldn't have. Nor should the board of supervisors have forwarded this complaint on you. It's dirty politics."

"The file says board of supervisor Arlo Davis's son worked for the county, too," I said, "in MIS. He downloaded pornography or looked at something he wasn't supposed to. It's unclear exactly what he did. At any rate, he was asked to resign rather than be prosecuted." I grabbed my purse for hard candy or another lozenge.

"What's MIS?"

"Oh sorry. It's Management Information System. It's the county's I.T. department—Information Technologies. They take care of our computers, networking, stuff like that. The board of supervisors is above MIS so we're looking at nepotism, I guess, but the boy didn't get prosecuted or fired for the illegal use of the computers. Instead, it looks like he was allowed to resign."

"Well, it's nepotism! And I'm amazed at this whole thing about the county administrator's wife, that they're taking her department away from you to save her job!"

I agreed. I didn't know the exact particulars of the law, but certainly it seemed the county administrator's wife's job was saved by the board of supervisors because she was married to the county administrator. I suspected Katherine no more hired her daughter than I'd hired Ashley. It was probably a human resource issue, just like in my case. In the case of Lynette, her job was saved because of whom she was married to. That sounded like nepotism to me.

"Okay, there's more, right?" Troy asked, standing up and going to his desk to look for something.

"Yes. There are notes here indicating that Katharine was being bullied by the board for bringing up Supervisor Chip Davis's conflict of interest issue regarding the IDS contract. Also it looks like there was at least one open meeting violation."

"Open meeting?" Troy asked.

"When the board makes decisions it's supposed to be done in a public meeting, not in secret. It looks like the IDS contract may have been discussed in a closed executive meeting rather than in the open. I accused the supervisors of open meeting violations when they took those ten employees of mine."

Troy nodded and took his seat on the barstool again. "Now, on to your case," he said, "I have bad news for you."

My throat constricted, but I willed myself to relax.

"I looked into the charge. It's a misdemeanor, as I told you, but there is no intent on your part required. So you didn't need to intend to break the law. Most laws have intention required, but this doesn't—that surprised me. You knew I wasn't familiar with this when I took the case. I told you I'd have to do some research on it."

I nodded. I hadn't hired my daughter, but did allowing her to work for the assessor's office violate the law? If it did, and if intent was not part of the law, I could still be guilty. *Damn it!* I swallowed hard.

"Also, here's the worst part," Fabio said as he opened up the file and located a piece of paper.

Shoot, I thought.

"You can be removed from office if you plead guilty or if you are found guilty." Troy rubbed his eyes. I wondered if he was tired. He appeared less sure of the case than he had on our previous visit. "I was stunned when I realized for a low-level misdemeanor like this they could remove you from your elected position."

You really are my hero, I thought. *If Troy hadn't represented me pro-bono, I would've pleaded guilty and taken the penalty. I would've been removed from office.* I had no clue that this was the board's way of getting me out—with the help of Dorky Dicky aka

"Bastardly Dastardly" and bulbous-headed Bill.

"So we can't go forward with this defense," Fabio continued. "I think there's too much risk. We might win if we prove it was Mike Park's mistake because he failed to provide competent legal advice to human resources. It's really negligence on his part. It's sort of ironic: he's responsible for providing competent legal advice, and he receives an anonymous complaint, discovers there's a law against your daughter working for the assessor's office, and turns it in for investigation. This would have never happened if he'd given the proper advice to begin with!"

"So let's fight it," I said.

"I just don't think it's worth the risk. If you lose, you'll be removed from office."

"But if I plead guilty?"

"No, here's what's offered. They'll do a deferred prosecution—that means you're not pleading guilty, but you're acknowledging Ashley worked for the county, and there was a law against it. At the end of the day, you're accountable even if it was human resources that messed up."

I nodded. That was true. Even if I wasn't guilty, I probably should be accountable. The buck stopped with me.

"I suggest," Fabio said, "you enter into a deferred prosecution and pay back your daughter's earnings, about $6,000. Don't commit any crimes for six months; then they'll dismiss the charges so nothing will be on your record and no one can remove you from office."

If I paid back everything Ashley had earned it would be as if she'd volunteered. So if she wasn't supposed to make money by working for the county, then this was fair to the taxpayers. It would alert the administration and human resources not to make this mistake again. It sounded reasonable. My mind whirled, *To pay back the salary, I'd have to dip into the money I'd set aside for my next campaign. That'd run me short. I'd worry about that later. At least they can't remove me from office for this. I'd sure dodged a bullet.*

My mind went to another problem. *If I don't certify the tax roll they probably will remove me.* My throat started to constrict again. *How could I approve the tax rolls? I couldn't if I didn't have control of the data that the board of supervisors' employees in the mapping and title departments were inputting.* I decided to worry about that another day; maybe the attorney general would provide the legal opinion I needed soon enough to allow me to fix things. *Today the supervisors couldn't remove me from office for allowing Ashley to work for the county.*

The first attempt to remove me from office failed. Check.

#

I pulled my blue Jeep Liberty into the parking lot in front of the County Building on Fair Street in Prescott. *I can't do this,* I thought, dreading my upcoming encounter with the attorney I called 'Dick Dastardly.' I turned towards the back seat, lifted my briefcase and set it on my lap.

Before I got out of the car, I looked at the red brick three-story building in front of me and reflected on my job as assessor and the dispute with the board of supervisors. *Value the agricultural properties at ten dollars and ten cents an acre or as high as eleven dollars an acre otherwise I would be punished,* I'd been warned. Now I was taking the punishment for refusing to do as they'd demanded.

The board of supervisors had taken ten employees from my staff. They'd seized equipment and torn down our conference room. They'd swept about a million dollars from the assessor's budget, taken six cars from our fleet, and forwarded an anonymous complaint of nepotism to the sheriff's office against me.

I fought back the tears as I thought about it. *Don't let them see you cry! Be confident and poised. You can do this.* I opened my car door and stood up, hoisting my briefcase straps over my shoulder. I sucked in my belly and walked towards the building. I'd done everything I could think of to push back against the illegal actions that crippled my office.

I'd already asked for an official legal opinion from Dick Dastardly on whether the supervisors had overstepped by taking the titling and mapping functions from me. Had they violated the state Constitution by usurping the assessor's authority? Dastardly had to admit he had a conflict of interest because he worked for the board of supervisors. He couldn't legally provide this requested opinion, so he had forwarded the question to the Maricopa County Attorney's Office in the Phoenix area.

The Maricopa County Attorney returned an opinion that this action *was unlawful* because it usurped the authority of the assessor and could prevent me from fulfilling my statutory duties. I'd been told by other assessors and some private attorneys that Dastardly should allow me to seek outside representation because he had a conflict of interest. Dick, in typical fashion, pretended not to understand and continued to refuse to allow me to pursue the issue with a separate legal counsel.

Every morning I walked through the double glass door. *Good posture. Smile as if nothing's wrong,* I told myself as I entered the assessor's department. I acknowledged the customer service employees with a nod. "Good morning," I said, faking a happy attitude and walking through the department towards my office.

After realizing that Dastardly wouldn't allow me to seek outside legal help, I'd filed a complaint with the Property Tax Oversight Commission (PTOC). I'd filed the complaint hoping that PTOC would force the issue or at least explain to the board of supervisors—and Dastardly—the board couldn't proceed with their reorganization of my office.

I also went to the Arizona Association of Assessing Officers. We composed a letter to the Arizona Attorney General. Twelve assessors, including me, signed it. We requested that the attorney general's office intervene and force the Yavapai County Board of Supervisors restore the resources I needed to perform the tasks I was elected to do.

Enormous problems would occur if I couldn't certify the assessment tax rolls due to the interference from the board. If I were unable to approve the tax rolls because of these barriers, all taxing jurisdictions, including the schools and fire districts, would not be able to obtain their share of tax revenue. They had to have a certified tax roll. The board of supervisors was playing chicken with the tax rolls, and they didn't seem too worried about it.

Overall, this was an impossible situation; several of my former employees complained that now that they were under the board of supervisors' control they were being harassed by the county administrator's wife and two of her minions.

It appeared that processing the assessor's work had taken a back seat to rubber band fights, flirting, eating, personal calls, and makeup applications. I had no power to write them up or to discipline them in any way. They were untouchable and even rude to me. Yet, I would be held accountable for their work if I certified the tax roll as I was required by law to do on December 20th. My heart contracted, and my stomach felt like it would revolt. *Breathe. It's okay. Today you don't have to certify a tax roll. Today you just have to deal with the Dick Dastardly interview,* I coached myself.

The Property Tax Oversight Commission asked if I'd remove my complaint if the attorney general agreed to issue a legal opinion on the issue. I'd agreed. The attorney general's office then contacted me and stated that if Dastardly asked for a legal opinion from their office regarding the situation, they'd be willing to issue one.

Dastardly decided to seek legal advice but claimed he'd have to interview all involved, to determine what his question would be. So here we were. *Why?* I wondered, disgusted with Dastardly. *What's so hard about asking if the board of supervisors usurped the authority of the assessor when they took these responsibilities away from the assessor's jurisdiction?*

In my office and seated at my desk, I looked through my office window at the spider web, now grown again, now conquering the entire lower corner of the window. The moth and fly caught in the web appeared dead, having long ago given up their struggle. I couldn't see the spider but decided after this meeting I'd sweep the window, clean off the web and spray the corner of the window with poison. Watching these spider victories had gotten old.

I turned my attention back to the issue at hand—getting the assessor's office fully restored. Today I was supposed to meet with Dastardly so he could interview me as to why I believed the current organization of employees made it impossible for me to fulfill my statutory obligations as the assessor. He needed to craft the question for a legal opinion from Mark Brnovich, State Attorney General.

I looked up from the paperwork strewn all over my desk. Dick Dastardly had arrived and now stood at my door. I motioned him to come in and take a seat. He gave me a pleased-with-himself smirk. I'm sure if he had a mustache, Dastardly would have twisted it between his fingers.

"So how does not having the map and title employees under you deny you the ability to do the job you were elected to do?" he asked, holding up the written opinion from the Maricopa County Attorney's Office that confirmed the changes were a usurpation of the assessor's responsibilities. He tossed the opinion towards me. The paper glided on my desk and landed in front of me. I picked it up and glanced at it.

"First, the job of the assessor is to identify, locate and value all properties in the county. Now, with the current changes, the mappers are locating properties under the board of supervisors' direction, not mine. And identification is being performed by the title department, which is now under the board of supervisors, not me. So the affidavits of value are being processed by the title staff— again, under the board of supervisors' jurisdiction. These critical forms aid my valuations." I took a breath, trying to appear in control and calm. "Basically the board of supervisors is now involved with about eighty percent of the statutory duties of the assessor. I'm expected to certify their work, but I have no assurances that the work is performed professionally." I waited. No response.

I continued. "So if you want examples of specific problems I'm having, here's an example: when the county administrator's wife and her staff were under me, they did pro-rations correctly. Now they do them wrong and refuse to do them the way I request. This alone will prevent me from certifying their work as I'm required by law to do on December 20th!"

My chief deputy, Jacob Brock, a tall youngish brunette, joined us in my office, taking a seat against the wall to my left. He folded his arms, and I was glad he was there to support me.

Dick nodded, acknowledging Jacob's presence, and jotted down a note on his notepad.

I explained further, "Second, Supervisor Arlo Davis's property increased in size about six acres after the map employees went under him. I can't be responsible for this math or conflict of interest. The department of revenue is over me, not over the board, and I report to them. There is no oversight regarding possible favors performed for the board of supervisors on their valuations, and the department of revenue is concerned about that." I located the letter I'd received from the department of revenue, stating their concerns over certifying the tax roll and my inability to add any kind of limiting condition to the certification. I handed the letter to Dastardly.

Jacob nodded his head and added, "The assessor's house, and all of the real estate she owns, is valued by the department of revenue—this way there is no conflict of interest. She doesn't value the property she owns, nor do employees she supervises value these properties." He raised his voice, trying to get Dastardly's attention. "But the department of revenue doesn't have the ability under the law to assess the board of supervisors' homes and properties! Now employees working under the board of supervisors change values of their properties. This is awkward, and really it's a conflict of interest issue."

Dastardly appeared to write down the points we'd made.

Jacob Brock continued, addressing Dastardly, "You've agreed you had a conflict of interest and could not provide a legal opinion as to whether or not the board of supervisors usurped the authority of the assessor by taking the mapping and title duties away from Pam. The Maricopa County Attorney returned with an answer of 'yes,' so how can you continue to deny that they're usurping Pam's authority?" By now he was looking frustrated, leaning in toward us.

I nodded in agreement.

Dastardly laughed awkwardly and replied, directing his remarks to me, "Well, the Maricopa County Attorney's opinion is that the changes might prevent you from fulfilling your statutory obligations. I'm here to determine if that's the case, so how is it preventing you from doing your job? I don't see it stopping you from doing your job. These employees do their tasks, answer to the board of supervisors, and the information is passed on to you. Seems fine to me."

I sucked in my breath, trying to focus on giving him information and not wanting to display my anger at his refusal to see how it was impossible for me to fulfill my statutory obligations with certitude and integrity without mapping and title duties.

It seemed that Dick just liked to play games with me, loved to see me beg and then refuse me what I needed, pretending not to understand my point. I figured he knew from the beginning the board of supervisors was acting illegally. Dick didn't care!

I shook my head, realizing it was probably over.

Out of the side of my eye, I saw Spidey had returned to his web. He was walking towards a little white moth—preparing to make a meal of him. *Don't look, don't look! Stay focused on Dastardly the Devil,* I reminded myself.

I answered Dick's absurd question. "There are issues with tax area codes. In the past, the employees would ask me for guidance, and I'd provide it. But now, they ask the clerk of the board and take directions from her—whether I agree or not. Yet, I'm the one that is held responsible. This is not legal!"

My chief deputy chimed in, "Yes, that's a good point. They have been ordered to continue to input information into the software, but if we disagreed with the interpretation, the staff should be instructed to do as the assessor requested. That isn't happening!" I could see his hands tremble, and I realized he was nervous. "We go back and forth, and in the end, the employees do it the way the board requests. Yet, these decisions impact the valuations that Assessor Pearsall has to certify!" *So much was at stake! How could Jacob not be nervous?*

"Another problem is the affidavits of value," I added. "The title staff aren't investigating the sales as they used to. They're slow to be processed, and scanning the documents isn't happening anymore."

I wanted to add the problems with the lack of supervision of the title employees I'd witnessed. I had also heard complaints of a hostile work environment, including vulgar language and inappropriate touching. I'd been appalled by the party atmosphere and lack of productivity. But I decided not to mention it at this point. Lynette was untouchable, that was understood, so there was no reason to bring it up. Dastardly must have seen the behavior. Anyone who walked through the new department saw it. It was on display all day, every day.

The map division was still behaving professionally, but the map workers were frustrated by the lack of discipline by the county administrator's wife and two members of her staff. Also, she had become a statewide embarrassment for me. On one occasion she'd attended a luncheon with all fifteen assessors' staffs from throughout the state. She'd shouted proudly that she was drinking "fucking alcohol" at this statewide meeting. When it was reported, I'd no power to hold her accountable.

"Yes, certification of the tax roll means I'm certifying that the tax roll is accurate. Legally I can't approve it if I know it is flawed. I understand you know this, Dick," I said looking directly at him. He consulted his notes as I continued to explain, "I'm telling you the system now is *flawed* and the more time that goes by with employees putting incorrect data into our database, the more flawed the tax roll will be! I can't be sure of the tax area codes, and ownership is being done by the board of supervisors now so I can't be sure of that either. I know for a fact that the affidavits of value have been incorrectly coded and entered into our software. The math on the pro-rations is wrong! For all these reasons, I won't be able to certify the tax rolls." *Could I make it any clearer?*

Dastardly jotted more notes in his notebook and asked if there was anything else we wanted him to consider when creating his question to the Attorney General.

I had to add one more thing before the Dorky Dick Bastardly Dastardly left. "Currently the boards' employees aren't processing tax roll corrections when they've made a mistake, and a refund is required. These taxpayers deserve immediate refunds on their overpayments. I understand hundreds are waiting to be processed!"

My throat now ached from all this talk. *I'll go home, take a pain pill and lay down as soon as I'm finished with this meeting,* I told myself. I placed my hand on my neck. The coolness of it felt nice. The vocal cord was twitching and twerking. I pictured Dastardly tied to a railroad track, a train blazing toward him. In my fantasy, Dick looks at me and begs, "Please untie me." I relent and untie him, but not until he'd vows to behave honorably. Then we'd have a happy ending.

It seemed to me that Dastardly was attempting to devise his questions in such a way as to get an answer helpful to his client, the board of supervisors. I hoped that wasn't true, but I suspected it was. How could it be possible to ask this question in such a way that the attorney general would say it was legal to take my employees away and render my work impossible?

10

TWISTED

2015

THE STAIRWELL IN THE COUNTY building had cinder block walls and a metal staircase with concrete casings. Stark, dimly lit, it reminded me of a prison. The stairs went from the bottom floor, where my offices were located, up four floors to the rooftop of the building. I took each step as slowly as I possibly could, and headed to the supervisors office on the third floor.

I felt doomed. I knew the current tax rolls were flawed. I'd asked the department of revenue if I could approve these rolls with a disclaimer stating that the work I was in charge of was credible, but I wouldn't take responsibility for the work of the board of supervisors or their employees.

The department of revenue responded that they couldn't find a law that allowed me to limit my approval. Here I was, with a law that said I must certify the tax rolls by December 20th and another law that said it was a crime to approve the tax rolls if I knew they were flawed. I'd assume personal liability for the tax rolls as soon as I certified them! I knew for a fact that the rolls contained many errors and lacked credibility due to the incorrect data the board of supervisors had inserted since May. *I'll turn this in, uncertified with a disclaimer. Then they'll remove me from office for failing to follow my statutory duties,* I thought. My throat burned, my eyes itched.

December 20th had fallen on a Sunday, so that bought me one extra day. I'd waited until the last possible day and prayed for a legal opinion from the attorney general's office before I had to submit the tax rolls. I'd be protected from removal if the attorney general indicated the board of supervisors usurped my authority by taking some key employees from my staff. No opinion had come, and now the tax rolls were due.

What does it look like to be removed from office? Do they call the police to come and drag you out of the building? Will the media be here to interview me and ask me questions like "How does it feel to lose your job?"

Instead of going to the supervisors office, I walked all the way up four flights to the rooftop landing and tried to open the roof door, but it was locked. I took a seat on the final steps of the landing and rocked back and forth. My chest felt like a refrigerator was resting on it. I couldn't escape from the constant pain. I imagined the headlines in the newspaper and the top of the hour radio news broadcasts: *Pearsall Didn't Do Her Job; Board of Supervisors Forced to Remove Her from Office.*

I'd refused to value the agricultural properties at the excessively low amount of ten dollars and ten cents and acre, going against the powerful figures in our community. By standing up and refusing to do as the board of supervisors had demanded I'd put myself in a position to be publicly destroyed.

I prayed, "Dear God, please, I don't want to turn in this uncertified tax roll, then be removed from office." *Why had I thought I wanted to be in a public position? My failure was now going to be just that—public, for all to see.*

I stood, sucked in my breath, and decided I couldn't procrastinate any longer. I headed down one level of stairs to the third floor and went to the board of supervisors office. There I turned in the tax rolls with a disclaimer attached: I took responsibility for the work my staff and I'd performed and then stated my concerns about the flaws on the rolls because of the board's interference. I refused any accountability for those errors.

I went right away to the elevator, wanting to get to my office as soon as I could. Seated at my desk, I waited for someone from the sheriff's office or the Prescott Police Department to show up and drag me to the parking lot—throwing me out as I'd beg to be heard. My window, now free of the spider web, moths, flies or bugs, looked empty. All was quiet. I waited.

At exactly five p.m., not fired from my post yet, I headed home. As soon as I got there, my cell phone notified me of an email from the State of Arizona's Attorney General's office. He'd issued an opinion in response to Dick Dastardly's twenty-three-page question that asked if the board of supervisors would be usurping the authority of the assessor if they took away employees and tasks.

Every point Dastardly made was answered in my favor: eighty statutes supported my position, and not one law supported Dorky Dick Dastardly's position! I grinned as I remembered how confused Dick pretended to be when I explained the issues and problems. *Now they wouldn't be able to remove me from office. In fact, the board of supervisors would have to give me these employees and tasks back or face a lawsuit that they'd surely lose. Another battle won!* I had to pinch myself.

On December 22nd, 2016, the headline in the *Daily Courier* read, "*Attorney General Says Supes Exceeded Authority,*" with a quote from Supervisor Chairman Craig Brown: "The Attorney General's opinion is just an opinion. It has no standing in law."

On January 8th, the headline read, "*Supervisors Reverse Course, Put Assessor's Office Back Together*" with a subtitle confirming that Pearsall refused to certify the faulty tax assessment rolls.

I hadn't refused to certify the tax rolls, but I couldn't confirm them because I knew they were flawed. Certifying meant they were credible and appropriate to be relied on by the taxing jurisdictions; they weren't, so I couldn't. I'd learned by now that headlines aren't always accurate. I was just thankful the headlines were not about my removal from office. The second opportunity to remove me from office failed. Check.

#

I could hear birds chirping as I inhaled the scent of the forest. Tyler and Robert, my son Mike's oldest boys, were demonstrating their best tricks on the trampoline as I sat watching from a patio chair in my backyard. In between clapping in delight at their incredible gymnastic feats, I dialed my sister's number.

"Hello?" She finally answered after letting it ring several times.

"I almost thought you were too busy for me," I responded.

"Never. So, wow! I read Toni Denis' article in the *Courier* today. Something about you 'receiving a gift and the board getting well-deserved coal.' Great article. So what's next?"

"I'd like to terminate Lynette for a lot of reasons, but the reorganization of the office isn't actually needed anymore so I can't really dismiss her—" I sucked in my breath and waited a few seconds to make my announcement as dramatic as I could. Then I finally I added, "But she put in her two-week notice, so she'll be leaving. At least she'll be leaving the assessor's office. I suspect she has another position in the county with a different department; I imagine Bulbous-Headed Bill has seen to that."

"Oh, that's good news, but I heard some news I'll tell you in a minute. Right now, as your official campaign manager, I need to tell you some gossip I heard about your campaign," Bev said, sounding serious.

"Grandma! Look!" the boys screamed in unison. I looked up to see them doing tumble tricks. I laughed—they reminded me so much of their dad at that age.

"Remember the rule—you're not allowed to get hurt at Grandma's house," I called out at them.

I turned back to the phone. "Okay, you can tell me the bad news, and then I'll catch you up with the rest of the story on Lynette." I stood up, walked to the garden hose and turned it on to just a drip then placed it on the rose garden. The roses would be incredible later in the year.

"Mattie is looking for a candidate to run against you. I was talking to someone from the contractors group, and they said that

Mattie was having meetings, trying to find someone who'd run for assessor."

"Oh, wow! I could have guessed that. So nice to be Mattie's B.F.F. (Best Friends Forever)," I said, trying to sound sarcastic. "I have something to tell you about that, too—" I added. Suddenly one grandson's foot connected with the other grandson's head. Screaming and crying ensued. I told Bev I'd have to let her go so I could handle the emergencies. I promised to call her back later. I tended to both kids, made them lunch and turned the Disney channel on to entertain them for a few minutes.

I heard a knock at the front door, ran to answer it. Surprised, I found Beverly standing in my doorway. "What are you doing here?" I asked, happy to see her.

"I was on my way to work when you called before. I thought I'd stop in and see Tyler and Robert. I have Tyler's birthday gift in the car," she answered as we walked into my kitchen. I made her a glass of iced tea. We went outside and sat on my back patio to finish our conversation.

"So, first Lynette—I told you she gave her two-week notice," I said, as Bev sipped her tea. "Well, typically I'd handle the action form because title will be back under my control before her two weeks are up. On the action form I could mark if she's eligible for re-hire in the county or not. Instead, human resources has let me know they'll be handling her action form!"

"Of course they will, because she has another job in a different department!" Bev said finishing, my thought and lighting a cigarette.

"Did you hear that she had a different position?" I asked

"Yep." Bev took a drag on her cigarette, then continued, "I heard it from a good friend that works in the county that she has a position—they didn't really want her in the department, but she's got it because of her connection with the county administrator," Bev said

The boys came out, took off their shoes and scrambled onto the trampoline to entertain us with their gymnastics.

"Was that it, or was there something about Mattie, too?" Bev asked.

"Oh yeah—the best part! I got a phone call from a guy claiming to live in Tucson. He said he was a rancher and he hates Mattie."

"So, a smart guy called you, please continue." Bev stood, walked towards the garden hose and moved it to the other side of the rose garden, cigarette dangling from her hand.

"He claimed that Mattie embezzled money from the Yavapai County Beef Association when she was an officer in that group, and she'd been caught. According to him, Mattie is making monthly payments to pay it all back."

"How much money did she steal?" Bev asked.

"I thought he said $65,000. But I ran into Bobbie Carson's husband—you remember Bobbie. She used to babysit for you and she's Mormon—her husband's the new president of the Yavapai ABA, I think. Anyhow, I asked him about it. He confirmed the embezzlement, and I believe he said it was $55,000. So I'm not sure how much money was stolen. Bobbie's husband stated that they didn't call the police or press charges but that it's not really a secret. Most people in agriculture know about it. When I spoke to another assessor, she confirmed that she'd also heard Mattie had embezzled money."

"So Mattie steals money, shoots pet Labrador Retrievers and drains the Verde River of all its water, killing the little fishies—some BFF you got yourself there!" Bev said, sitting back down and clapping her hands in amazement for Tyler's last trick on the trampoline.

"Another fun fact about Mattie—you know the Yavapai County ABA lawsuit on the updated values?"

"No, really—you? Updated agricultural values?" Bev said with sarcasm.

"Her ranch has some high-quality grassland along the Verde River. We're valuing the grazing land now based on its animal unit carrying capacity, so high grass pasture land is now valued at about $40 an acre, while dirt that has mostly rocks and not much growth down by Wickenburg is about $4 an acre. It averages $18 an acre, but it's all different, based on how many cows can be fed on a section of land,"

"The point? Remember this is about Mattie, not math,"

"The lawsuit that settled recently at ten dollars and a few cents an acre is a reduction for Mattie's ranch, so she'll be getting some refunds. However, it's an increase for some people in the lawsuit. Some will owe money to the county 'cuz of the settlement agreement! *Thanks Mattie*," I said.

How can the attorney for the beef people argue for an increase for some of his clients? Why would they agree to that? Plus the lawsuits probably cost them more than a quarter of a million dollars so far—did the ABA pay for that or did Mattie or did they all pitch in, you think?" Bev asked, her green eyes wide.

"I believe they all pitched in evenly regardless of the size of ranch or the value per acre." I said.

"Oh, wow! Remember how Grandma used to always say 'give them enough rope, they'll hang themselves?' This is a perfect example of what she meant. Between Mattie's embezzlement and this lawsuit they'll be seeing her for what she is!" Bev stood up and gave me a hug. "Gotta go to work."

The boys climbed off the trampoline, ran over and gave her a hug, too. Then we walked her to her car so she could give Tyler his birthday gift. We waved goodbye as she pulled out of the driveway.

Driving off, Bev leaned her head out of her black Escalade and hollered, "By the way, it's development services at the county that Lynette's going to work for!" With that, she backed out of the driveway and left.

I hadn't seen a position advertised for development services. *I don't think there's an opening. Wow, even with a sexual harassment or hostile work complaint against Lynette they'll find her a job. Probably created it for her. They barely hide the favors for Lynette and Bulbous Bill. Now that is nepotism at it's finest.*

I soon received a couple more two-week notices from title staff members, making it a loss of three people out of the five-person department I was getting back. Lynette, the supervisor, and one of her staff members, left to work in the county's development service department, and the third person went to work for a title agency.

I couldn't estimate how much all of this ended up costing the taxpayers. I could only guess it was expensive.

#

1992

I loaded my genealogy notebooks into my second suitcase. *Bev will probably moan, tell me how boring I am,* I thought as I shoved my suitcase closed and latched it. I loved family history. My cousin Sharon had managed to trace and document several generations of our family. I wanted to help, so I'd put together all her work and was now off to make discoveries of my own in Texas.

My grandmother's line was from Brenham, Texas. *Maybe if I had time I could look up that branch and do some research while I was there.* I seldom had time without the kids, and Bev could help. She'd tease, maybe call me Molly Mormon, but it was her family, too, and she might get into it.

"Mom, come watch this," eight-year-old Mike called from down the hallway. I turned from my suitcase and towards my son, but he was already gone—not a good sign.

When asked to watch something, my response usually was to scream "No, stop, don't!" because when Mike invited me to come see something, it typically was some trick he had thought up and dared Nick to try. If Nick, now six, could safely navigate the trick several times, then Mike would try it out himself. Unfortunately, Nick usually tumbled; bumps and bruises would be the result. I ran down the hall, praying for no broken bones.

Once outside, I saw that the boys had taken a shovel and industriously made their own bike trail. They'd dug ditches and piled mounds of dirt. It was quite impressive. They must have worked on it for hours. My mother sat on a folding chair in the back yard reading a book, smoking cigarettes, and watching the boys. Now she walked over to me.

We both watched as Nick got ready to tackle the track with tricks to impress. I gave my usual response, "Wait, stop, don't!" I

wanted to take a minute and look the track over for any dangers—
but Nick went for it. He started peddling as fast as he could. Up a
hump, down a hump, successful leap—and then, there it was. I saw
it in slow motion—a rope had been tied from the edge of the roof
to a pine tree. The last leap put Nick's neck even to the rope.

Nick jumped his bike high enough that his neck hit the rope,
catching him by the neck as the bike continued down the track. He
tumbled to the ground. I tore off in a run, praying he'd be okay. He
seemed stunned but stood up as if unhurt. "Are you okay?" I asked.
His eyes were wide and round and glistening. He said nothing.

"That was so cool!" Mike said. "Almost like that kid in the
movie 'Home Alone!'" Mike patted his brother on the back, and
Nick grinned ear to ear, still saying nothing.

I examined Nick's neck. There was a red band already forming.
"That's going to leave a rope burn. Come inside and I'll put some
aloe vera on it." I looked at my mom. "Have fun," I said, trying to
sound sarcastic.

"A rope burn, wow!" Nick said, finally getting his wind back,
"The kids at school will think that's neat."

"No more tricks while I'm gone," I said, instructing the boys
and my mom. Mother laughed. She loved all their tricks. She wasn't
always the innocent bystander. Her laughter often accelerated their
attempted adventures. I didn't want her encouraging their antics
and having an emergency to deal with while I was out of town.

It had been decided that once Gil Sieling was released from
the hospital in Texas, he'd come to my house to recover for a couple
of weeks. His house was in Camp Verde, his mother, a brother and
sister, all lived there too. The doctor wanted Gil to stay near a large
hospital after he'd be released. Since I lived in Glendale, Arizona,
near several large hospitals, I was asked if he could stay with me,
just for a few weeks. I agreed. *That's what Jesus would want. Right?*

Mom had offered to help Bob with my kids while I was in
Texas with Bev, and she'd also agreed to help me take care of Gil
when he came to my house to recover. That was huge because
Mom hated Gil. I was impressed that she was willing to help me
with him, and glad she'd be there to help. She was a better cook and

better caregiver than I was, and I was afraid: open heart surgery! What if something happened? What if he choked on my cooking or something?

#

2016

I walked into my office, took a seat at my desk and scanned the emails on my computer. Lorrie, my ever loyal and super assistant, peeked into the room. "You have to make a police report!" she said.

I looked up to see several staff members standing behind Lorrie at my door. Alarmed, I stood. *Was someone at the front counter that needed to be restrained?* We had plenty of that over the years. Once a man had stripped down naked because he was hot—apparently, he was on drugs. The police had responded and removed the man from the building. After that, we'd installed a panic button underneath the customer service counter.

Over the years there'd been people with guns on their hips who'd threatened and screamed because they believed they were "Americans," not citizens of the United States; being a citizen was something they thought you volunteered to do. They'd read a book with instructions on how to be a sovereign citizen free from taxation. It was misguided, of course, but these "Americans" believed it. Their book cited statutes and the Constitution to support its claims. Whoever sold that book and tricked these people had caused us some issues over the years.

The panic button was the best I could do since the board of supervisors believed strongly in gun rights. I did, too—but leave the weapon in your car if you're ticked off at me. These "Americans"—who didn't belong to the United States—believed I was harassing them.

The county also had people who'd wanted to make citizens' arrests. They'd claimed government employees were domestic terrorists. We had one religious group that refused to give their name because their philosophy was that God owns everything, including the land, and He shouldn't have to pay property taxes.

When the treasurer sold "God's land" for back taxes, it made them angry. Their ignorant stand made me sad.

I'd even had a four million dollar lien recorded against me by one of the "Americans" because he was tired of my harassing letters. He'd typed my name on the lien, stated on the document that this typed signature was a "true and authentic signature." Next, he recorded the lien, and it showed up on my credit report. The claim went up on their website. Dick Dastardly told me he'd take care of it. Later when I looked at my credit report, the lien was gone. To my surprise Mike Parks (AKA Dorky Dick Dastardly) had actually done as he'd promised and helped me with this. *Maybe he wasn't full of vile and free of any trace of humanity after all.*

"Call the police? Why, what's up?" I asked, walking towards Lorrie and the staff members behind her.

"It's your email. That Republican-Viking-with-an-ax is threatening you again."

I stifled a giggle and went back to my seat and looked through my email to find his threat. For the last year or so every time my name made KYCA, the local talk show radio station, or the *Daily Courier*, supportive citizens would send me beautiful notes of encouragement, sometimes even flowers or candy and photos of themselves. They'd tell me to stay the course. They knew I was leading with integrity and that it was difficult, so they sent great uplifting notes of encouragement.

On the other hand, there was one vocal person who hated me. He'd sent threatening emails signed, "Republican with an Ax" every single time I made headlines. His threats had escalated to threats against my staff and me. He used vulgar language to punctuate his hatred.

I found his latest email. Viking had plans for me—in language colored with vulgarities. I looked up at Lorrie. My insides now felt like jelly.

"Muttley told me you should do two things," Lorrie said. "First, email the Republican-with-an-ax and tell him not to contact you again unless he has a particular issue with his valuation. Tell him he's not to threaten you or your staff anymore. Then make a police report. The threat needs to be documented."

"But, I don't call the police over craziness," I said, surprised that Muttley felt this threat rose to the level of a police report.

"His speech is escalating. It might not be anything, but Muttley said it still needs to be reported," Lorrie said. The staff behind her nodded in unison.

I called the Prescott Police Department. As I waited for them to arrive at my office in response to my call, I reflected on the threats, perceived and real, I'd faced over the last seven years. *Life had been exciting for sure.*

A young blonde Prescott Police officer showed up at my office and took the report on the Viking-Republican-with-an-ax. "I think I know who he is. He lives in a mobile home park over by Abia Judd School. I'll talk to him," he said.

I looked at Lorrie and gave her the look: *Wow! How creepy is that? The ax guy lived in a mobile home park by a grade school? That sounded like a scary movie—wonder if he has lots of cats?*

#

1992

It was a dreary day in Texas, similar to a day you'd see in a movie when vampires jump out unexpectedly—gray clouds, rain, the perfect day to head to a cemetery. I would usually have loved this sort of experience because we were headed to the Yellow Fever Cemetery. However, today I had a headache, and I just wanted to be back in the motel bed, where it was dark and quiet, and I could hold my throbbing head. But Bev wanted to go hunting for ancestors. So here we were driving around, looking for the cemetery.

We'd waited in the Texas Heart Institute last week for hours while Gil had surgery. He'd done well. Now we were only allowed to visit each morning at 9 a.m. and again at 6 p.m. for a half an hour, giving us abundant time to explore.

I'd pulled the genealogy materials out of my suitcase before Bev and I did our morning visit. Then we headed off to Brenham, a little more than an hour away, straight down Highway 290—easy to get to, easy to navigate back.

We scoured courthouse records, returning to the Institute in time for our evening visit. The next day we did the same. In fact, we'd done this for a week.

Today, we paid our quick visit to Gil, who looked pale and weak but grateful to see us. After the visit, Bev and I were off to find the Yellow Fever Cemetery—an adventure during scary cemetery weather. *If only my headache would ease up.*

I wasn't worried about Gil recovering in ICU. I knew he'd be okay. Mom told Bev and me just before we left, "Don't worry, he's such a jerk he'll be fine. He's going to outlive me, just to spite me."

Yesterday the lady at the courthouse gave us directions to the cemetery, where we had ancestors buried, but I couldn't understand the directions, and we came to a dead end. The throbbing headache wasn't helping matters. We saw no cemetery. Instead, we were in a neighborhood with ranch homes, even an occasional horse or cow.

Nothing made sense. We were driving in circles: North Park Street, Pecan Circle Drive, Northview Circle Drive. I kept returning to North Park Street over and over again. It seemed like we were in a monster movie and I was being punked. *This wasn't fun.* My headache pounded as the rain fell. I wanted to go back to the motel. "It's impossible! Let's just go back to the motel and watch a movie," I finally said.

"But, if our ancestors are dead in some spirit world, and if they want us to find them, then we shouldn't give up. We'll probably never have a chance to get back in this area," my sister argued. Bev seemed to be having fun. She'd teased me about how boring my genealogy hobby was; now she'd discovered how fun family history could be—finding their stories, learning how they'd dealt with issues.

The gray cloudy weather, with the constant drizzle and occasional burst of thunder, continued—reflecting both my mood and my throbbing head. I hoped our ancestors were aware of us and wanted their stories known. That's what I believed, but today my head hurt, and I wasn't in a spiritual mood.

Bev looked at me wide-eyed with a huge grin and said, "Let's say a prayer and ask to be led to the cemetery. If all this is real, we'll be prompted or led. I know they want us to find them! They know we only have this chance." Her eyes shone green and clear.

I was the sister that was active in church, taught classes, volunteered, and read my scriptures daily. Bev not so much. She had not remained active in the church. I'd played the role of the good girl while she was the silly, fun one. Now Bev was showing earnest spiritual interest, a moment that could make or break her belief in the teachings of the Mormon Church.

How could I explain to Bev it didn't work like that? You pray and maybe have a good feeling—maybe nothing—and rarely was there a miracle or . . . I tried to put words together in my head to explain it.

"You offer the prayer," Bev said, interrupting my explanation. "Then tell me where they say to go—straight, left, or right; I'll drive where they tell you." She asked me to pull the car over to the side of the road. We switched places. She then folded her arms and bowed her head waiting for me to offer a prayer. She looked so sincere; how could I let her down softly without destroying her desire to learn more about our ancestors?

I voiced a powerful prayer; there was no way for Bev to know I was faking it. It sounded sincere and confident. The prayer was even full of *thou's,* and *thee's* to impress her. At the same time, I said a more casual prayer silently in my heart to a Heavenly Father I believed knew Beverly and me. *Please, I'm sorry, let her testimony survive this disappointment.*

Bev said "Amen" at the end of my fantastically faked prayer. Then, grinning, she started the car and began to drive. At the first stop sign, she looked at me and waited for instructions that supposedly I'd receive from the spirit world or perhaps from God.

"Left," I said, as if I'd received guidance. At the next stop sign, she again paused until I called out an instruction. This continued for about fifteen minutes, and I kept wondering how long it would take until she realized I had no clue how to get to the cemetery, and I wasn't getting any help from unseen ancestors. Finally, Bev pulled the car over to the side of the road. Apartments sat to our right, and to our left was a field with barbed-wire fencing and a "no trespassing" sign.

"Oh, it's here!" Bev shouted. She jumped out of the car, ran to the fence, pulled the wire loop up and over the gatepost, opened the section and dropped it to the ground. Then she ran into the field.

Crap, crap, crap, I thought, *we're gonna get arrested for trespassing.* I grabbed my notebook and purse with camera and credit cards. *I can bail us out with the credit cards and try to explain to the police that we thought the field looked like a cemetery or matched our directions or something.*

The rain stopped. I ran after Bev, trying to catch up. My pounding headache lifted. "This isn't it," I yelled, but my voice failed me as always. Bev couldn't hear me. I'd run for about 300 feet before I saw it—a headstone, like you'd see in the movies. It stood as high as my knees. I stopped and stared. Trees, vines, and brush grew all around, weaving in and through everything. It was winter and nothing was blooming, but I wondered if the vines were roses.

I stood in amazement until I heard Bev—way out in front of me—screaming, "They're over here, they're here!" I followed the sound of her voice deep into the Yellow Fever Cemetery towards the northeast. When I caught up, she said, "Here he is," and pointed. A headstone had fallen over, but you could clearly read the words chiseled on it: *"Lindsay P. Rucker."*

"They're so sad he's gone. He was such a good friend, a good dad, a great pastor," Bev said, as if she were aware of the emotions of the people attending the funeral held so many years ago when they laid Lindsay P. Rucker to rest. "This is his wife, and I'll take you to a different thing." I followed her. "You don't have these people in your records, but they are related to us. Write their names down." She pointed at a section that had wrought-iron fencing around it. Inside the plot were six graves.

I did as she said, feeling confused. *How had I guided her here?* "This was their baby, died at two years old. It hurt so bad to lose her," Bev continued, talking as if she knew the parents.

I wrote as Bev told me stories and pointed out gravesites of ancestors. The camera was in my purse. I pulled it out and took photos. Bev and I traipsed around the cemetery for an hour. She provided information that I didn't have, and I documented what she said.

"That was weird," Bev said, stopping her stories and looking at me as if she had just awakened.

I then spotted a fire pit, some old beer cans and a dead dog that had been burned. I felt goosebumps on my arms, and the hair on the back of my neck stood up. I couldn't swallow. My heart started to pound. I could smell the dead barbecued dog. With the background of the gray clouds above the old cemetery, the image of the dog was terrifying.

Bev turned her head to see what I was looking at. "Teenagers have partied here, pretending to be badasses. They even attempted some witchcraft—some evil stuff," she said, swinging her arms like she was trying to shake off something. "Let's go, I don't feel safe!"

When we got to the gate, I held up the wooden post, and Beverly placed the barbed-wire loop back, securing the fence. In the car, Bev explained she'd seen people standing around Lindsay P. Rucker's grave. She felt their sorrow at his death and sensed their stories.

I felt humbled. Whatever the spirit world is, surrounding God or a Supreme Being, I decided that faking it didn't fool Him or our ancestors. Bev's sincere desire for answers to our prayer were given to her from somewhere beyond our reality.

Everything Bev told me, I later was able to verify with other sources.

\#

2016

Do they have takeout? They must or how can they stay in business? I wondered, looking around the empty Pizza Hut. Sitting in a booth, I stared out the window at a deserted parking lot. From this vantage point, I'd be able to see my friends when they pulled up.

The time on my cell phone indicated I was twenty minutes early. "I'll have iced tea," I said to the waitress as she walked up. I smiled and tried to look pleasant. *Does she recognize me from all the publicity?* I wondered. My opponent had negative commercials about me on five channels, airing constantly. I felt exposed, vulnerable; the ads spewed lies. CHUD (**C**annibalistic **H**umanoid **U**nderground **D**weller), my opponent, lied when his lips moved.

There was no way for me to defend myself publicly, and it seemed plenty of people were being persuaded. I checked my texts and then read Muttley's email with its shocking message that they were replacing Kate, our fantastic brunette attorney, whom I thought would look great as a redheaded attorney, with some guy named Jim Sousa! This was the Phoenix Cement appeal case. *Why the hell would they replace Kate mid-stream in this case? This makes no sense!* I spouted foul words to myself. *The supervisors are crazy; who in their right mind would fire the best attorney in Arizona specializing in property tax issues for some unknown that none of the assessors have even heard of?*

I crossed my legs and started to shake my left foot back and forth, attempting to release some of the pent-up anger I was feeling. I fantasized that I could knock the county administrator's head off. I'd get a flyswatter, walk into Bill Drone's office and smash that spider head of his into a mishmash.

Using my cell phone I called Muttley. "Why are they firing Kate?" I asked as soon as he answered, not identifying myself or wasting time on idle chit chat.

"Jim's a good attorney and they, uh, they think Kate's too aggressive," Muttley answered. "I'll let her know later today. Just wanted to let you know first."

It was professional of him to let me know, but he had to know the board of supervisors was setting up the county for failures. The air felt hot. "So is the county saving money by using someone else? What reason do they have to fire Kate when she's done nothing but win?" I asked.

"Jim's good. He's both an accountant and an attorney," Muttley said, not addressing my question about why the board voted to fire a competent attorney in the middle of a claim.

It was sabotage, and it made no sense at all unless they were working against everyone except the litigants. They were supposed to work for the taxpayers, but midstream in a lawsuit, they'd fired an attorney that had a stellar reputation throughout the state with all the assessors! Kate had served our county with win after win.

I figured the board wanted to please the owners of rock quarries and certainly the owner of the Phoenix concrete plant. In my opinion, the board had long since stopped working for the regular taxpayers and now were the puppets of special interest groups. *They want to lose these lawsuits! How sick is that?* I ended the conversation abruptly and called Kate.

"Hi there, how are you doing?" Kate said, in the friendly manner I'd grown accustomed to. The waitress brought my tea, and I told her thanks as she walked away. I took a long sip. It was cold and hit the spot. I rubbed my fingers over the cold droplets of water accumulating on the outside of the glass and put my cool hand on my neck.

"I just found out that the board of supervisors has decided to replace you on the Phoenix Cement case with some guy named Jim Sousa," I answered, and waited for a response. I suspected I'd caught her off guard, so I continued, "I'm sorry. I hadn't seen this coming, but I wanted you to know about it as soon as possible. I found out maybe fifteen minutes ago."

After a moment, Kate responded, "They really did? This is odd. I know Sousa. He's less experienced than I am and certainly isn't as recognized in the property tax—"

"I've told you they're misogynistic men. They don't respect women . . . and I don't think they want to win these cases," I interrupted.

"You know, it's not worth the fight. I'd rather quit all the cases I currently have representing Yavapai County. I don't want to work for people who don't respect what I can do . . . I do like you, though, and I don't want to let you down."

"You're going to quit the Arizona Beef Association's case?" I asked, sucking my breath in. The ABA had continued to file lawsuits every year of valuations, and they needed to be confronted. But I didn't blame Kate for her decision. I'd refuse to work with these guys, too. I'd quit as their attorney and tell them where to stick their lawsuits.

The board of supervisors should just settle lawsuits and not pay attorney fees for court cases they didn't want to win. Why pay lawyers if they didn't want to aggressively defend their positions? Why not settle lawsuits out in the open for voters to see? Instead, it looked like they wanted to set up property tax cases by not putting forth the best cases possible. Then they'd pretend the county was on the wrong side legally when a judge ruled against them. Obviously, a lawyer would want to work for clients that rooted for the win, rather than wanting failure. I wished the taxpayers knew how underhanded these supervisors were.

"I think I'll quit the ABA case. Unless you don't want me to. I don't want to hurt you. But for me, I don't need their work. I have plenty of cases without them."

"No, I understand," I said. "They don't want you to win; they want the county to lose. It's weird, but it's what I believe. The board wants the beef association and the cement company to win, and they couldn't care less about the tax shifts to their constituents." We continued with small talk until my friends arrived at the restaurant, and I let Kate go.

Toni and Kristy joined me in the restaurant booth. I told them about the board's decision to fire Kate, and we discussed my upcoming campaign to serve another term.

"So, um—," I said, getting their full attention, "I'm done. I don't see winning the election now. CHUD and company have created another anonymous complaint about my work. They've sent it to the county and the county forwarded it for investigation. News media got some kind of package on it and they'll be playing the story tomorrow."

"What's the complaint?" Kristy asked, then looked up at the waitress. "I'll have a Coke." The waitress nodded, seemed to hesitate, then walked away.

"The 'anonymous complaint,'" I said, making quote marks in the air, "states that I hired a relative for the assessor's office."

"Another one, or is this your daughter again?" Toni asked.

"Another one. This hiring was about seven years ago, and it's a niece-in-law," I said. "I didn't hire her, of course, and you know I didn't hire my daughter either, but the *Courier* is going to run the story as another nepotism accusation." I fought back the tears. *Breathe.*

"You said it's an anonymous complaint, but it came from CHUD's team? That's dark!" Kristy said.

I agreed. My opponent, along with his campaign team, were underhanded. They'd win at any cost. I hadn't told Kristy or even my sister of the envelope Barney had threatened me with four years ago when he hadn't wanted me to run. He'd done a background check and found the information on Gil Sieling. He'd threatened it would all come out if I ran again. It wouldn't have done anything but embarrass me and wouldn't have helped defeat me in an election. Time had proved Scott right when he predicted I'd be attacked from all sides, and I knew Mattie and Boe were the puppet masters, along with Barney pulling the strings for CHUD.

Over the years, I'd lost sleep worrying that Barney would release information on Gil Sieling and cause embarrassment to my mother and sister. Typing anonymous complaints and forwarding them to the county was nothing in comparison.

"Yep, it's dark but what do you expect from a Cannibalistic Humanoid Underground Dweller and the minions?" I said and laughed.

Kristy laughed, too. "So you think you'll lose?"

"I might win, but he's spending 500% more than we are. He's played dirty—which we can't do and keep our integrity, so he's got us there." I took a sip of my iced tea. My throat was hurting, and I needed to go home and lie down. Maybe put an icepack on my neck.

"What would you do if integrity didn't matter and you could

play dirty?" she asked with a chuckle.

"These are just happy thoughts, and I won't actually do them, but I'll let you know my darkest fantasies if you want." I leaned in to whisper as if I had some deep dark secrets to share. "First, because CHUD's Jewish, I'd like to go to his synagogue or temple and on his car's bumper I'd put the bumper sticker, 'Jesus is my co-pilot.' Or maybe, just because he's a jerk, the bumper sticker should say, 'Don't follow me cuz I do stupid shit.'" Grinning, I took another swallow of tea. "Actually, now that I think about it, I'd put a 'Don't drink and drive. You might hit a bump and spill your drink' bumper sticker on Rowle's car."

Kristy and Toni laughed. I needed that.

"Yep, you're in a dark place, a real dark place for a Mormon," Toni said, laughing.

I quieted down and finished lunch, and I felt better. I might lose this election, but I knew CHUD's team was responsible for the anonymous complaints that made up crap about me. If I lost, I'd make sure people saw what kind of guy CHUD and his puppet masters were . . . I might even write a book!

#

1993

It was a warm spring day in May, just after Mother's Day in 1993. I stood in the garage as Bob demonstrated the baseball he'd installed. It dangled from the ceiling. If I pulled the Suburban in to touch it, I'd be in far enough to shut the garage door and avoid hitting the shelf on the wall . . . again.

The garage phone rang, and I ran to catch it.

"He's dead," Bev said, sounding calm.

"Who?" I asked, knowing it was bad news—the "dead" part being a clue. I sat on the stool next to Bob's workbench and pulled my hair up into a ponytail, using the rubber band on my wrist. The phone was cradled between my shoulder and ear.

"Gil Sieling," Bev answered, just as Mom walked into the garage carrying my oldest daughter. Heather was crying, her knees scuffed. Seeing me on the phone, Mom left the garage with Heather in her arms. She'd take care of the knee injury.

My heart cramped, my hands started to tremble. Gil couldn't be dead! Mom had sworn he'd outlive her for spite, and she was usually correct in the things she predicted.

"How?" I asked, fighting back the tears and sucking in my breath. I'd really thought he'd be fine. After his heart surgery, he'd come to my house where Mom and I had taken care of him. As soon as he was ready, he'd gone home to Camp Verde.

After Gil recovered, Mom moved to Bev's house to take care of her because Bev was pregnant with twins, and it was a difficult pregnancy. Then the twins were born prematurely. My focus had returned back to Cub Scouts, church, my job at Bank of America, Bev's health issues and the twins. Everyone was finally doing fine.

Gil had come to visit often, and Mom again refused to be in the same room with him.

"It was his heart," Bev said. "The tenants found him in his bedroom on his bed."

I looked over at Bob, who gave me a smile but looked concerned. He may have overheard something or could see from my face and shaking hands that it was bad news.

Mom returned to the garage and sat in her lawn chair just outside. She lit a cigarette and returned to reading her book. I heard Bob say something to her, but didn't hear what he said. She got up and walked over to me. "Gil Sieling is dead," I said. "I guess it was his heart."

Mom sucked in air loudly. Bob remained calm and gave me a hug.

"Can you meet me at his house?" Bev asked. "You sound like you're okay with it."

Gil had kept his house in Camp Verde. I was the executrix of the estate and I had his will. Gil and I had taken care of that a year ago before he'd gone to Texas for heart surgery. So even though his mom, sister and brother lived in Camp Verde near him, I'd be the person responsible for all the funeral arrangements and paperwork needed.

"Yes. It'll take me a couple hours," I said. Bev lived in Prescott Valley, an hour's drive away from Gil's house, while I still lived in Glendale. We agreed to meet at Gil's house in Camp Verde that afternoon. "I think I'm just surprised, but I expect it'll seem real in a minute."

My pain increased when I told my boys and saw their anguish over the news. They were close to their grandpa. He'd been very active with them over the last year. He swam in our pool with them. Caught balls in the yard. Rolled around on the floor wrestling and tossing them into the air. Played board games, taught them how to play chess, and watched every bike or pool trick they came up with, clapping and showing how impressed he was by their most colossal tricks. They didn't know our history. To them, he was just their grandpa, and he'd been a very attentive, loving one. This was their first experience with death. When I told them we hugged. I wished I could take away their pain but there was nothing to do. They cried and went to their rooms to be alone.

"I'm so mad at him for causing this pain," Mom said. "I know he can't help he died, but it does piss me off." She stood in the living room, pointing down the hall towards my boys' bedrooms. I knew she could hear how unreasonable that sounded and I had to laugh. She went on, "It's weird, knowing he's dead. Now nice memories about him are coming back. Things I'd forgotten."

I looked at her, and my mouth dropped. She'd never said a nice thing about him all these years. Nice memories? Was that even possible? Poor Mom, this had to cause her such mixed emotions. She'd been married to him seven years, and he was the source of so many problems during that marriage, but there must have been good times and good memories. Also to his credit, the entire time since he'd been out of prison he'd remained sober and repentant.

Looking back, I see he'd accepted whatever was dished out from us. He never got angry but understood that any relationship or trust would come slowly, if at all. Gil never backed down. He wanted a relationship, and he did whatever he could to achieve one. I realize now he'd done the best he could with what he had. In a drunken blackout or a mental breakdown—whichever it was—the attack on us set his course, and he dealt with the aftermath with authenticity. He never pretended to be something he wasn't. I mourned his death and miss him even now.

#

2016

The weather on the covered patio was perfect, not too hot and not too cold. *Does it ever get really cold here in Phoenix?* I wondered. The pool sparkled blue. Birds chirped. Flowers bloomed. I felt tranquility in the air and sat perfectly still, leaning against the stucco wall of the covered patio.

My husband's cousins, Roger and Vicki, had asked if I'd like to stay at their home in Phoenix while they went to Europe for three weeks. I'd jumped at the chance. I wanted to be alone, to think, to figure out what was next. It seemed like there was no next. So I just sat, trying not to think much about anything, but of course thoughts raced through my mind.

The pain of knowing the voters had rejected me was more than I'd expected. For days my heart felt like it had compressed down to the size of a prune, but now it felt broken. My eyes felt gritty; it hurt to blink. I'd lost the election by 4%. I'd thought the voters would know better or see through it all. But how would they? I'd not defended myself. I'd been determined to not go negative and stay positive. I'd run a campaign touting my qualifications and ignored CHUD's lies.

Strangers, friends, relatives had been exposed to his lies for months. Even the best of friends believed I'd illegally hired my daughter. They'd say things to me trying to lift me up—things like "We all make mistakes, but you owned up to it, took responsibility, and it was such a minor thing." My life's been full of errors, but hiring my daughter wasn't one of them.

I even stopped responding to these lies. I blamed my silence on my voice and told myself I didn't have enough vocal power to keep addressing these accusations. But in reality, I just wanted to hide somewhere. I felt overwhelmed knowing that people believed

I'd do the things I was accused of. I felt tired, buried under the lies even before I'd lost.

I'd never dealt with being bullied by falsehoods before. These lies were whispered at meetings I attended. They were on television commercials, radio commercials, even on mailers sent to registered voters—including my husband and me. There was no way to get away from the gnawing at my reputation and my soul. Record amounts of money had been spent destroying my character.

I sat for days on the covered patio in Phoenix, not moving. I'd go in the house, eat, then sleep. The next day I'd repeat my vigil on the patio. My husband came down from Prescott to Phoenix to be with me, but he kept to himself and allowed me to sit and sulk on my own.

My cell phone rang. I ignored most calls, wanting to be invisible or not exist at all. The caller ID revealed it was my son, Nick, now in his early thirties. I had to answer. *Nick might need something.* It may be an emergency. I'd never ignore a call from my mom, sister or children—even if I didn't want to talk.

"Hello," I said

"How are you?" Nick asked.

I looked at the patio. *How was I? Well, I was great, sitting on this patio looking at the pool and the beautiful flowers. But my spirit was broken. I'd have no job in a few months. Rejected and no longer respected.* I tried to explain it to Nick, but it became the emotional dump of everything I'd held in.

After a few minutes, Nick said, "Mom, can I ask you something?"

There it is, He has an emergency, and here I've been going on and on about me and the embarrassment of losing. Add 'mother that sucks' to the list of my achievements this year.

"Sure, Nick, what's up?"

"My question is this: do you think it's more important to be a good person or is it more important to have people think you're a good person?"

The answer was clear. Of course, I'd want my children to know that being a good person is more important. He had me there. I'd wanted both—to be good and to have people believe I was good. I knew I could be a better person. I'd thought mean thoughts about people. I'd missed church a lot the last several years. But at the heart of it, I knew I wasn't a bad person. I was imperfect for sure, but basically I was a good person. "To be good," I answered.

Standing up and stretching, I noticed that my back was starting to hurt from all the sitting with bad posture in this stucco seat built into the patio wall.

"Does it matter what anyone thinks, really? Their thoughts don't define you—do they?" I thought of Jesus, of course, and also Joan of Arc and Joseph Smith. Many people belittled and persecuted them. That certainly did not define them. In fact, all three had been murdered by those that hated them. I wondered if it bothered them to be thought of harshly? Or, if they were above caring about what others thought.

What a question. Did I care what others thought of me? Heck, yes, I cared! That's why I studied so hard and got good grades—so people would think I was smart. That's why I went to church a lot of the time. It was for everyone to see I was devout and loved God. That's why I did most things that I did. Yep, Nick, what others think totally matters, I thought, but I didn't want to admit I was that shallow to my son.

"I'm not sure. I do want people to think well of me, but at the end of the day, I guess I agree with you. It shouldn't matter as long as you're living with integrity and not hurting other people," I said.

"That's what I thought. So it's the taxpayer's loss to choose CHUD over you. Honestly, we both know in reality you were the better selection and that he's not qualified." He paused.

As I waited for him to continue, I moved into a patio furniture chair made with wooden palm fronds.

Still silence from Nick. I wondered if we'd been disconnected, but then Nick continued, "You're okay, it's going to work out."

With that, I knew he was right. My heart lifted. I felt joy and realized I hadn't felt happy for a while. It was better that I lost and could get away from all the toxic pressure I'd been under. It didn't matter what others thought, and it was time for me to stand up, dust off, go buy some Necco candies and get back to life. Because I knew *in the end it'll be okay, if it isn't okay, it isn't the end.*

EPILOGUE

Bevery is healthy and free of cancer.

Lawyer Kate resigned from the ABA lawsuit, as she said she would. The Phoenix Cement lawsuit appeal is either waiting for its day in court or by now has been settled.

David Boisvert (Boe) was hired by assessor-elect Judd Simmons (CHUD) as the new chief deputy of the Yavapai County Assessor's Office. All five Yavapai County Board of Supervisors voted to approve the advanced range and step pay requested by Mr. Simmons—that means that David Boisvert came in as a chief deputy at a higher pay than the outgoing chief deputy—despite the fact that the outgoing chief deputy had a higher level appraisal license and more experience. In my opinion, this proves the predictive powers of my old friend Scott. It was all part of the plan he'd tell me—if he were here.

Additional Information

Okay, now you've read the book, and you feel like you want more, or need to contact me, or maybe you have your own book to write and want to find out the process I used—if any of that is your intention, then these websites are for you:

- www.pinterest.com/pampearsa/book
- www.pampearsall.com
- www.facebook.com/assessorpampearsall

Believe it or not, I've actually had wack-a-doos friend me on Facebook. If you're a wack-a-doo or one of the creeps mentioned in my book, please disregard the links above—they aren't for you. Notice I said *please*! That should impress my sister Beverly with how polite I am.

Have a great day! If it were in my power, I'd grant you a fantastic life—but, hey, if your life has been challenging—I suggest you write a book.

Acknowledgements

Vicki King, my cousin, first urged me to write this book. Elaine Jordan subsequently worked with me as an editor and became a dear friend. Elaine's help was invaluable. Maria Lynam worked as a final reader, volunteering her time and talent to make this book what it is.

My mother answered questions openly. This book would not exist if it weren't for her willingness to always support my decisions.

About the Author

Pamela J. Pearsall was born in Phoenix, Arizona, and is a third generation Arizonan. Elected in 2009 she served eight years as the Yavapai County Assessor.

She earned her real estate license in 1980. Pamela is a General Certified Appraiser, certified by the Arizona State Board of Appraisal, and was a certified appraiser through the Arizona Department of Revenue. While assessor, her office earned the Certificate of Excellence with the International Association of Assessing Officers.

She now works as an audit lead manager for Tax Management Associates, Inc. Pam is the mother of four, and grandmother of eight.

CPSIA information can be obtained
at www.ICGtesting.com
Printed in the USA
FSHW012037020720
71837FS